our school

our school

*The Inspiring Story of Two Teachers,
One Big Idea, and the
School that Beat the Odds*

Joanne Jacobs

OUR SCHOOL
Copyright © Joanne Jacobs, 2005.

First published 2005 by
PALGRAVE MACMILLAN™
175 Fifth Avenue, New York, N.Y. 10010 and
Houndmills, Basingstoke, Hampshire, England RG21 6XS.
Companies and representatives throughout the world.

PALGRAVE MACMILLAN is the global academic imprint of the Palgrave Macmillan division of St. Martin's Press, LLC and of Palgrave Macmillan Ltd. Macmillan® is a registered trademark in the United States, United Kingdom and other countries. Palgrave is a registered trademark in the European Union and other countries.

ISBN 1-4039-7023-8 hardback

Library of Congress Cataloging-in-Publication Data

Jacobs, Joanne.
   Our school : the inspiring story of two teachers, one big idea, and the school that beat the odds / by Joanne Jacobs.
      p.   cm.
   includes bibliographical references and index.
   ISBN 1-4039-7023-8
   1. Charter schools—California—Case studies.   2. Mexican Americans—Education—California—Case studies.   3. Minorities—Education—California—Case studies.   I. Title.

LB2806.36.J33   2005
371.01—dc22   2005048869

A catalogue record for this book is available from the British Library.

Design by Letra Libre

First edition: December 2005
10   9   8   7   6   5   4   3   2   1

Printed in the United States of America

contents

acknowledgments

I'd like to thank all the people who encouraged me and helped me to turn this idea into a book: Charlotte Gusay, who advised me on refining the proposal; my agent, Scott Mendel; my editor, Amanda Johnson; and Elias Castillo, who was invaluable.

I'm very grateful to the Downtown College Prep leaders and teachers who let me observe them at work and answered my questions. In particular, Greg Lippman, Jennifer Andaluz, Jill Case, Alicia Gallegos, Laura DeRoche, Shawn Gerth, Vicky Evans, and Irene Zuniga took time to talk to me and tolerated me when I was in the way. I have enormous respect for their dedication to their students. Maria Lozano helped me find former students.

I had moments when I thought I'd made a colossal mistake by leaving my very good newspaper job to undertake this project. My daughter, Allison, told me that I'd made the right decision and that I'd make it work. She said she was proud of me. That meant a lot to me, Allison. This book is dedicated to you.

John, thank you for the tech support and for your love.

introduction

Only the educated are free.

—*Epictetus*

Grandpa Sol came to America 100 years ago because his father wanted more than a Hebrew school education for his children, and the Russian schools didn't want Jewish children. In New York City's public schools, my grandfather and his brothers and sisters received an education that enabled them to be successful in America.

When my mother was in high school in Chicago, some of her friends transferred to private school. Grandpa Sol's candy business was doing well. (If you like Whoppers, those malted milk balls sold in a milk carton, thank Grandpa Sol.) He could afford the tuition. But he wouldn't consider it. "Why would you go to private school?" he asked. "This is America! You can go to public school."

America's public schools are supposed to be the escalators of democracy, giving all children an equal opportunity for success in our society. Any child—in my day it was "any boy"—can grow up to be president of the country or of her own company.

But it doesn't really work that way.

There are good public schools for families who can afford to buy a home in the right neighborhood. I went to excellent public schools in Highland Park, Illinois, after my parents moved from Chicago to the suburbs "for the sake of the children."

Highland Park public schools were set up to teach students from educated, middle-class, two-parent families. Expectations were high and classes were challenging. Miss Anderson, who taught Great Books and Latin, had studied classics in Greece. She had a wonderful story about sneaking into Troy—closed for Turkish naval exercises—and being arrested as a spy. My high school offered a philosophy class, too, taught by a visiting college professor. When I took Western Civilization at Stanford, it was review: I'd read two-thirds of the reading list in high school.

My classmates became doctors and lawyers. I became an editorial writer and op-ed columnist for the *San Jose Mercury News*.

My daughter went to public schools in Palo Alto, California, an upper-middle-class town where students start thinking about college before they've finished the Beezus and Ramona series.

Parents who have money can exercise school choice, either by buying a home in an area with good public schools or by paying tuition.

But less-affluent parents are stuck with what they get. If the local school is led by a distant bureaucrat, staffed by inexperienced or burned-out teachers, whipsawed by education fads, and dominated by bullies, parents are told reforms are on the way: Just wait a few years, and then a few more.

If the school is just second-rate, parents are fed happy talk about how everyone's special and those nasty test scores don't indicate the real learning kids are doing. Why, they're going to be lifelong learners! It doesn't matter that they've learned nothing so far. They can look it up on the Internet.

Nobody says: "Juan can't read or write well enough to fill out a job application; he doesn't have the math to qualify as an apprentice carpenter, electrician, or plumber. He can go to community college, because they'll take anybody with a pulse. But he'll be stuck in remedial classes to learn what he was supposed to learn in elementary or middle school. The odds are he'll get discouraged and quit." That, they don't say.

As an editorial writer and columnist, I covered education for more than 15 years. I saw school districts adopt upbeat mottoes: "All children can learn" is the most popular. But principals and teachers at schools in low-income and working-class neighborhoods kept telling me that many of their students were doomed to fail because of circumstances beyond the school's control. Students didn't speak English. They were growing up in homes where the TV was blaring all day, and nobody ever read a book or had a conversation. They joined gangs, dropped out to take low-paying jobs, got pregnant, gave up. Many educators were angry at their students' parents, whom they described as uncaring, uneducated, and incompetent. If they weren't blaming the parents, they were blaming each other. Teachers told me stories of know-nothing principals. Principals told me about do-nothing teachers. It was depressing.

Finally, I began to meet people who *didn't* want to talk about how much blame to lay on incompetent parents versus idiot principals, chintzy taxpayers, and, of course, the media. I met people who had ideas about how to educate students and involve parents, and wanted the freedom to give their ideas a try. They were starting charter schools.

When I started working on this book in early 2001, I knew the theory of charter schools. I was curious about how it works in real life, when idealism meets the plumbing in the boys' restroom.

I quit my newspaper job. I started volunteering at Downtown College Prep, then in its first year, and at East Palo Alto Charter School, a K–8 school. Both schools serve children from low-income, minority families; most parents have immigrated from Mexico, searching for opportunity.

Originally, I planned to follow a first-year charter school from the planning process through the first year. I couldn't get the access I needed at the first two schools I tried. First-year teachers were afraid I'd get in the way or catch them saying something stupid.

By the time I talked to Greg Lippman and Jennifer Andaluz, the founders of Downtown College Prep (DCP), about writing about their school, DCP was starting its second year. But I'd seen some of the first year as a volunteer in Andaluz's Mock Trial class, in which students built their reading, speaking, and argumentation skills by acting as lawyers and witnesses.

Most importantly, Lippman and Andaluz gave me full access to every aspect of the school. They believe it's essential for their school to be open to public scrutiny. They told me that if I liked what I saw, great. If I had criticisms, they'd consider them feedback. But my opinions weren't going to rock their world, one way or the other. What mattered to them was what the parents felt about their children's education.

"Our parents believe in this school," said Lippman. "That's what counts for us."

I spent a year observing classes, following Lippman and Andaluz, helping with the Mock Trial team, and tutoring a ninth grader, who is called Lisa in this book. I sat in on staff meetings, disciplinary committee meetings, an expulsion hearing, teacher interviews and evaluations, parent education classes, a Parent Council meeting, and a board of trustees' meeting.

Thanks to the founders' example of openness, DCP staff and teachers also were open, honest, and tolerant of my presence in their crowded classrooms. I began to appreciate how incredibly difficult it is to teach a class of 20 students, all with different abilities, personalities, and fluency in English.

Parents also were welcoming, despite my limited Spanish and, in many cases, their limited English. Later, I asked a Spanish-speaking friend to help me interview parents more fully.

The students were great. They talked to me, let me use their writing in this book, and allowed me to observe them in their good and not-so-good moments. With a few exceptions, I liked DCP's students, even as I admired their teachers' patience.

I remember Larissa's pride when she returned to school after having her baby with all her homework neatly done. I think of Pedro playing Lady Macbeth and cracking up at the line "I have given suck." Or Lorenzo explaining why ninth graders study the Aztecs: "Because they're dead!" There was Barbara fighting a girl six inches taller for a rebound, Roberto giving a speech at Open House in English, Lisa borrowing a calculator to multiply 3 times 9.

This book depicts DCP in its second year; the final chapter tells about the students who graduated and went on to college and those who didn't make it. There are lessons to be learned from DCP's successes and failures that can be applied to traditional schools, as well as charters. Above all, there is hope.

With the exception of the name of the girl who gave the graduation speech, I've changed the names of students mentioned in this book, although they begged to be included under their real name. "You might not like what I write about you," I told Hector, who'd let me sit in on his disciplinary committee hearing. "What if you were reading it ten years from now and it describes something stupid you did in ninth grade?"

"Well, if I did it, that's on me," he said.

I did not change the names of adults.

There are no composite characters, no quotes from imagined conversations. Real students wrote the poems, letters, and essays I've included.

The school is changing as it grows, and as its leaders figure out what works and what doesn't. By the time you read this, DCP will be doing many things differently to achieve its goal: educational opportunity for all.

1

crossing over

After eight hours of school, the ninth and tenth graders burst out of the shabby church, shouting, flirting, joking, shoving, waving *adios* as they climb into battered pickups and vans, jockeying for sidewalk space for their skateboards. Most are Mexican-American, with a few whites and even fewer blacks or Asians. All wear the white, black, or gray polo shirts of San Jose's Downtown College Prep over khaki pants or skirts.

Darting through the crowd is Greg Lippman, principal and cofounder of DCP. At 32, the dark-haired Lippman would look like someone's older brother without his navy-blue jacket and striped tie. He pauses to shake a small, plump boy's hand. "Do you still want a tutor? Are you ready to show respect this time?"

The boy nods.

"OK, I'll put you on the list for a new tutor," Lippman says.

The boy lost his original tutor because he failed to show respect, Lippman explains. "The tutor told him to put his juice box away, and he didn't do it." He is entirely serious. Disrespect to a tutor is disrespect to the school community. It is a failure of *ganas*, the school's highest value. *Ganas* means "desire," also translated as "motivation," "willpower," "spirit," "heart," or "true grit." DCP will be a place of *ganas*—or it will fail.

In the charter high school's first year, with one class of 100 freshmen, Lippman tried to shake each student's hand every day. With nearly 200 students in the school's second year, Lippman can't do that. But he tries, standing outside every afternoon at five o'clock to shepherd students home, praise, exhort, nag, joke, and connect.

DCP is a charter school. That means it's a free public school that operates similarly to a private school, setting its own rules, hiring its own teachers, and controlling its own budget.

The school's mission is to prepare underachieving students to succeed at four-year colleges and universities. The typical DCP student is a Mexican-American living in downtown San Jose who starts ninth grade with fifth-grade reading and math skills. Lippman and his cofounder, Jennifer Andaluz, believe their school can move students from the drop-out slide to the college track.

Inspired by the dream and curious about the reality, I'm standing with Lippman on a warm fall day in 2001 outside Saint Paul's Methodist Church in downtown San Jose. Now in its second year, DCP has no building of its own for its ninth and tenth graders. The school rents space at Saint Paul's and at a former YWCA fitness center eight blocks away.

As a politician works a factory gate, Lippman works the crowd.

He shakes hands with sumo-sized Buddy, who has to hurry home to comply with the terms of his probation. Buddy was expelled from his large high school after a gang fight. In the shadow of 9/11, Buddy's worried about his father, serving on an aircraft carrier en route to the Persian Gulf.

Lippman shakes hands with slender Selena, an honor roll student, who is "Original DCP," the principal says. When she was in middle school, he recruited her for the first Summer Bridge tutoring program, which Lippman and Andaluz used to test their education ideas and gauge interest in a charter high school. Selena feared being labeled a "schoolgirl," a taunt Hispanic students sometimes use to put down each other for trying too hard. Lippman told her she could go to college—he guaranteed it—if she was willing to do the work. Now, "she bleeds orange and purple," DCP's colors, he says proudly. Selena's mother, who had a first-grade education in Mexico, works two or three jobs at a time as a janitor and seamstress to support her children. Selena cooks, cleans, and cares for her younger siblings, while studying to maintain an A average.

Like the bar in *Cheers,* DCP is a place where everybody knows your name. Lippman seems to know every student's name, class schedule, grade point average, and middle school record. He knows who's feuding with Mom, whose Dad moved back to Mexico, whose cousins moved in, whose brother was arrested. When a student who's never done homework turns in several assignments in a row, Lippman hears about it and lets the student know he knows.

Lippman shakes hands with tall, impatient Larissa and with small, nervous Gil, both repeating ninth grade, and with Byron, an outgoing boy who also is Original DCP.

Lippman points to a boy whose hair sticks up in gelled spikes, a popular style. "He's crossed over from the Dark Side," the principal tells me. "That girl, too. And those two at the corner. They've crossed over."

He doesn't mean they're reformed gang members, though some students do have gang ties they're supposed to cut. "Crossover students" have left behind their apathy. To use another DCP metaphor, they've emerged from "the tunnel of F's," or, at least, seen the light at the end of the tunnel. For the first time since kindergarten, they're serious about school.

Another crossover student, Pedro, gives the principal a big grin and a hand, then swaggers down the sidewalk. Pedro went to a nearby high school as a freshman but cut 90 percent of the time. "He was too busy selling marijuana to go to class," says Lippman. Pedro agreed to enroll in DCP in the school's first year, even though it meant repeating ninth grade, hoping for a fresh start. It was a tough year, but he started to improve halfway through and made it to tenth grade. His grades continue to rise; referrals to the office are down. "He was a very angry kid when he came last year," says Lippman. "Now I think he's going to make it. I have visions of him as an art major at San Jose State." Pedro, who sees himself as a rapper, has signed up to perform at the school's upcoming Talent Night.

Lippman shakes the hand of a weathered man who's picking up his daughter. "She's doing better," Lippman says. "*Muy buena.*"

A former high school English teacher, Lippman didn't know Spanish when the school opened, but he's been learning, and he likes to use the language as often as possible with parents. His broken Spanish makes many parents feel less embarrassed about their English. I suspect Lippman of exaggerating his difficulties when he speaks Spanish with immigrant students, who spend the eight-hour school day struggling to learn in English. Lippman asks them to correct his Spanish and teach him new words. He laughs at his own clumsiness. His implicit message is that you don't have to be good. You just have to keep trying to improve. It's DCP's unspoken motto: We're not good now, but we're getting better.

A bright-eyed girl bounces up to Lippman. "Ms. Robinson says I'm too good for Math Reasoning!" she announces, with a Roo-like series of leaps. All ninth graders take algebra; low-skilled students also take the remedial Math Reasoning (MR) class instead of an elective. Lippman shakes her hand and congratulates her. He already knows about it and is working on her schedule change.

A glowering ninth-grade girl drags her mother to Lippman. In Spanish, English, and sign language, with reluctant translation help, Lippman tries to explain why he confiscated Rosita's hooded sweatshirt. Although students may think hoodies are just a fashion, DCP considers them to be gang clothing.

"No gangs!" says Rosita's mother, with enthusiasm. Not for her daughter.

Rosita's glower fades into a pout. She barely musters the energy for a shrug of her shoulders. *So boring,* she mimes. Lippman dashes inside to his office, retrieves the sweatshirt, runs back out, and hands it back. "Next time I'll keep it till June," he tells Rosita. She allows her limp hand to be shaken, then drags her mother away.

A small boy named Henry skitters down the sidewalk, avoiding Lippman's outstretched hand. Henry has admitted vandalizing the bus that shuttles students between the church, which houses math and science classes, and the Y, which contains English and history. Henry is supposed to work off the $800 vandalism bill by sweeping and other cleanup chores. Though he can be charming and childish, Henry is prone to fits of rage. Lippman worries about his lack of self-control. He worries even more about the students who saw him vandalize the bus and did nothing.

"You know what phrase I hate?" he says. "I hate it when people say, 'It's all good.'" He mocks the phrase in a bright, empty voice. "*It's all good.*" He points at the departing students. "It's *not* all good," he says. "It's *not!*"

The school's target student isn't a troublemaker, says Lippman. He's a trouble follower. In a large high school, he'll drift along, doing what's expected, which is not much. At DCP, immersed in a culture that honors grades and determination, the target student will follow the academic leaders all the way to college. That's the promise DCP has made to parents: If your children graduate from this school, they'll qualify for a four-year college or university. DCP doesn't guarantee Stanford, half an hour away, or

Berkeley or Cal Tech. San Jose State, just across the street, is a challenging goal for most students.

At DCP, low achievers aren't told they're doing well; they're told they can do better, if they work hard. The school doesn't boost self-esteem with empty praise. Instead, Lippman and his teachers encourage what's known as "efficacious thinking," the belief that what a person does has an effect. If you study, you'll do better on the test than if you goof off. Work hard in school, and you can get to college. You have control over your future. So, stop making excuses and start getting your act together. The complete absence of sugarcoating may seem harsh to outsiders, but students seem to appreciate the honesty.

The students are dispersing now: the small, round ninth graders who haven't hit puberty; tall goateed boys who are a year or two old for their grade; slender girls in tight pants; heavyset girls in baggy pants.

Lippman's day is not over. He'll confer with Jesse Robinson, one of the math teachers, about her plans for Geometry Mystery Night: Students will make up matrix problems for their parents and other visitors to solve. It's a way to lure parents into the school to applaud their children's achievements. He'll call the parents of problem students and talk with Andaluz, who's trying to get San Jose State to supply land for DCP's dream, a real school building. Lippman will run home to have a quick dinner with his wife, who's expecting their first child, and then return to coach the Mock Trial team.

The handshaking ritual has energized Lippman. It's not all good. But it can get better.

Talent Night gave students a chance to shine in front of classmates and parents, and let the staff show another side of themselves. One student performed with his mariachi band, all in black suits with silver buttons and white ruffled shirts. Four girls sang "My Guy." Two girls danced and lip-synched to a song by Brandy.

Teachers also took the stage: Jesse Robinson impressed students with her ability to balance ten spoons on her nose, lip, eye socket, and chin. Lippman and the ninth-grade English teacher, Angela Hensley, sang "Ain't No Sunshine When She's Gone."

The math department—Robinson, Aaron Srugis, and Dan Greene—sang "Don't Think Twice, It's All Right."

Pedro and his cousin performed a rap that Pedro had written about giving up drugs and alcohol. This is an excerpt, with his spelling:

Just come to me
I'll do my best to make it better
But if ya need any of that stuff
Ima havta see ya later
Cause I aint for that G
I don't wanna be
caught up in hand cuffs
that just aint me.
Once I had anamosity against drug and alcohol addicts
Then I found myself doin' that same shiznit
I was goin through some rough times
wasn't loc't back then
I didn't even like to write rhymes
And if I didn't change
I was headed to the pen
I decided to change
Not to be cool
I had to maintain
and not stay a dumb fool . . .

At a national level:

Hispanic and black students in the twelfth grade read and compute at the same levels as white students in the eighth grade.[1]

High school graduation rates averaged 72 percent in 2002: 78 percent for whites, 56 percent for blacks, and 52 percent for Hispanics. Of those who earned a diploma, 40 percent of whites, 23 percent of blacks, and 20 percent of Hispanics were ready to attend a four-year college on the basis of their course work and grades.[2]

In California:

More than 85 percent of Hispanic students in Silicon Valley (portions of Alameda, Santa Clara, and San Mateo Counties) are *not* enrolled in mathematic courses beyond algebra.[3]

Among native-born Californians ages 25 to 29, 13 percent of Hispanics, 15 percent of blacks, 31 percent of non-Hispanic whites, and 62 percent of Asian Americans have a college degree.[4]

On California's Standardized Testing and Reporting (STAR) exam, which is taken by students in second through eleventh grade, 70 percent of Hispanic ninth graders are performing *below* grade-level in math; 68 percent of Hispanic students are performing *below* grade level in reading.[5] On the part of the test linked to state standards, Hispanic and black eleventh graders score below white seventh graders in reading.[6]

Of every 100 Hispanic students entering kindergarten, only 61 finish high school, 31 complete some college, and fewer than 10 obtain a bachelor's degree.[7]

Only 12 percent of Hispanic students and 14 percent of blacks who start ninth grade will graduate in four years with the course work and grades required for admission to California's public four-year universities.[8]

2

fighting the blob

From the morass of red tape, regulations, forms, files, work rules, and mission statements, a huge monster arose. "The Blob,"[1] so named by the former secretary of education, William Bennett, is the impenetrable mass of bureaucracy that crushes creativity, chokes innovation, and gobbles up education funds. For years, education reformers from Chester E. Finn, Jr., to Joe Nathan and Theodore Sizer have tried to beat back the Blob. It kept growing. So they looked to charter schools as a way around it.

Oddly enough, it was a union leader who popularized the idea of charter schools. In a 1988 National Press Club speech, Albert Shanker, the dynamic leader of the American Federation of Teachers, proposed shaking up the system.[2] Let groups of teachers design their own schools. Give them a charter to run their school as they see fit. If the school doesn't achieve its goals, close it.

Other union leaders feared Shanker's idea would open the door to nonunion schools, but education reformers were excited by the concept, which they expanded to include schools designed by alliances of parents, educators, academics, community activists, and business leaders.

The first charter school opened in Minnesota in 1992, and the movement quickly grew. In 40 states and the District of Columbia, "grumpy optimists," as DCP's founders call themselves, are starting their own schools. By 2005, nearly a million students were enrolled in 3,400 charter schools across the country.[3]

As a public school, a charter is funded by tax dollars, though typically charters receive less money than district-run schools. According to a 2005 analysis, the average charter school is allotted only 78 percent of the funding of a traditional public school.[4]

Charters must be free and open to all students. Like a private school, a charter is run by its own board and is exempt from some state regulations, though many still apply. Depending on state law, a charter may be created by teachers, parents, academics, community activists, or business leaders. The students are there by choice. So are the teachers, who usually are young, willing to work long hours, and not unionized.

Though charter founders can't choose their students, a school may focus on educating a specific group, such as dropouts, pregnant teens, home-schoolers, learning disabled students, gifted students, artists, or budding scientists. Although charters can't discriminate on the basis of race, ethnicity, or religion, some are designed to serve the needs and interests of disadvantaged black, Hispanic, or Native American students.

Some charter schools offer an alternative approach to education: learn-through-doing, learn-through-technology, learn-through-the-arts, learn-at-your-own-pace, and so on. Many are traditional schools—perhaps more traditional in curriculum and discipline rules than the district-run public schools in their area.

Sometimes existing schools convert to charter status, either because teachers want to save an effective program threatened by district control or because the school is doing so badly that the school board is happy to let someone else try. In both cases, a conversion charter school tends to resemble the district-run school that preceded it: Inertia is a powerful force. Despite the challenges of hiring a new staff and recruiting students, a school that starts from scratch, like DCP, finds it much easier to chart its own course.

In most states, a charter school doesn't need a brick-and-mortar building. Cybercharters, which often are for-profit organizations, have sprung up to deliver instruction online to students working with a parent "coach" at home. Some cybercharters specialize in students who have been expelled, have dropped out, or have left to take a job or raise a child; these students usually don't have a parent guiding their education and tend to do quite poorly.

As the movement grows, all sorts of people are starting schools, including the tennis star Andre Agassi in Las Vegas, the boxer Oscar De La Hoya in Los Angeles, and the basketball star Kevin Johnson in Sacramento. A Chicago law firm is starting a charter school; there are even a few run by teachers' unions. In some cases, districts start their own charter schools to escape burdensome state regulations.

Nationwide, charter schools educate more low-income students and significantly more blacks than traditional public schools do, but fewer special education students, concluded a 2004 U.S. Department of Education report.[5] The proportion of students who aren't fluent in English is about the same.

"While 28 percent of [charter] schools report targeting low-income and low-performing students, 74 percent reported attracting these groups of students," the report found. "Similarly, less than one-quarter of charter schools targeted gifted and talented or special education students, but more than half of the schools attracted these students."

Poverty data is based on eligibility for a free or reduced-price lunch. But a third of charters don't participate in the federal lunch program,[6] because of the regulatory burdens, so charters' share of poor students may be undercounted.

Despite Shanker's belief in independent (teacher-run) schools, the education unions are wary of charters. But the unions don't dislike charters as much as they hate vouchers, which give parents total say about how to spend tax dollars to educate their children. At least charters are part of the public system, and most are not-for-profit operations.

In California, as in many states, charter schools were offered as a way to stave off voucher plans. The educrats—state bureaucrats, district administrators, school boards, and the powerful teachers' unions—went along with charter legislation, while lobbying Democratic lawmakers to limit the number of charters and restrict their independence.

California's charter law, passed in 1992, made it easy for school boards to prevent the creation of new schools. Only 100 charters could be granted statewide, but that was more than enough. Only 9 received school board and state approval the first year.

The state's first charter went to an experimental school chartered by San Carlos Elementary District in a middle-class suburb of San Francisco. Working near the venture capital center of Silicon Valley, San Carlos Superintendent Don Shalvey, the charter's champion, had imbibed a more entrepreneurial spirit than most public superintendents, who tend to be staunch defenders of the status quo. "Choice is reality," Shalvey says. "We have choice in everything else. Why not schools?"

Shalvey worked with parents who wanted an unstructured, "child-centered" school. The first few months were rocky. Unstructured turned out to be chaotic. However, unlike a conventional school, the San Carlos charter school had to please parents or lose its students and its financing. Parents, teachers, and administrators revised the school's design in midyear to solve the problems. The school thrived, attracting students and posting high test scores.

In the 1990s, high-tech entrepreneurs became increasingly worried about the quality of local schools. As the Internet boom drove up the cost of housing, luring new talent to Silicon Valley became harder. Business leaders wanted to tout public schools good enough for the children of the world's best engineers. They also wanted to be able to hire locals, who already had housing or at least had a family to live with until they could afford $2,000 for a two-bedroom apartment. Joint Venture Silicon Valley's education committee began offering large grants to school districts willing to follow a business model: Set a goal, measure progress toward the goal, continuously improve the process.[7]

In a meeting with Joint Venture executives, Shalvey met a high-tech millionaire named Reed Hastings, who'd taught school before launching a business career. Hastings believed charter schools would energize public education. He partnered with Shalvey to write an initiative removing the limits on charter schools and making it harder for school boards to block competition. With Hastings's money and high-tech connections, it was a sure winner.[8] So Democrats, who dominate the California legislature, cut a deal with Hastings and Shalvey: The Democratic leaders agreed to pass a new state law that included most of what the charter school advocates wanted; in exchange, the initiative was dropped. In short, legislators saw the school choice train was leaving the station and hopped on board. California now says a school board *must* approve a new charter unless it can find an educational or financial reason to deny it; the County Office of Education or the charter-friendly state board of education may approve petitions denied locally.

The state school board became even more procharter when Hastings was named a board member by Governor Gray Davis. He became the board president. Also named to the state board was Donald Fisher, founder of The Gap, who'd donated money to help open new charter schools and train charter principals, and Susan Hammer, former mayor of San Jose, whose son, Matt

Hammer, works for the grassroots group People Acting in Community To-gether (PACT), lobbying for small, parent-controlled schools. Her daughter-in-law, Michelle Longosz, later became DCP's photography teacher.

Hastings, who went on to found Netflix, lost his seat on the state school board in 2005 when Hispanic Democrats blocked his reappointment, an-gered by Hastings's insistence that bilingual classes use English at least two and a half hours a day.[9]

After the law changed, charter schools started to spring up all over the state to provide alternatives to dissatisfied parents, serve students with spe-cial needs, or rescue students in especially bad school districts. Most are run by not-for-profit boards, but California law allows for-profit operators such as Edison Schools Inc. to run charter schools as well.

Don Shalvey quit his school district job and started Aspire Public Schools, a not-for-profit devoted to running charter schools. His dream was to create a network of 100 charter schools. Aspire opened charters in the Central Valley, where Shalvey had started his teaching career, and in Oak-land, which desperately needed decent schools. In 2001, Aspire partnered with the Stanford University School of Education to open a charter high school in East Palo Alto, a predominantly low-income, minority commu-nity; an existing charter K–8 in East Palo Alto joined the Aspire network. By fall 2005, Aspire had grown to 14 schools.

Of course, as the charter movement grew, so did the opposition.

Critics complained that charters take money from district-run schools. School funding formulas vary from state to state; usually schools lose per-student funding when they lose students but still have to pay fixed costs, such as central administration. In areas where enrollment is rising, a new charter school may save the district money by taking students who'd other-wise require a new school; if enrollment falls because of a new charter, dis-tricts must make the politically unpopular decision to close a school.

California now requires a district to provide or fund classroom space for all students who'd otherwise attend district schools, even if they enroll in a charter, but most states don't provide facilities for charter schools and spend less per student than in district-run schools. Charters must raise extra fund-ing from private donors or do without; most run a bare-bones operation.

There's no question that charter schools threaten to shake up existing school districts, especially those with many very low-performing schools. In Detroit, public school enrollment has plunged as parents choose charter alternatives or move to the suburbs for better schools. In Dayton, Ohio, the most charter-intensive city in the country, 26 percent of public school students attend charters.[10] Charter schools also are taking students from district-run schools in Washington, D.C., which has the nation's highest per-pupil spending and the lowest test scores. These districts have been forced to cut costs and close schools. On the other hand, is that so bad? The purpose of public education funding is to educate students, not to maintain the school district as is. Charters flourish where the traditional public school system has failed to meet the needs of some—or all—students. Whether districts will learn to compete to prevent students from leaving is an open question.

Charter Schools, 1995–2005	
1995	100
1996	255
1997	428
1998	790
1999	1,100
2000	1,700
2001	2,110
2002	2,431
2003	2,700
2004	2,996
2005	3,400
—Center for Education Reform, 2005[11]	

3

a school of our own

San Jose's Gunderson High was in the throes of "whole school" reform. That meant endless, mind-numbing meetings to talk about the process of change.

Teachers hashed out a mission statement: "A Gunderson High School diploma gives students the technological, critical thinking, and business skills necessary for success in an increasingly interdependent world. A Gunderson diploma will be a passport to the Global Community."

In reality, teachers couldn't agree on the school's mission, much less the strategy for turning out self-esteeming, diversity-loving, community-minded lifelong learners who could pass college classes or qualify for a job. Reformers and traditionalists feuded endlessly.

"It was the Rebel Alliance versus Darth Vader," says Greg Lippman, then a Gunderson English teacher.

"It was ridiculous," says Jennifer Andaluz, who taught history. "People couldn't disagree without thinking the other person was a bad person."

At the southern end of Silicon Valley, San Jose is a city of nearly a million people ranging from well-paid engineers and programmers to very poor immigrants from Mexico and Vietnam. Overall, it has the highest median household income, $76,181, of any major U.S. city and the lowest crime rate. Some 33 percent of San Jose residents hold a bachelor's or graduate degree; 20 percent didn't complete high school. No one ethnic or racial group dominates: 34 percent are non-Hispanic white, 31 percent are Hispanic, 28 percent Asian American and less than 3 percent black. Forty-five percent of families speak English at home, while 25 percent speak Spanish, and 23 percent speak an Asian language.[1]

In school, Vietnamese American and other Asian American students have done very well, even those growing up in low-income, non-English-speaking families. As a result, the generation educated in the United States has moved rapidly into the middle class. By contrast, Hispanics have much less success in school and much less social mobility.

Gunderson High is an ethnically and economically diverse school of more than 1,200 students. Some students—usually the children of educated, middle-class, and/or Asian parents—do well enough to go on to college. Others—usually the children of poorly educated Hispanic parents—drop out or just barely make it to a diploma. Overall, test scores are near the California average.

As young teachers, Lippman and Andaluz created programs in the humanities and American Studies, hoping to get Hispanic students to college. One day, they asked themselves a question: If these programs didn't exist, how many of our students would go to college?

"All of them," Andaluz concluded. "We were working with Hispanic students who were doing well coming in to high school and were going to college with us or without us. We weren't making a difference."

Meanwhile, Hispanic students from downtown—kids from poor and blue-collar immigrant families—were lost in the system. Half dropped out before they earned a "passport to the Global Community."

Lippman and Andaluz coached basketball and discovered many of their players had no college plans. They pushed everyone to apply, helped them all to complete the paperwork, and sent them off to college. But that didn't make a difference either. "Within six months, they were all back home," says Andaluz. "They weren't prepared to do college work."

The 50 percent of Hispanic students who earned a Gunderson diploma rarely went much further in their education. Some enrolled in community college but usually had to take remedial classes. Overall, only 2 percent of Gunderson's Hispanic graduates went on to the University of California, and 8 percent to San Jose State or other California State University campuses. Even in that top 10 percent, a majority had to take remedial English or math—or both—in college. Many never completed a degree.

Successful students from low-income Hispanic immigrant families were like needles in a haystack, Andaluz and Lippman concluded. They didn't want to spend their careers sharpening a few needles. "We wanted to educate the haystack," says Andaluz.

What if downtown students were pushed through a rigorous college prep curriculum, with lots of extra help to make sure they kept up? What if they were held to real standards? Forced to develop strong work habits? Linked to opportunities for internships and scholarships?

Lippman and Andaluz couldn't make a difference at Gunderson. It was too big. They needed their own school.

Jennifer Andaluz was raised by her divorced mother in a blue-collar neighborhood in Pleasanton, a small town east of San Jose. Her mother, who worked as a saleswoman, had moved to California after reading about the community college system. She wanted her four children to have a chance to go to college. But Jennifer's older brothers never tried, and her sister dropped in and out for years before earning a degree. Jennifer, the baby of the family, didn't seem to be college material either. She was a mediocre student, sleepwalking through school. Some days in middle school, she'd cut class, go home, and watch *All My Children*. It was more interesting than anything that might happen in class. Only sports motivated her to show up.

One day, when she was 15 years old, a former exchange student talked to her Spanish class about living in Europe. It sounded cool. Jennifer applied to Youth for Understanding. Someone must have seen some potential in her that had gone unnoticed up until that point. To her surprise, she was accepted.

Before she'd thought about what she was getting into, she was in Spain, living in a book-filled house with an educated, cosmopolitan family. Her American family watched TV. Her Spanish family talked about politics, about ideas, about the world. She was embarrassed that they knew more about American politics than she did, that they owned Hemingway novels and she'd never heard of him. She was miserable, but she was intrigued. Jennifer realized that it was possible to have ideas that related to something larger than you and your friends and your favorite TV star. And she started to read books. She fell in love with reading.

Back in Pleasanton, she combined high school and community college classes to graduate in one year, despite the school's refusal to recognize the credits she'd earned in Spain. She wanted to go to UC-Santa Cruz because it was by the beach, but couldn't get in with a 2.5 grade point average (GPA) and below-average SAT scores. (She'd never heard of the SATs till her counselor told her she needed to take the test.)

So she went to a Santa Cruz community college, working as a waitress and a house cleaner to pay for rent and food. No longer a sleepwalker, she earned excellent grades.

She'd known since her time in Spain that she wanted to be a teacher, like her host mother. She transferred to UC-Santa Cruz, where she earned a history degree and a teaching credential.

In Spain, Andalusians had praised her lisp. "You're a real Andaluz," they said. In honor of her life-changing year, she chose to be Jennifer Andaluz, and began her new life with a new name.

Greg Lippman grew up in the Carmel Valley, one of three children in an educated, affluent family of Jewish ethnicity. He went to an elite private school and then on to Princeton.

Not till his first semester in college did Lippman discover what failure feels like. The low point occurred the day he broke up with his girlfriend and discovered he'd earned the lowest score of anyone in his organic chemistry section. It was humiliating. Then he tried to buy 20 cents of detergent; the machine took his quarter and gave him no change. "I wanted to go home," he recalls. "I called my mother to complain." He mimics an adolescent whine, "Princeton won't give me my nickel!"

Lippman stuck it out, confident even in the depths of misery that he could handle Princeton. "I had the crazy presumption that I would survive," he says.

It occurred to him that he didn't have to take organic chemistry, having long since abandoned the idea of following his father into medicine.

Lippman thought he wanted to be a novelist, but he was rejected three times when he applied for admission to a creative writing seminar. So he chose an unfashionable career for Princetonians: high school teacher. "I had 'O captain, my captain' fantasies of going into a ghetto neighborhood and saving everyone," he says.

Teaching was a way to ground those fantasies in reality. After graduating with a degree in English literature, he earned a master's degree in education at Stanford.

He went to Budapest to teach English for two years. There, in the country his relatives had fled in 1956, he met his future wife. They moved to San Jose, and Lippman took a job teaching at Gunderson.

In his second year, he noticed an outrageously outspoken new teacher at a faculty meeting. He invited Jennifer Andaluz for ice cream.

Despite their different backgrounds, they were both confident, impatient, adventurous, and willing to make waves. Both believed the system was failing its most vulnerable students. And they thought they could do something about it.

"Some would say we're arrogant," says Andaluz.

Many of their Gunderson colleagues did say that. Most of the rest said they were crazy.

After four years at Gunderson, Lippman left to teach at Eastside Prep, a no-tuition private school in all-minority East Palo Alto, and to study education administration at Stanford.

Eastside Prep is the vision of a fanatically determined man named Chris Bischof. While a Stanford student, Bischof started a basketball and tutoring program to motivate black and Hispanic students. He earned a teaching credential and became a middle-school teacher in East Palo Alto. But he saw that his students and his basketball players weren't ready for high school. They'd be bused to whiter, richer towns—East Palo Alto's only high school had closed in the 1970s—where most would drop out. Bischof raised money from Silicon Valley philanthropists to start a private high school featuring very small classes—and a very good basketball team. In 2000, all eight students in the graduating class went on to four-year colleges. One got a full scholarship to Stanford.

Lippman saw hope at Eastside Prep. With high expectations and hard work, low-income minority students could master tough academic classes and go on to college. But it wasn't going to happen in a big high school staffed by bickering teachers. Not without a real consensus on the school's goals, priorities, and strategies. Not without buy-in from parents, students, and teachers.

Lippman and Andaluz met in coffee shops to plan the revolution. It was 1999, the peak of the Silicon Valley boom. All around them, enterprising people were turning their ideas into high-tech start-ups. "There was all that start-up excitement in the air," says Andaluz. "We thought: We can do this. It was a crazy idea."

The two teachers decided to start a charter high school to prepare San Jose's underachieving Hispanic students for four-year colleges. Andaluz was 27 years old; Lippman was 30.

Unlike Eastside Prep, which takes students who are the most likely to succeed because of their motivation and academic skills, a charter school would have to take all comers. But, as a public school, it wouldn't face Bischof's massive fund-raising burden.

By creating a charter, Lippman and Andaluz hoped to have the best of both worlds: the independence of a private school and the tax dollars of a public school. California law had been amended to make it easier to open a charter school. Lippman and Andaluz read up on charters. They'd need to persuade San Jose Unified School District or another district to grant a five-year charter to run a high school. The state would provide about $5,000 per student, then the average state funding at the high school level. They figured they'd need to double that through their own fund-raising to pay for 20-student classes, an eight-hour school day, counselors, tutorials, college field trips, and space in high-priced downtown San Jose.

Lippman and Andaluz started by gauging community support. Did anybody want the kind of school they wanted to create? They went to Father Mateo Sheedy, a community activist and pastor of Sacred Heart parish, which serves poor and working-class Hispanic families in central San Jose. Sheedy's church also had a building that might be turned into a school.

Sheedy told Lippman and Andaluz that he'd badgered the Jesuits at Santa Clara University to grant an annual scholarship for a student in his parish—and then searched in vain for a graduating senior who qualified for Santa Clara. Few children of Mexican immigrants were taking college-prep classes. Most weren't graduating from high school.

His dream was to use his building to start a Catholic middle school to keep Sacred Heart boys out of gangs and on track for college. If he could send them on to a small, character-driven, academic school geared to Hispanic students, maybe Santa Clara would have to make good on that scholarship offer. Sheedy didn't care that the charter school would be public, not Catholic. He told Lippman and Andaluz that their idea was the answer to his prayer.

The priest was a sick man, fighting a losing battle with lung cancer. But he had the heart to work for a better future for his parishioners' children. He didn't give Downtown College Prep just his blessing: he gave the school organizers vital help in reaching Hispanic parents, community leaders, politicians, and philanthropists. After Lippman and Andaluz talked to Sheedy, the DCP idea wasn't so crazy anymore. "Father Mateo decided this school would happen," says Lippman.

To connect with potential students and parents and try out their ideas, Lippman and Andaluz organized Summer Bridge, a free skill-building program for underachieving middle schoolers. Lippman's parents donated the money for the program; San Jose State provided classroom space. Middle school counselors in San Jose recommended students, mostly Hispanic, who were struggling in school.

Expecting the usual summer school snooze, Bridge students found themselves sweating through reading and math skills in an academic boot camp with Lippman and Andaluz as their drill sergeants. But, once they got over the shock, students got hooked on the attention and the sense of purpose. Their parents wanted more. Bridge parents began meeting with Lippman and Andaluz to discuss a charter high school.

The two teachers quit their jobs to work on the charter plans full time. Lippman lived on the salary of his wife, a financial analyst. Andaluz drew $700 a month from grants she'd raised and drew down her savings. They set about writing a charter they could sell to San Jose Unified's school board.

DCP's office was a corner table at a downtown Starbucks. They'd sit with a laptop computer and work on the unglamorous details of creating a school with the academic rigor of Eastside Prep that would be open to students who weren't going to make it at a large high school. They also were inspired by Deborah Meier's work in East Harlem, where she created a small high school that sent 90 percent of its low-income minority students to college. They read up on the small schools' movement, which advocates creating schools with a sense of community, in which students and teachers know each other and nobody can get lost in the shuffle.

Lippman and Andaluz decided to carve out separate roles.

As executive director, Andaluz would run the Across the Bridge Foundation, which would be the school's parent organization. She'd serve as DCP's financial manager, fund-raiser, and spokeswoman. She'd be the boss.

Lippman would be principal, running the daily operations of the school, meeting with parents and students, hiring and supervising teachers.

They agreed on the basics. Downtown College Prep would be a small school with 400 students. Its mission would be to prepare underachievers to succeed at four-year universities. The school would recruit Mexican-American students in downtown's poor and working-class neighborhoods with less than a C average and students who'd be the first in the family to go to college. The school's culture would value hard work and academic achievement. DCP would pay its nonunion teachers salaries comparable to San Jose Unified's pay but would ask them to work an eight-hour school day.

Working Father Sheedy's network, Lippman and Andaluz recruited powerful allies to DCP's advisory board.

Ron Gonzales, San Jose's first Mexican-American mayor, had coordinated Hewlett-Packard's education philanthropy. He too had fantasized about starting a school for Hispanic students. Gonzales promised city loans to help with start-up costs.[2]

Robert Caret, president of San Jose State University (SJSU), was interested. Half of SJSU freshmen must take remedial English and/or remedial math; the numbers are higher for Hispanics. Caret wanted more Hispanic students who were prepared to succeed and saw Downtown College Prep as a natural partner for his downtown university.

Tony Ridder, CEO of Knight Ridder Corporation, donated money and linked Andaluz to Silicon Valley executives and foundations. Eventually, he agreed to serve on the board of trustees.[3]

With strong political connections and the backing of their Summer Bridge students' parents, the founders made their pitch to San Jose Unified Superintendent Linda Murray and Assistant Superintendent Joanne Mendoza.

San Jose Unified is a banana-shaped district of 32,000 students attending 45 elementary, middle, and high schools. In the north, which includes the downtown area, most students come from low- and moderate-income Hispanic families; in the suburban south, middle- and upper-middle-class white and Asian-American families predominate. Students on the east and west sides of the city attend schools in several dozen smaller districts, a legacy of San Jose's rapid growth by annexation.

In 1985, Mexican American parents won a desegregation lawsuit against San Jose Unified, which created magnet schools to encourage voluntary integration. The plaintiffs agreed to return to neighborhood elementary schools in 1998 in exchange for initiatives to boost the achievement of Hispanic students, who now make up half the enrollment.

When they met with district administrators, Andaluz and Lippman admitted DCP would take students and therefore per-student funding from the district. But it would take the high-cost, high-aggravation students: kids earning D's and F's, kids still struggling with English. If the school worked, San Jose Unified could brag about the success of its Hispanic students. If it flopped, the district could blame the charter. Not that Andaluz put it that way exactly. She'd learned tact—belatedly—in the Gunderson school reform wars. She sold DCP as a partner, not a competitor, in San Jose Unified's search for educational excellence. Murray and Mendoza bought it. Later, Mendoza became deputy state superintendent, giving DCP a friend in California's Department of Education.

Many superintendents and school board members feel threatened by a charter school, especially one that is implicitly criticizing the district's education of minority students. They're not used to competing for students and believe they're locked in by rules that the charter doesn't have to follow. If a charter takes students, and the state funding that goes with them, the district still has its fixed costs for administration but fewer dollars. When too many students opt out, the district has the political agony of closing a school.

In states where only a school district can approve a charter in its territory, very few charter schools are created. If the new school is chartered without district approval, district staff may obstruct the search for a building, recruitment of students, and grant applications. Sometimes, state funding isn't passed along in time: In 2004, a coalition of seven charter schools sued Los Angeles Unified to get special education funding passed through without large deductions for services the district wasn't providing.[4] Charter founders are bombarded with paperwork and legal quibbles. District administrators can make life hell for an unwanted charter school.

That didn't happen in San Jose. Superintendent Murray, frustrated by the poor performance of Hispanic students and eager to try something new, gave DCP genuine support and encouraged the district staff to see DCP as a source of pride for San Jose Unified. She urged the board to grant a charter.

Late in 1999, Andaluz presented the school's budget to the board. In addition to state funding, geared to the average per-student spending at the high school level, DCP would need to raise $811,000 in grants and donations to fulfill its mission. She already had raised most of the money.

The teachers' union grumbled but spent no political capital trying to stop a done deal. DCP had the superintendent and the mayor, Silicon Valley and Sacred Heart, the *San Jose Mercury News,* and parents named Ramirez, Resendez, Ruiz, Fernandez, and Flores, who asked in Spanish and English for a school designed for their children. On a unanimous vote, the school board granted the charter.

Now DCP's founders needed to persuade the parents of 100 ninth graders to take a chance on a school that didn't yet exist. They had a group of parents whose kids had been involved in Summer Bridge; they had cousins and friends of Bridge students. But they needed more.

Lippman and Andaluz turned to Sacred Heart's bookkeeper, Florina Gallegos, a woman with a passion for education and a valuable network. If Father Mateo Sheedy was the patron saint of DCP, Florina Gallegos became its godmother.

She was 15 when she moved from Mexico to San Jose. Her father had abandoned the family; her mother had died. Speaking no English, she was placed in low-level high school classes that ended her dream of a college education.

Florina married Lawrence Gallegos, who'd been a classmate at Lincoln High. They started their oldest child in public school and went faithfully to PTA meetings but eventually gave up on making a difference in the public school system. Florina's Sacred Heart job helped pay Catholic school tuition for their three children. Lawrence worked two jobs, as a county social worker and airline baggage loader. They stayed in their low-income neighborhood and invested in their children's schooling.

Lawrence and Florina Gallegos became founding members of People Acting in Community Together (PACT), a church-based group that lobbies for better schools, after-school tutoring programs, housing, and other local needs. They helped start Biblioteca Latinoamericana, the city's Spanish-language library.

Florina Gallegos knew how to organize. She arranged for Andaluz to speak at Mass on Sunday at Sacred Heart and other churches. She set up a series of coffees at which Lippman and Andaluz ate Mexican pastries with prospective parents. Most importantly, DCP became part of Florina's family network.

She talked her sister, Irene Zuniga, into helping stuff DCP information in Sacred Heart's church bulletin. After a few hours working with Lippman and Andaluz, Zuniga decided DCP was the right school for her oldest son—and for the students she met at the dentist's office where she was a receptionist. Whenever a family entered the office with an eighth grader, Zuniga asked about the child's high school plans and made a pitch for DCP. "I recruited a dozen students for that first class," she says.

She recruited herself, too: Irene Zuniga left the dentist's office to work for Lippman as school secretary and office manager. Her husband, Ruben Zuniga, became a DCP board member.

Finally, Florina Gallegos found DCP a key teacher, her daughter, Alicia. Alicia Gallegos, 24, was completing a master's degree in education policy at Harvard. She wanted to be an education advocate or policy maker, not a teacher. Home for spring break, she gave in to her mother's nagging and met Lippman for coffee at Starbucks. Not knowing it was a job interview at DCP's unofficial office, she wore blue jeans.

Lippman asked Alicia Gallegos to create and teach DCP's most critical course. College Readiness would teach underachievers the habits and skills of serious students: how to take effective notes, how to summarize a reading, how to plan study time, how to organize a research paper—and whatever else Gallegos thought students would need to succeed in high school and college.

Gallegos wavered. Studying education at Harvard was no preparation for teaching at a start-up charter school in San Jose. But, like Lippman and Andaluz, Gallegos wanted to make a difference.

Her mother told her to take the job, but it was Sheedy who persuaded her. "I'm here because Padre Mateo wanted me to be here," Gallegos says. She became the only Mexican American teaching the academic core, the only teacher who'd grown up in the neighborhood.

DCP found an experienced math teacher, Aaron Srugis, at a New York City magnet school. Lippman and Andaluz couldn't afford to fly him out, so they offered him a job over the phone. Frustrated by the bureaucracy in New York, Srugis took it.

The school's dean of students, Jill Case, was a veteran middle-school counselor who'd steered students to Summer Bridge. Her contacts with other counselors proved invaluable in recruiting students, especially those with learning problems.

DCP's other teachers were a few years or a few months out of college. Lippman and Andaluz hired for brains, energy, and a commitment to the school's mission. Few applications were from Mexican American teachers. Except for Gallegos and the science teacher, a black man named Na'eem Salaam, their academic teachers were white.

However, at a recreation program called Inner City Games, Lippman found Jose Arreola, who was hired to teach physical education, organize activities, and do anything else that needed to be done. Arreola had started out in a tough neighborhood in Southern California. His parents sent him to Catholic school to keep him out of trouble. When they could afford to, they moved to a white middle-class area with better schools. In high school, a counselor urged Arreola not to take advanced classes. "I realized then that, because I'm Hispanic, I'd have to fight to get a first-rate education," he says. He did. While Arreola's friends from the old neighborhood ended up in gangs, he went to San Jose State. A natural leader, Arreola became a key part of the administration team.

DCP couldn't stay at Starbucks forever. Andaluz spent months looking for affordable space. But Silicon Valley was booming, and she couldn't pay dotcom rents.

Finally, she rented office space from the YWCA, which had folded its fitness center. But the YWCA building, which also included transitional housing for homeless women and children, wasn't big enough.

Andaluz discovered an evening law school that was willing to help out with classrooms that were empty during the day. She thought she had a deal. A real estate agent on the board warned her the landlord wouldn't want a bunch of teenagers in the building. She didn't listen. In midsummer, under pressure from the landlord, the law school backed out. It seemed to be a disaster.

But a few weeks before school was set to open, Andaluz reached a deal with Saint Paul's Methodist Church, eight blocks from the Y and across the street from San Jose State. Saint Paul's had several classrooms that had been used as a day-care center, and space that could be turned into classrooms with the use of curtains. If the Y's former fitness center also was divided into classrooms, there'd be room for 100 students.

Lippman, the principal, could set up an office at the church; Andaluz would remain at the Y.

DCP would have to bus or walk students between the two buildings during two 20-minute transport periods and lunch. The school would need more staff to supervise two sites and keep track of students. It was a huge headache, but Andaluz made the most of it. When students walked between Saint Paul's and the Y, they could check out the San Jose State campus, their goal.

Saint Paul's was a mess. That turned into a plus too. Dozens of parents, students, and DCP supporters showed up on a weekend to scrub restrooms, paint the walls, scrape ancient grease in the kitchen, and pull weeds in the scrubby patch of ground by the front door.

Betsy Doss, the mayor's education policy adviser and a DCP board member, cleaned the kitchen with Selena's mother, a janitor. Irene Zuniga led the weed-choppers' brigade. Painting was supervised by a father who was a painting contractor.

A year later, Andaluz and Lippman could name every person who had showed up at Saint Paul's, and the job he or she had done to get the building ready. A bond had been forged.

"Where DCP Stands" is the school's credo:

1. High expectations for all: DCP's school model is characterized by high standards, a rigorous curriculum, a strict code of conduct, and a commitment to college success for all students.
2. Small school structure promotes a uniform school culture: DCP's learning environment stands in stark contrast to that of the large, urban public school. DCP's Culture of Achievement is defined by specific values—personalization, accountability, and *ganas*—the will to be successful.
3. Parent involvement: DCP parents are involved in all aspects of the school—student discipline, academic support, teacher and student recruitment, and community advocacy. DCP's parent education program helps parents learn about DCP's academic program, college opportunities, and adolescent development.

4

downtown college purgatory

Downtown College Prep staged an opening fiesta on August 30, 2000. Mayor Gonzales welcomed the first class of 102 ninth graders and their parents. A mariachi band serenaded Silicon Valley leaders as balloons floated into the smoggy sky. The honored speaker was Father Mateo Sheedy, now nearing the end of his long battle with cancer. He died six weeks later.

That first year was "collective insanity," says Lippman.

"We didn't know if the school would make it," says Andaluz.

With Summer Bridge, word of mouth at Sacred Heart, referrals from middle-school counselors, and Zuniga's dental patients, DCP got the students it wanted: Eighty-three percent of the first class was Hispanic, with white and mixed-ethnic students, a few blacks, and a few Asians making up the remainder.

Most students had earned D's and F's in middle school; some were repeating ninth grade. Some had been labeled learning disabled, hyperactive, or emotionally disordered. Nearly half were "English learners," meaning they weren't completely fluent in English; a few spoke no English at all. Most also fit the second target category: They'd be the first in their family to go to college. "We wanted Hispanic students who were failing in school but weren't in jail," says Lippman.

Some students chose DCP because they wanted a chance at college, or because their parents wanted them to go to college. For many, the draw was a small school that would pay attention to their needs, a safe school with no gangs or drugs, a fresh chance after failing elsewhere. But, by and large, the pioneer class was ambivalent, at best, about DCP. Their friends were going to Lincoln High or Willow Glen or San Jose Academy, and they wanted to go along with the crowd. Mostly they came because their parents made them.

Lippman and Andaluz quickly realized they'd underestimated their students' academic problems: Most students read at the fourth- through sixth-grade level; some students had made it to high school with second- or third-grade reading skills.

Jorge, the youngest of ten children, stumbled over the phrase "ride the carousel" on a test of English language skills, reading it as "ride the carrot salad." It didn't make sense, but Jorge was accustomed to reading things that made no sense to him.

By then, Lippman, Andaluz, and their teachers felt as if they were hip-deep in carrot salad. Rejecting despair, they turned to humor. Jorge's misreading became the informal school motto. The lead math teacher, Aaron Srugis, proposed printing a T-shirt: "Downtown College Purgatory: Ride the Carrot Salad!"

Srugis was trying to teach algebra to students who couldn't do simple arithmetic. The clunky old calculators—long obsolete before they were donated—didn't help. Many students didn't know when to add or multiply, where the lowest common denominator might be lurking, or why they should care. They didn't know why $2 \times 1/2 = 1$; negative numbers were a mystery. "Sometimes I'm teaching first-grade math," Srugis said. "Here's the ones column. This is the tens column." A few students had solid math skills and number sense. For most, it was all carrot salad.

Lippman and Andaluz set aside their dream that all DCP students would take Advanced Placement (AP) calculus in twelfth grade. Their new dream was that all DCP students would pass algebra by the end of tenth grade, with the help of summer school.

As progressive educators, they disliked tracking and believed all students should take college-prep classes, regardless of their reading level or English proficiency. All students took College Readiness, English, History of the Americas, algebra, science, and Spanish, plus technology, physical education, and a weekly Mock Trial class to build critical thinking skills.

Literacy was the priority in every class. Teachers followed a structured plan developed by a consultant to build students' reading, writing, and analytical skills. Even in math and science, students wrote "accordion paragraphs"—they folded the paper in accordion-style pleats when first learning the format—that required a thesis supported by facts and summed up with a conclusion. To improve students' comprehension, teachers taught vocabulary words in every class; the week's words were posted on white boards in the halls. (When students were told to supply their own graph paper or pay a nickel for the teacher's graph paper, a student wrote that Srugis was demanding "tribute," a History of the Americas word.)

Students who spoke little English were clustered in the same class and immersed in English. Roberto, who'd learned almost no English in two years at a San Jose middle school, was suffering visibly as he tried to keep up. Larissa, newly arrived from Mexico with no English at all, was driving teachers crazy.

At first, the school provided no extra instruction for students with limited English, not wanting to pull them out of mainstream classes. "Big mistake," says Lippman. By midyear, DCP hired an English as a Second Language tutor to work with non-English-speaking students outside class time.

Homework is to DCP what rice is to China. Teachers in every class assigned homework every day. Students needed to build strong work habits to have any hope of catching up academically and preparing for college-level work. Yet, with a few exceptions, incoming ninth graders weren't used to doing homework regularly. Some hadn't done homework ever. Somehow they'd been passed along anyhow, with no work habits and a string of F's. Again and again, Lippman and his teachers hammered in their simple message: Do your homework. Every day, you'll have homework. You have to do it every day. You can't pass your classes and go to college if you're not willing to do your homework. So, do your homework.

DCP teachers called home when a student missed two assignments— and three assignments, and four, five, and six assignments. Students were supposed to get a parent to sign their daily homework log, showing what was due in each class. Soon, every teacher was calling almost every parent.

Students built up endless detentions for not doing homework, for not doing the homework log, and for not going to detention, which met before school at 8:00 A.M.

"We made a lot of mistakes that first year," says Lippman. "We threw everything at our ninth graders right from the start. Students had homework in six different academic classes. We nearly killed them."

Virtually every DCP student tells the same story: "I hated it, at first. I wanted to quit, but my mother told me to keep trying. After a while, I got used to it."

Once students crossed over—sometimes in a few months, sometimes at the end of the year—and started to do their homework, they started to improve. But they began so far behind that it was a long, hard trek to reach a C-, the minimum acceptable grade in an academic class.

At the end of the first semester, nearly half the class was on academic probation with less than a 1.0 (D) grade point average. While 11 students were on the honor roll with a B average or better, another 11 had a perfect 0.0.

"I'm afraid the students hate us," said Lippman halfway through the first year. "So many of them are failing. They're trying harder than they ever did before, and they're still failing."

One day, volunteering in a Mock Trial class, I asked Gil whether he'd read the witness statement. "He can't read," a friend of his said. "No, really. He can't." Gil shrugged. He was failing every class.

Gina, a round-faced girl, would raise her hand, then say she'd forgotten what she wanted to say or didn't know how to say it in English.

"Say it in Spanish," Andaluz said.

"Um, I don't have the words in Spanish either," Gina said.

I ran into Srugis in the hall on a bad day. "They don't think," he said of a particularly frustrating math class. "They don't *want* to think. They don't think they *need* to think." He laughed at his own moment of despair and moved on to his next class.

Srugis and the other teachers kept trying to find ways to wake up their sleepwalking students. With each other, they were brutally honest about the problems they faced, in the faith that defining a problem correctly would be the first step to solving it. The ethos of the school demanded honesty. In front of their students, they hid their doubts and preached persistence, resilience, *ganas, ganas,* and more *ganas.*

Lippman began talking about "the five-year plan." DCP would spend the first year preparing students for ninth grade, then four more years teaching a college-prep curriculum. But so many students were already a year or two behind. It wasn't possible to ask them to stay in high school till they were 20, he decided.

So he concentrated on closing the gap. If ninth graders starting acting and thinking like serious students, they'd make it to a four-year college with a decent chance for a degree. DCP wasn't prepping students for Stanford, Lippman reminded himself. The goal was San Jose State or another California State University school, with the best students going to Santa Clara, Cal Poly, UC-Santa Cruz, maybe UC-Davis. That was realistic.

I asked Andaluz whether she felt that some DCP students might be better off at a school that prepared them for a union apprenticeship or a vocational program in the community college system. "They all want to qualify for a good job," I said. "But it seems like a lot of your students would like to do it with as little classroom time as possible."

"If someone else wants to start a vocational high school in San Jose, we'll help them in any way we can," said Andaluz. "But that's not our thing. We need to stick to our mission and not dilute it."

Discipline was tight. "Some people think we're protofascist here," Lippman said. He shrugged. "We'll do whatever it takes," he said.

All students wore uniforms, with a ban on red and blue, gang colors, and such gang fashions as stuffing an extra sock under the tongue of a sneaker. They hated the uniforms, which they associated with elementary school. But parents appreciated the school's vigilant attempts to keep out gang influences.

About two dozen in the first class were problem students, frequently in trouble for scrawling gang graffiti on walls, for rude language, and for disrespect. DCP's most rigorous student contract—one referral means suspension; two mean expulsion—was named after the worst offender. The contract's namesake was expelled.

Toward the end of the school year, just as ninth graders seemed to be adjusting to the role of serious student, eight students were caught drinking on campus. They were put on independent study and banned from school grounds for the remainder of the year.

Not all charters are run like DCP. In the book *Upstart Startup,* James Nehring describes his tenure as principal of a "democratic" charter school near Boston with 12- to 14-year-old students. One morning, he saw a "large, ornate '69' with sperm swimming happily around it" chalked on the sidewalk in front of the school. He consulted several teachers before deciding that it was indeed "inappropriate." In addition to marking a sidewalk that served other tenants, "the explicit sexuality of the drawing will be offensive to some" and "the act of making a drawing of such an obviously controversial nature in such a prominent location without having first discussed it with anyone charged with responsibility for the school is presumptuous and insensitive." Nehring called the whole school together so the adults could "bear witness" that the drawing violated school norms. But his teachers weren't willing to condemn the drawing, while students defended the image as "free speech." There was no consensus that the adults were in charge.[1]

DCP doesn't promise to be a democracy. The adults are in charge. Greg Lippman, Jennifer Andaluz, and their staff don't tolerate a scrap of paper on the ground, much less a lewd drawing. When they started the school, creating a community of learners was the top priority, and they believed order was necessary to do it. Students who didn't want what DCP had to offer were told they could go elsewhere. But they also were asked to give it a try, and most did stick with it. Even students who resented DCP's rules and resisted homework loved the attention they got there.

Even in the year of carrot salad, there were signs of hope. One girl got one D and a bunch of F's on her first report card. She decided to start doing homework; she asked her parents to quiz her on vocabulary words. She was a B student by the end of the year.

DCP fielded a coed soccer team but couldn't afford uniforms for everyone. So playing time was determined by grade point average. Several soccer-mad students raised their grades to get on the field.

The school took students to the Oregon Shakespeare Festival (OSF) in Ashland. At a discussion about one of the plays, an OSF staffer asked about the social stratification at their school. Did students group themselves by ethnicity or social class? Who was on top of the social scale?

To Andaluz's delight, students said grades determine status at DCP. "They said the top kids were on the honor roll." These were kids who'd jeered diligent students as "schoolboy" or "schoolgirl" in middle school, who'd thought academics were reserved for whites or Asians. No Mexicans need apply themselves. "It's cool to make honor roll here," says Andaluz. "That just blew me away."

Encouraged by Bob Grimm, the retired high-tech executive who chairs DCP's board, four boys—Rico, Rajiv, and brothers Adam and Bill—entered a countywide competition called the Tech Challenge, which attracts top public and private schools. The team had to build a remote-controlled car that could climb a ramp. Competing against older students, the DCP team came in fourth.

As a volunteer aide in Andaluz's Monday Mock Trial class, I started to see students transform themselves.

Roberto sat with Gil and two other boys at a table in the back. Whenever there was a group assignment, Roberto did 90 percent of the work, despite knowing the least English. When students had to practice cross-examination, Roberto played the lawyer, questioning the witness in English. "Look at Roberto," Andaluz told the other students with limited English. "If he can do it, you can do it." His back-table buddies did very little work and made little progress. Slowly and painfully, Roberto learned to speak and write English.

Then there was Selma. She always had her hand up, asking for help, so I spent a lot of time with her. A tiny girl with mascara-black eyelashes, blue eyelids, and bright red lips, she claimed to understand nothing. I'd explain and explain, and, finally, I'd just show her what questions the prosecution could ask an expert witness or what key points the defense needed to make.

Eventually, I realized that Selma was playing me. Helplessness was her strategy: All her intelligence was devoted to getting *me* to do her work. I tried to resist, but Selma was too clever for me. Of course, she was getting D's and F's. Her strategy wasn't really effective. But it was all she had.

Then one day, Selma crossed over. She asked me a question, listened to the answer, and started doing the work. No more questions. No more helpless act. And, I noticed, less makeup. From that day forward, Selma did her own work. She was a student. She began her climb to a C average.

In spring, students took the statewide exams: Only 23 percent were reading at or above the national average; 29 percent were average or above in math. However, they'd moved up on San Jose Unified's reading exam from a median fifth-grade reading level to a seventh-grade level, gaining two years in less than a year. The best news was from the high school graduation exam: Sixty-four percent passed the English language arts portion, better than other downtown high schools and equal to the state average.

The honor roll doubled to 22 students.

Lippman and Andaluz decided to add Verbal Reasoning (remedial English), Math Reasoning (remedial math), and English as a Second Language classes for ninth graders in the school's second year.

Many students had to go to summer school to raise D's and F's to C's, if possible. The University of California and the second-tier California State University system don't accept grades lower than C in college-prep courses. After summer school, 40 percent of students were told they'd have to repeat algebra. Nine would have to repeat the ninth grade, including Larissa and Gil. All agreed to repeat. DCP believed they could learn, and, despite their frustrations, they wanted to believe, too. One boy showed up in September with a gang tattoo on his face and was not allowed to enroll unless he removed it. He chose the tattoo.

Roberto, now speaking English, passed to tenth grade, just barely. So did Pedro. Barbara, one of the group suspended for drinking, returned for tenth grade.

Alicia Gallegos had bet the science teacher, Na'eem Salaam, that she'd quit teaching. She wasn't sure she'd survive the year. He left DCP to prep for medical school. She signed on for DCP's second year.

DCP demographics 2001–2002
Hispanic: 83 percent
Multiethnic: 7 percent
White: 5 percent
Black: 2 percent
Asian American: 2 percent

At the end of DCP's first year, a consultant surveyed students and talked to them in focus groups. Students said they felt pressured by teachers and by their parents to work harder than ever before. Most took pride in meeting the challenge; some complained it was too much on top of their family responsibilities.

Focus Groups: Students' Perspectives after Their First Year

How is DCP different from the school you used to attend?

- They expect more of you here. They notice more. They're on you to get your grades up. People notice faster.

- You're always being watched. You're under more surveillance than at a regular school. Everyone knows you. Any small thing you do you can get in trouble because they are always looking over you.
- It's stricter here! Definitely.

About homework:

- In my middle school I did not do homework. My teachers didn't care. The teachers didn't check it.
- They push you. They make you realize that you have to do it. We have no other choice. If you don't do it you fail, and the people don't want you to fail here—the teachers, the students, everyone.
- I changed. At first semester I didn't do my homework. I was just talking in classes. I got F's the first semester in math, history, and science. . . . In the second semester I started studying to do well. I went from F to a B in math. I got a C in science and a C in history.

At home:

- They (parents) ask about your homework and whether you did it or not. It's kind of uncomfortable because there are always people on your back. First you have your teachers; then you have your parents. It kind of gets annoying.
- Parents got our PSAT [Preliminary SAT] scores and they were low and then they went crazy. They were afraid it goes on your permanent record.
- Over here they get the parents more involved. They make them know what we're doing. If you don't tell them, anyway they're going to find out. We thought our parents wouldn't find out about our grades, but the school told them the grades are coming at a meeting.
- They sort of cheer me on. One side of my family went to college. My other side, they are losers. I guess that's where I get my laziness from. They cheer me on and say I can do it.

Friends outside DCP:

- My friends think it's stupid. They say, if you don't get into college, it was a waste of time.
- My friends may have A's and B's. I have some D's and C's and my friend says, "Ha, ha, I got better grades than you." But they don't learn as much. We're already learning physics and genetics!

We know you came here with the idea of going to college. Has the way you now imagine the future changed from when you first came to DCP?

- When I came here I thought it would be really hard to get into college. Now I think it's really simple. I know what to do: Have a good GPA; do activities. I didn't think GPA was a big deal. Now that I know, I can raise it.
- My parents want me to get a job. My family needs money now. I have no time. I have to help around the house.
- I used to think I'd work at McDonald's or Burger King. But now I think I will be a professional.

5

this is dcp!

"Yesterday, I had to clean up excrement smeared on the wall of the boys' bathroom," Greg Lippman tells his staff at a weekly meeting in the fall of 2001. "At first, I thought: 'What am I doing here? I'm the principal!' But then I realized that it's part of my job description. I have to deal with the crap they hand out, literally and figuratively."

Everyone laughs. A bit nervously, perhaps, but at least they're laughing.

In truth, Lippman and Andaluz are worried. They devoted the first year to creating a community where failing students could succeed. Now that hard-won learning environment is at risk. The second year's ninth graders have far more emotional and behavioral problems than the pioneer class. Disrespect for teachers, vandalism, and theft are plaguing the school.

Lippman sits at one end of the shoved-together tables in a classroom called Cal Poly. All the classrooms are named after universities. At 32, he is one of the oldest people in the room.

Most DCP teachers are in their twenties and have zero, one, or two years of classroom experience. None has a California teaching credential; most take night classes at San Jose State, across the street, to meet the requirements.

Alicia Gallegos, math teacher Aaron Srugis, and the ninth-grade humanities team, Angela Hensley and Jessica Rigby, are back for their second year teaching at DCP. Dan Greene, teaching math and an art/technology elective called Multi-Media, was an Americorps volunteer in the charter's first year. Laura DeRoche was a Teach for America English teacher for one year at Compton High in Los Angeles, before the chaos drove her to DCP. Her tenth-grade humanities partner, Shawn Gerth, taught history for a year at a 4,000-student high school in East San Jose. Math teacher Jesse Robinson taught for a year in New York City. Biology teacher Omar Safie and Integrated Science teacher Jeff Fox are novices.

Photography teacher Michelle Longosz has grassroots and high-level political connections, as well as a gift for connecting with students. She was involved in Oakland's push for charter schools and small schools with her husband, PACT organizer Matt Hammer, who's now working for small charter schools in heavily Hispanic East San Jose. Longosz's mother-in-law, Susan Hammer, is on the state board of education; her father-in-law, Phil Hammer, is a former San Jose Unified board member.

Rounding out the teaching staff are Itziar Aperribay, an elegant Basque woman who teaches Spanish, and sad-eyed Francisco Lopez, who teaches English as a Second Language, Spanish, and Verbal Reasoning.

Jose Arreola, now dean of activities, is back, along with counselor Jill Case, the dean of students. Steve Smith, a half-time counselor and half-time fund-raiser, has joined from Eastside Prep, the free all-minority private school that's a model for DCP. Vicky Evans, the unpaid college counselor, helped out at her children's upper-middle-class high school till she decided to lend her talents to a school that wasn't awash in volunteer help.

Lippman reminds the staff that last year's freshmen were no angels. He and Andaluz trade horror stories to illustrate what DCP already has survived. "Nobody here now is as crazy as James was last year," he says. He turns to Gallegos. "Remember, Alicia, when he was spinning around and around in a chair, with a paper bag on his head, screaming? Now he's on the Student Council."

"Our turning point last year was when we expelled Joshua for marijuana possession," says Andaluz. "He was a popular boy." "When he had to leave, that sent a message to the rest of the class. They knew we were serious."

Joshua's expulsion was Lippman's worst experience as principal, he says. He didn't sleep the night before the meeting that confirmed the expulsion, worrying that he was letting down Joshua's mother, who'd turned her son in after finding marijuana in his backpack and said, "I trust you to do the right thing." But he couldn't tolerate a little drug use in his school. Joshua had to go to protect the school community.

DCP's "affirmative discipline" resembles the "broken windows" theory of crime control. If the little things are let slide, Lippman warns, the big thing—turning F students into college students—will be impossible.

He stresses that students must be in the DCP uniform at all times: a black, white or gray polo shirt and khaki pants. If a student's sneakers have a red or blue stripe, it must be covered by masking tape. No gang color or symbol or style or attitude will be tolerated. "I don't want to see hooded sweatshirts," says Lippman.

Students are supposed to put their backpacks on the floor, out of the way, not piled on the tables. Sloppiness is a dangerous habit, Lippman tells the teachers. "I don't want to walk in your classroom and see seven back-packs on the table—then you wonder why your classroom is disorderly," says Lippman. "I shouldn't see kids in the back row dorking around."

Every day ends with a 60- or 75-minute tutorial period. Students must work for the entire period. "I see students packing up their books five minutes early," Lippman says. "That's not acceptable." Don't let students get away with anything, he warns. It all matters. It's not all good.

But Lippman also reminds teachers not to get angry in front of the students. "There is a curtain. Behind the curtain you can be whoever you are. But don't show your anger. We have broken kids here."

With a few exceptions, DCP students are the kids nobody else wanted, the kids nobody really believes can make it. The ninth graders ignore home-work assignments, then cut detention for failing to do homework. They carve on the tables, scribble graffiti on the walls, and rip the expensive di-viders that split space into classrooms. They watch Henry vandalize the bus.

"Kids aren't seeing this as *their* space," says Andaluz. "It's not *their* ta-bles, *their* chairs. The DCP experience is a transition from chaos to *this is mine*. We need to make kids feel responsible for what we are, where we are."

Not every student can be saved. But they all deserve a chance. "Re-member," says Lippman. "The kids who drive us nuts are the kids we want to be here."

Larissa drove everyone nuts in the school's first year. She'd arrived from Mexico with no English and no self-control. Teachers begged Lippman to expel her. But she stayed at DCP and returned to repeat ninth grade. The new Larissa is responsible, hard-working, committed to going to college—

and pregnant, Counselor Jill Case announces. In fact, though she doesn't look as if she's carrying any extra pounds, Larissa is eight months pregnant.

Her boyfriend has walked out, but her mother will help with the baby, Case says. Larissa wants to stay at DCP. The school will try to make it possible, without encouraging other girls to think that combining teen motherhood and school is easy.

"She won't be allowed to bring the baby to school," says Andaluz. "We don't want kids making a big fuss over how cute the baby is."

In Mexican villages, school ends with sixth grade. It's common for girls to marry and start a family in their teens. In San Jose, Hispanic girls who get pregnant in high school usually don't earn a diploma, though there are alternative schools for them. Alum Rock, an elementary district in East San Jose, has a program for "pregnant and parenting" girls in the sixth, seventh, and eighth grades.

DCP aims to give girls a reason to avoid teenage pregnancy, as well as information. Case promises to develop a sex ed program, perhaps as part of "advisory," a weekly discussion with a staff member and a group of 12 to 15 students.

Advisory hasn't been working well, so Case and Smith have reshuffled the groups to mix ninth and tenth graders. They hope the sophomores will pass on some of their maturity to the newcomers.

In the first mixed advisory, students were supposed to name their role models, and draw a symbol of each.

"James had Gandhi and Martin Luther King," says Gallegos. "Pedro had Hugh Hefner, which meant all the freshman boys decided *they* wanted Hefner. And Rajiv drew a picture of a chick and said his role model was Byron, because 'he's a chick magnet.'"

With that, it's time for the weekly assembly, which runs for 30 minutes. It's the only time all the students are together in one place. Under Arreola's direction, Leadership Club students have set up folding chairs in the church's multipurpose room.

The walls are decorated with giant "cell simile" posters from Omar Safie's biology class, which meets in the room. In one poster, the cell is a car with the Golgi complex as the gas tank, endoreticulum as the muffler, vacuole as the oil filter, nucleus as the engine, cell wall as the paint, ribosome as the pistons, and mitochondria as the gas pedal.

Another poster compares the cell to the human body with clothes as the cell wall.

A third poster describes the cell as a shopping mall.

At every assembly, students are honored for schoolwork, especially for progress. For this one, Andaluz reads the names of students who've done all their homework in two or more classes. As requested, students hold their applause. But when she calls Pedro's name, cheering breaks out. Students are amazed: Pedro did his homework? All his homework?

Pedro walks across the stage with a rolling gait that reminds me of a pirate—a jolly pirate: Pedro grins broadly and bows to the audience.

The good news: Students are cheering classmates for doing homework.

The bad news: At this point, only four of 200 students have done all their homework in all their classes.

The teachers perform a skit at the assembly. Safie, who coaches the four-man cross-country team, plays a track coach. Some of his runners are naturally speedy, he says. Others are not as talented, but they have *ganas*. Srugis, DeRoche, Robinson, and Greene have fun playing lazy, rude, cocky hares: "Can I go to the bathroom?" they whine repeatedly. Gallegos plays the hardworking turtle. In the first practice—a run around the room—she finishes last. But in the big race, supposedly a year later, Gallegos is the winner, while the lazy hares collapse in exhaustion before the finish.

"It's your fault," whines Greene to the coach. "You didn't train us properly."

His teammates correct him. He lost because he lacked *ganas* and didn't work hard.

Safie sums it up: "You can decide whether you have *ganas* or not. This isn't running. This is your life."

Subtlety is not a strong suit in DCP skits.

After the skit, Lippman speaks: "This school was founded to be something different, a place where people can trust each other. There are people on this campus who are breaking that trust. The values of this school are going to prevail. Those who are defacing the school, stealing out of backpacks, and showing disrespect for yourselves by disrespecting others will change or leave."

Four students come on stage. A girl says her cousin, who speaks little English, doesn't want to take her calculator to school because she's afraid it will be stolen. A boy says while he was at cross-country practice, his skateboard was stolen. Speaking for the Student Council, Byron and James urge students to trust each other and be trustworthy.

Then Jessica Rigby, the ninth-grade history teacher, speaks. "I taught in Los Angeles," she says. "The school was tagged all over the place; the bathrooms were disgusting. They had to lock everything up to prevent theft. People didn't care about the school. . . . I want to teach in a place where people know each other, where I can leave my backpack, where I can call your parents and they care. I drive here from San Francisco every day, two hours every day, with Ms. Robinson. We put so much time and energy into this place. . . . I had money and credit cards stolen from my wallet. . . . I want to leave my backpack out. This is DCP!"

Byron, tall, handsome, and cool, Rajiv's model of a chick magnet, concludes: "If you're brave enough to steal, are you brave enough to admit it? I doubt it. Be DCP! Be original."

The students erupt in applause that sounds genuine.

Then Lippman wraps up with another reminder that DCP is supposed to be a community. Usually, assembly ends with DCP's rhythmic clap, which goes from slow to fast. Gallegos took it from the farm workers' movement. "Instead of doing the clap, I want you to take 30 seconds to reflect on how to make DCP a better place," says Lippman. A room full of nearly 200 students on folding chairs becomes so still the only sound is the scratch of my pen. Students bow their heads as though they're praying. Henry looks as if he's praying for a miracle. Then the 30 seconds is up and the noisy, jostling horde of khaki-clad students stacks the plastic chairs and heads for class.

Half stay at Saint Paul's for math, science, Spanish, College Readiness, Multi-Media (graphic design), English as a Second Language, and Verbal Reasoning (VR). The rest walk to the Y for English, history, photography, advanced Spanish, and Critical Thinking (social issues).

To shoehorn 200 students into the two sites, PE was dropped so the church's largest room, used as the assembly room, lunchroom, and library, also could be used as a classroom for biology and VR. There was no room set aside for teachers; they sometimes ate or read in Lippman's small office as he worked.

At the Y, the copier was moved to create an oddly shaped teaching space. A small room used as a teacher's break room became a classroom several periods a day.

At both sites, some teachers float from room to room, so no space goes unused.

When students break into small groups for the weekly advisory session, several groups at the Y meet on the second-floor patio, also used for lunch in good weather. In the rainy season, groups meet in a small space with a couch at the foot of the steep stairs leading up to the classrooms or in the second-floor hallway; students eat lunch in their classrooms. At the church, small groups use either end of the back hallway or meet outside at rickety picnic tables set on a former driveway, now fenced off.

Case, who shares a tiny office with Evans at the Y, and Smith, who shares a similar office with Arreola, often take students outside to the picnic tables or patio for counseling sessions. It is impossible to have a private conversation inside at either site.

The crowding adds enormous stress to teachers' days, but sharing space also prevents the isolation that's common at many schools. Teachers don't close their doors and do their own thing in their own room. Most have no door to close and no room of their own.

Students grouse about having to set up, carry, and break down the lunch tables every day at the church, but they accept the crowded classrooms without complaint. When San Jose rents soared during the high-tech boom, low-income families doubled or tripled up in apartments; a family of five might live in a garage. DCP students are good at making do with very little space.

Andaluz and Lippman considered putting sophomores at the Y and freshmen at Saint Paul's. In the end, though, they decided it was more important to mix the rackety freshmen with the more focused sophomores. Last year's hard cases had grown into this year's role models.

Normally, a bus shuttles students between the sites during twice-daily transport periods. But on Wednesday, after the all-school assembly at the church, there are too many students to bus. So, 80 students and their teachers walk past the San Jose State campus to get to classes at the Y. DCP's uniformed students looked positively military compared to the college students shuffling along in T-shirts and baggy shorts.

To their right, they pass a giant campus parking garage and then concrete-heavy academic buildings surrounded by green lawns. On their left, they see scruffy student apartments, cottages, an occasional Victorian house, a 7-Eleven, a liquor store, and a tiny all-Vietnamese shopping center with a shoe store, a laundromat, a pool hall, and a deli favored by teachers. Near the Y, they go by a few panhandlers on the corner.

Sometimes, the walk leader takes the alternate route, cutting through the San Jose State campus, then past Jack in the Box and McDonald's, before reaching the Y.

DCP's dual campus also is within walking distance of The Tech (the city's high-tech museum), the San Jose Art Museum, the Center for the Performing Arts, and San Jose Repertory Theater. DCP photography students helped create a photo mural on one downtown wall. They are intensely proud of the mark they've made.

Andaluz, who leads today's walk to the Y, reminds students that San Jose State's campus is within their reach, if they do their homework and raise their grades. The Wednesday Walk may be an inconvenience, but it has become a DCP tradition.

Roberto gave a short speech at Open House:

"My brothers brought me from Mexico. They wanted me to have what they didn't have, education. My brother found out about DCP. I didn't want to come here. The main idea I didn't want to come was I didn't speak English. Now you see I am speaking English. (He pauses till the applause dies down.) I want to go to college. I have to take advantage of these opportunities. I want to say thank you to my brothers. I want you to be proud of what I'm doing."

6

vamos, caballeros

Alicia Gallegos comes in early on November 1 to help students who've volunteered to set up the Dia de los Muertos display in the assembly room. On the Mexican Day of the Dead, it's traditional to leave gifts for departed relatives. Gallegos has expanded the tradition to include students' photos, mementos, and writing to honor living people they admire, as well as the dead.

Neary brought her mother's photo; her essay praised the *ganas* that enabled her mother to escape from Cambodia.

Gil wrote: "Picture of my friends that died in stab or gun wounds. They were good friends to me and never did nothing wrong to me. . . . It feels weird and different when you don't see them no more."

Gallegos honors Father Mateo Sheedy, who helped the charter school get its start and died a few months after its opening. He was her parish priest at Sacred Heart; he was also her friend.

Gallegos is one of only two Mexican American teachers in the school's second year. It's important to her to represent Mexican culture in a positive light. Gallegos grew up in a neighborhood where only 1 percent of students graduate from college. She knows many DCP families from the neighborhood or from church; three students are her cousins, the office manager at the Saint Paul's site is her aunt, and her uncle is on the board.

At Santa Clara University, Gallegos majored in political science and minored in ethnic studies and Spanish. She envisioned herself working for a nonprofit agency or for the city—not teaching. But when she had a chance to go to Harvard Education School, she thought, "I might as well try it." Her master's focus was on education policy, administration, and planning.

Then her mother talked her into meeting with Lippman, and Father Mateo told her to bring her education back to her neighborhood. So, Gallegos found herself creating and teaching DCP's College Readiness class for ninth graders. "Really, it's high school readiness," she says. Students learn to take "coded" notes and summarize what they've read. She explicitly teaches them how to plan their time and study for tests. Gallegos uses the same reading comprehension and writing techniques used in English, history, math, science, and Spanish classes, including the infamous accordion paragraph. She throws in logic games and crossword puzzles for fun.

The climax of the year for Gallegos and her students is the Dinner Party: Each student must research a famous person—Frida Kahlo, Nellie Bly, Franklin Roosevelt, Leonardo Da Vinci, Diego Rivera, Sally Ride, Cesar Chavez, or another—write a biography, create a poster, and finally design a dinner plate. The idea is to engage students through art, which isn't dependent on English fluency, while also requiring them to do Internet research and practice their writing.

Her challenge is to enable students to learn elementary skills, such as writing a book report, without making the class so remedial that it bores students who are capable of more. She tries to get students to analyze their own learning style, so they develop a sense of what they can do to improve.

Gallegos doesn't have a classroom of her own, or a desk, or a place to hang a jacket or purse. She moves from room to room throughout the day, dragging her teaching materials in a wheeled backpack.

Her fifth-period class meets four times a week in Penn, a small space with a curtain at one end separating it from a slighter larger space used for remedial math or Spanish or, for one period, College Readiness.

Sound travels easily through the curtain. I find it distracting to hear Jesse Robinson talk about decimal points while Gallegos is explaining how to organize an outline, but the students don't seem to mind.

A poster on the wall done by English as a Second Language (ESL) students proclaims: "Latino students have to go to college because that is why we the Latinos came to Merica, to work hard and achieve a lot of great things."

There's also a behavior-and-consequences chart that a group of Gallegos's students did at the start of the year. In each of her classes, students discussed what sort of behavior was unacceptable, and why. Did unacceptable behavior reflect a lack of *ganas,* that is, poor motivation, or disrespect for the class, or both? Gallegos wanted students to take responsibility for class rules, instead of imposing them from above. She hoped students would think about how to create a place where they could learn. Posting the chart reminds students of the promises they made, and the draconian punishments they proposed.

Behavior	No Ganas or Disrespect?	Consequence
Distractive	Both	Write one-page essay
No homework	No ganas	Double homework
Bad language	Disrespect	Tape on mouth
Tardy	Both	Stay after school
Yelling	Disrespect	Sock in mouth

Of course, Gallegos doesn't use tape or socks; nor does she assign double homework. The real consequence for distracting the class is temporary exile from the room, usually five minutes sitting in a chair in the hall. Defiance may lead to a "referral" to the principal. After five referrals, a student and at least one parent or guardian must meet with the discipline committee. Offenses may lead to detention, which requires going an hour early to school, or to school service, usually sweeping up.

Near the door, Gallegos has posted homework charts for her Penn classes with stars showing each completed assignment. All DCP teachers assign homework four times a week, post the homework chart, and call parents if a student misses two assignments in a six-week grading period.

I sit in the back. There's almost no room for an extra person in Penn.

As every DCP teacher does, Gallegos posts her agenda for the class so students can see what they're supposed to be learning. Today she writes on the mobile white board in the front of the room:

- Problem solving
- Four-step summary
- Vocabulary

One of her 19 students in this period's class was working at grade level from the start, a quiet girl named Carolina who'd attended private school.

An unusually large number were in ninth grade last year, too, either at DCP or at another school.

Buddy sits in front, taking up a large percentage of the space in the room. Buddy was kicked out of his former high school for a gang fight and is now on parole. "He made some bad choices last year," says Gallegos, tactfully. Next to Buddy are tall, charming Lorenzo, repeating DCP's ninth grade, and Teresa, who hides behind a perpetual sneer and the dark, heavy makeup of a *chola,* a tough girl.

The class clown, a skinny boy with stick-out ears, sits at the next table. Dennis is bright, curious, good-humored—and nearly impossible to shut up. Despite his obvious intelligence, he's also repeating ninth grade, after transferring from a large high school. He enjoys flirting with Lisa, my tutee, and sometimes he can draw a smile from Heather, a girl with a hair-trigger temper.

Larissa, who's still struggling with English, sits in the back at a badly scarred table. (All the furniture is donated; the dotcom bust is starting to make better-quality office furniture available, but Penn hasn't been upgraded yet.) Two weeks before her due date, Larissa does not look pregnant, but her normal exuberance is subdued.

Felipe and Art also sit in back. Felipe suffers from what Gallegos calls Pencil Disease. He seems incapable of picking up a pencil and writing. He rarely talks, moves, or changes the haughty expression on his handsome Indian face. Art's face is animated, but its usual expression is confusion.

"Vamos, caballeros," says Gallegos. She asks, "What is Dia de los Muertos?"

"It's a Mexican tradition when the dead come to life," says Lorenzo, who often shows his intelligence in class but rarely does homework. Gallegos looks startled to get a correct answer so quickly.

She moves on to the logic exercise. Students are supposed to come up with an answer to her prompt: Although she was the star basketball player, Kisha did not play in the championship game. Why not?

While students are writing answers, Gallegos does the daily uniform check. She can see that all the students are wearing DCP's uniform, though Lorenzo, as always, is sporting a shirt from the office with *LOANER* written on it in orange letters. On most students, the shirt is too big, but it fits Lorenzo perfectly, and he wears it with his usual flair.

Gallegos checks that there's no red or blue showing on shoes or backpacks.

She also checks homework logs: Students are supposed to write down the assignment for each class and get a parent to sign off on the daily log. This simple step is a challenge for many DCP students. They aren't used to doing homework, so they're not in the habit of writing down assignments. Gallegos says a few quiet words to each student who's left gaps on the log. She will remind them a hundred times, if necessary, without losing her patience. She is relentless.

With another "Vamos, caballeros," Gallegos asks students for their answers to the exercise, which is supposed to make them read a sentence carefully and think logically. Why didn't Kisha, the star player, play in the championship game?

"She found out she was pregnant," one student says.

This is a logical answer, but it reflects expectations that Gallegos hopes to change. She suppresses a wince.

"She dreamed she was champion, but woke up."

"She was run over the day before."

"Good," says Gallegos. "She *couldn't play* because she *was run over.*"

"She went to a rock and roll concert."

"She was embarrassed to play in front of her boyfriend."

Gallegos shakes her head sadly. One of her goals is to get girls from Mexican immigrant families to work to achieve their own goals, without being held back by what a boyfriend might want.

"She was kicked off the team."

"She punched the coach in the nose."

"She was too old."

"Her daughter graduated."

Gallegos looks puzzled, but goes on.

"Her coach found out she was doing drugs."

"Her coach found out she was doing drugs," Gallegos echoes. "That's the *reason* she didn't play."

"She forgot to shave her legs."

Gallegos has accepted illogical answers without protest, but finally she objects. "She missed the game because she forgot to shave her legs? Does that make sense?" The student shrugs.

"She'd rather go skateboarding."

"She was at band practice."

About half the students haven't come up with a logical reason why a star basketball player would miss the championship game. They're still trying to slide through school without thinking. Gallegos has a lot more patience than I have.

Gallegos asks Buddy to collect the homework. He towers over classmates who are slow to produce work, looking like a loan shark's enforcer collecting payments.

Buddy was a troublemaker at first. Exasperated, Gallegos made him teach the class one day. He proved to be an enthusiastic teacher—and a strict disciplinarian. Ever since, controlling Buddy has been easy for Gallegos. Given the slightest bit of authority, he becomes her loyal aide.

Students have read about *Mendez v. Westminster:* In 1946, five Mexican American families sued because their children were barred from "whites only" schools; as a result, school segregation was ended in California seven years before *Brown v. Board of Education.* The assignment was to write an accordion paragraph answering three questions: Why did Mendez sue four Orange County school districts? Would you have sued? Why or why not?

Students start with a "green" sentence stating the thesis. Then they back it up with several "yellow" sentences, giving reasons and facts, and "reds," explanation and examples. DCP students write accordion paragraphs in every class for every writing assignment, of which there are many.

"Vamos, caballeros," Gallegos says. It's time for another ninth-grade staple, the four-step summary. Students are supposed to summarize the *Mendez v. Westminster* reading, using three examples.

- Step 1: Name it. (What's the title?)
- Step 2. Verb it. (Use a verb such as *describes, summarizes, explains, exhibits, demonstrates.*)
- Step 3. Give the big picture. (What's it about?)
- Step 4. Put it together. (Combine steps 1, 2, and 3 in a paragraph.)

Gallegos leads students through the four steps. They've mastered Name It and Verb It by now, but the Big Picture frequently gets lost in a fog of minor details. Asked a question, Felipe sits in perfect silence and stillness till Gallegos moves on. Art has a hunted look on his face. Gallegos can't call on Carolina to answer every question. Finally, Lisa hazards an answer good enough to be written on the board. Art sighs with relief. Felipe resembles a Zen devotee waiting patiently for enlightenment.

In quiet moments, I can hear Jesse Robinson teaching Math Reasoning on the other side of the pleated divider. Her class is learning positive and negative numbers by walking +2 steps forward, −1 step back, and so forth. The student chosen to demonstrate has a heavy tread. "Clomp! Clomp!" There's a pause. "Clomp!"

"It's *negative* one," says Robinson.

Another pause. "Clomp!"

"Good!"

It's hard to concentrate, waiting for the next clomp from the other side of the curtain.

Gallegos hands out an example of a four-step summary—this one of a Roald Dahl short story—done by a student in another class. DCP teachers try to give students concrete examples. Despite some grammatical errors, this one is marked "Excellent!"

Gallegos explains exactly what's going to be on the upcoming quiz. Her primary goal is not really to see whether students understand *Mendez v. Westminster,* though she'd like them to see education as a right to be fought for and cherished. Her primary goal is for students to understand how to study for a quiz. After students take the quiz, they'll fill out a sheet on how they prepared: Did they ask themselves questions, get others to quiz them, and so on?

Going over the homework, Gallegos is thrilled to see that Art did an outline of the Roald Dahl story. "It's not great but he almost never does homework," she tells me. "He's got the basic idea." She gives him extra credit. "He's getting all F's but when someone like Art does work, that's huge," she says.

The *caballeros* move on to the week's vocabulary words. In keeping with the popular "multiple intelligences" theory, DCP teachers ask students to draw pictures and design posters, in addition to writing, to use talents that otherwise might be ignored. In this case, students will have to write a synonym for each word, draw a picture, and write two sentences on their own. Gallegos shows them exactly how to do the exercise, though they've done it before.

"Teresa, what's a synonym for *intelligent?*"

There is a very long pause. "*Smart?*" says Teresa.

"What might be a symbol for *intelligent?*"

"A brain," says Heather.

"A book," says Lorenzo.

Gallegos demonstrates how to write the sentences. "Carolina is very intelligent because . . ."

"Because she gets good grades," says Carolina.

"Dennis is hilarious because he says irrelevant things," Gallegos says, knowing that Dennis loves attention.

"I'm hindering the class!" says Dennis, delighted to be bandying words with the teacher. *Hinder* is last week's vocabulary word.

"Dennis is very hilarious, but not very diligent," says Gallegos.

Dennis grins. He likes to think he's hilarious, not merely annoying. He looks at the vocabulary list, searching for more words he can use.

Gallegos hands out paperback dictionaries to help students do the assignment in class. But she doesn't have enough for every table, much less for every student. (Later, I bought some used paperback dictionaries and thesauri online and gave them to Gallegos.) Larissa shares a Spanish-English dictionary with her table mate.

"My mom is very precious to me because she is nice," writes Lisa. "My dad is very precious because he raises me." I tutor Lisa once a week, so I take the liberty of pointing to one of her sentences. "My brother is cautious because he hits me." I shake my head. "It means danger?" she asks. After I explain, she borrows Wite Out, paints over the sentence, lets it dry, and tries again. I've failed to persuade her whiting out mistakes is unnecessarily time-consuming. "I am cautious with my brother because he might hit me," she writes. "I am cautious not to catch a disease." She pauses to think. "My brother is not diligent, because he is 22 years old and does not have a job."

Heather has written: "Dennis is intelligent in his odd, little planet."

For once, Teresa is working: "I'm very precious. My mom loves me."

So is Lorenzo: "I'm cautious with my looks because I want to look good." He's wearing woolen gloves, a fashion allowed by the dress code.

Dennis is chattering to Lisa.

"Dennis, you're hindering our ability to learn," says Gallegos.

"I'll be more diligent," says Dennis, without missing a beat. He's been looking for a chance to get back in the game.

"And less loquacious," says Gallegos. "What's the meaning of *loquacious?*"

"Disturbing?" says Buddy.

"Talkative!" says Dennis, gleefully. He should know.

Felipe has done *intelligent,* but stops there.

Art is working steadily, though with much erasing. He asks me for a synonym for *precious.* I get him a dictionary from Carolina's table. To represent *precious,* he draws a picture of his skateboard.

Knowing that native Spanish speakers will interchange *v* and *b,* Gallegos makes the class practice pronouncing *chivalrous.*

"Shibboleth," the students chorus.

"Chi-val-rous," says Gallegos.

"Shi-bo-less," say the students.

"Chi-*v*al-rous."

"Chi-bal-rous."

Dennis gets in a laughing fit and is sent out of class. Gallegos has set a chair outside for exiles.

At the close of the 80-minute period, students stay in Penn for Sustained Silent Reading, a 40-minute period for free reading that occurs twice a week in DCP's complex, rotating schedule.

Buddy reads a boxing book called *Rope Burns* from the tiny room's only shelf. Lorenzo looks at a Spiderman comic. Larissa has a Spanish language novel about Chicano street gangs. Carolina pulls a Harry Potter book out of her backpack.

Most students don't carry a book with them—they only read during the reading period—and don't bother to check the shelf. Gallegos passes out copies of *National Geographic* for bookless students. Dennis, back from exile, takes one eagerly, hoping for an animal story: He wants to be a zoologist—or a cop. Lisa puts her head down on the table, her long hair flowing in front of her face, and peers sideways at her magazine. Teresa, a martyr to ennui, talks to Lorenzo till Gallegos makes her sit in the hall. Art stares at a photo. Felipe sits motionless with the unopened magazine on the table in front of him, as if posing for a portrait.

Gallegos handed out a four-step summary done by a student so students could see a concrete example of what they were supposed to be doing.

Step 1

NAME IT	VERB IT	BIG PICTURE
"The Hitchhiker"	describes	A hitchhiker who has a talent to pickpocket people without the person knowing.

Step 2

The story "The Hitchhiker" by Roald Dahl, describes about a hitchhiker with a talent to pickpocket people.

Step 3

- The man drives a BMW and picks up a hitchhiker.
- They speed over the limit and gets pulled over by a cop. The cop writes down information in one notebook and a ticket in another notebook.
- The cop drives away, and they start driving again. The driver finds out that the hitchhiker is a pickpocket because he stole the two notebooks from the cop.

Step 4

In the story "The Hitchhiker" by Roald Dahl describes a man with a talent to pickpocket people. The man drives a BMW and picks up a hitchhiker. They speed over the limit and gets stopped by a cop. The cop pulls out two notebooks, one for information, and the other for tickets. The police gives the driver a ticket and drives away. The driver drives again and finds out that the hitchhiker is a pickpocket because he stole the two notebooks that belonged to the cop. In conclusion, this is what "The Hitchhiker" describes.

College Readiness students complete this checklist to evaluate their study habits after each quiz and test.

Study Checklist

____ Completed the worksheet
____ Quizzed myself
____ Quizzed others
____ Rewrote answers in my own words

7

conflict and resolution

Over at the Y, sophomore World History students are learning vocabulary: *Exploitation, animosity, economics, colonialism.*

A girl tries to use a vocabulary word in a sentence: "The rich animositied the poor."

"No," says Shawn Gerth, reluctantly.

A boy pulls in current events: "The economics is doing bad because of the war."

That leads to a lively discussion about the effects of September 11 on the economy. Production has slowed. Because of anthrax, people are afraid to get mail. Stocks are down. People face layoffs. Some students' parents have lost their jobs.

"*Economics* is not a verb," Gerth says. "It is a . . ."

"Noun," says a ragged chorus of voices.

One of her students tries another word: "The U.S. *colonialism* is with the other states."

"That's a little off," says Gerth.

A classmate helps out: "*Colonialism* once existed, but now it doesn't."

Gerth wavers for a second, then lets the answer stand.

Students fill out a vocabulary chart with the correct definition of each word, but often they need the words in the definition explained. They also draw a graphic for each word as a memory aid and a bow to "multiple intelligences" theory.

"My Plans for the Future"—posters made by students at the start of the year—are taped to the tops of the dividers that separate Gerth's space from the space used by Laura DeRoche, who teaches English. In their posters, students describe their hopes for good grades, a good job, and an education at Stanford, Berkeley, or San Jose State. Gerth constantly reminds students that they're preparing for college; they must live up to a higher standard as sophomores and be role models for the ninth graders.

(In fact, the sophomores do look like model students compared to the freshmen: Most don't need to be told at the beginning of every class to sit down, pull out homework, and start the "Do Now" problem on the board. I always can tell a tenth-grade class by students' purposeful behavior.)

Lower down, Gerth has posted students' grades to date, the homework completion chart for each class, and checklists for reading and writing assignments. Some teachers code the grade chart, but Gerth uses their names. She wants students to be proud of earning good grades or of raising an F to a D or a D to a C. At DCP, a low grade is a starting point, a sign that hard work will be required to improve.

Just for inspiration, there's a World War I poster of a crashed plane with the motto: "Consider the Possible Consequences If You Are Careless in Your Work."

Gerth and DeRoche have worked together to create a tenth-grade humanities curriculum using the theme "Conflict and Resolution." They decided to use *Lord of the Flies, Animal Farm,* and *Macbeth,* all classic texts for high school sophomores, plus Elie Wiesel's *Night,* Anna Deavere Smith's *Fires in the Mirror* on the black-Jewish riots in Crown Heights, Brooklyn, and Monster Kody Scott's *Autobiography of a LA Gang Member.* (Later, the Scott book was dropped when classes fell behind schedule; it had the least literary merit.) Gerth is teaching modern world history, as defined by state standards, which call for covering the period from the French Revolution through the world wars, hitting the rise of democratic ideals, industrialism, and imperialism. Gerth and DeRoche spend much of their time on reading comprehension and writing skills, preparing students to write college essays.

Because the dividers extend only partway to the ceiling, Gerth's students can hear DeRoche teaching English on the other side, and vice versa. Sitting at the end of the divider, I can see and hear Gerth and DeRoche at the same time.

The ninth-grade humanities team also has logistics problems. To get to Jessica Rigby's History of the Americas room, it's necessary to walk through Angela Hensley's English I space, which also is used for advanced Spanish. The school's computer center—a collection of donated Macs of dubious reliability—is next to Hensley's space with no divider at all. In the rare moments when the Conflict and Resolution classes are silent, I can hear Hensley teaching *Romeo and Juliet* or *To Kill a Mockingbird*. Once again, I'm amazed at students' ability to tune out the distractions.

In DeRoche's space, a poster reminds students of reading comprehension strategies they're supposed to use:

- Think While You Read
- Visualize
- Predict
- Make Connections
- Note Confusion
- Use Fix-up Strategies

DeRoche also posts a homework chart with stars for each assignment turned in on time. Her grade chart uses numbers so students can check their own grades but not read everyone else's.

Her space has an ell to one side, where the photocopier was in the school's first year. On the list of room names from the previous year, DeRoche's space is called "Copier." At the back is an open area with three computers, used mostly by teachers, and some shelves. She has some table space but no desk.

DeRoche is trying to get students to figure out the meaning of *Lord of the Flies* vocabulary words—*whimpered, thrust, tremulous, glowered*—from the context of the book, which deals with a group of schoolboys, stranded on an island after a wartime plane crash, who fear a mysterious beast in the jungle.

For *whimper,* students guess "cry," "whine," "talk," "bug," and "complain."

DeRoche asks whether a *cry* is a noun or a verb. Students have trouble with this. There's action in *cry,* Barbara says, so maybe it's a verb.

"It's always a noun if *a* or *the* comes before it," DeRoche says.

For *thrust,* students guess "put on," "throw," and "pass." Noun or a verb? "It's a verb," says Adam confidently. He and his brother Bill were home-schooled for four years by their college-educated mother; they are among the best students in the class.

The class looks at a new sentence: "Jack's voice went up, tremulous yet determined." Nobody's close. They guess "loud," "yelling," "angry," and "unwilling."

The official definition is "trembling" or "quivering." *Quivering* is clearly an unfamiliar word, too.

They do better on *glowered,* coming up with "look up" and "glance." A girl guesses "went together," by which she means squinted.

Sitting in the back, Hayden Engelhart, a literacy consultant, observes how DeRoche is using the teaching strategies Engelhart taught teachers before school started. Looking at the text and predicting what comes next are the keys to comprehension for all subjects, including math and science, says Engelhart. Predicting requires students to think.

DeRoche uses another of Engelhart's strategies. She tells students to identify four ways to answer questions about their reading:

- Right There: Answer is right there in the text.
- Putting It Together: Answer is in different parts of text, such as "Who is discussing what to do about the beast?"
- Text and Me: Author provides clues that help answer the question, such as "What does Ralph think about the hunters hunting the beast?"
- On My Own: Answer not found in text but I can use the text to answer it. May start with *should, could, would,* etc. Text could be one piece of the evidence in your answer. This should be a discussion question. For example: Are humans basically good or evil?

On the other side of the divider, Gerth moves on to the main event: "The Great War: The World in Upheaval."

She has written the goal of the class on a white board: "To learn how to read a textbook." She gives the prereading and postreading questions to check their comprehension.

- Write down major subheadings.
- Predict what the text will say.
- What do photos and other things tell you about the context of the text?

Gerth worries sometimes that students aren't learning the content of history, because she spends so much time on reading and writing skills. But they're not going to learn much history if they can't read. And the accordion paragraph, which requires students to support their assertions with evidence, makes them think about history.

Today, students are supposed to write an essay comparing the causes of conflict, such as competition for limited resources, in *Lord of the Flies* and World War I. "In an accordion paragraph, what's the green sentence?" Gerth asks.

Green is the main topic sentence, the sophomores tell her.

"How many assertions do I want? How many yellows? Use one green, three yellows, and how ever many reds you need to support your point." Yellows are reasons; reds are facts or examples.

A girl asks what *assertion* means, then translates the answer for a Spanish-speaking friend.

The sophomores have no time in their schedule for English as a Second Language, though several are still learning English. They struggle along as best they can, often interspersing Spanish words with their limited English. Gerth agonizes when she grades their papers. She wants to be fair to students who've only been using English for a few years or less. But she also wants to be honest with them about their abilities. In a few more years, they'll be in college. If she's too easy on them, they won't be prepared.

A Seattle native, Shawn Gerth earned a B.A. in history at Duke and a master's at Stanford, then taught for a year at Independence High, on San Jose's East Side, which has many Mexican, Vietnamese, and Filipino immigrants, plus neighborhoods of middle-class engineers and programmers. With 4,400 students and 220 teachers, Independence is an easy place to get lost. Gerth came to DCP seeking a sense of community and a common sense of purpose.

Laura DeRoche, slim and very blonde, left Wisconsin to major in English at Pomona. After graduation, she joined Teach for America, which recruits graduates of elite colleges, gives them a summer's worth of training, and places them in schools that can't find enough certified teachers. DeRoche became an English teacher at Compton High near Los Angeles. It was a disaster. The huge, all-minority school was in chaos with hundreds of students wandering around campus during class time. "Me trying to get 300 students to go to class," she recalls. "That didn't work." Nobody else was even trying.

She got little direction from her superiors on how or what to teach, and what she did get was useless. "I'd get writing prompts from the district office with words misspelled."

DeRoche didn't even get a key to the staff restroom for her first three months. Finally, she criticized the administration at a staff meeting. "The union rep slipped me a key as a reward."

Sometimes, she'd sit in her empty classroom at the end of the day and cry. DeRoche had made a two-year commitment to Teach for America, but she refused to return to Compton. It was impossible to make a difference there. She followed her fiancé, a middle-school teacher, to San Jose, and went to work at DCP.

A week later, I'm back at the Y, sitting in a wheeled swivel chair at the divider between World History and English II. (Once DCP was filled with wheeled office chairs, donated by bankrupt dotcoms. Letting teenagers have chairs with wheels proved to be a mistake. To discourage games of bumper chair, and save space, most of the office chairs were exchanged for ordinary plastic chairs.)

"I'm talking to your math teachers about POWs [problems of the week]," Gerth says. "We'll do a humanities POW. You need to work on coming up with evidence to support your ideas. . . . Ms. DeRoche worked on your essays. She found a problem: You have quotes left hanging that don't back up your points."

DCP teachers are supposed to show students specific models of what to do and not do. Gerth shows them a sample essay and asks them to find the flaws:

My name is . . .

Students identify that as irrelevant fluff.

I'm here today to talk about . . .

Students look puzzled. "Don't use *I* in an essay," Gerth says.

I hope you enjoy this essay . . .

Students spot that right away: Fluff!
People are evil. They do bad things . . .
Not specific, Gerth says. "You need examples."
DeRoche's voice is audible: "People are essentially evil when they . . ."
Gerth points to a better example and asks Pedro, "What is good or bad about this introduction?"

It's one of Pedro's good days. "It's got *Lord of the Flies* and imperialism and the transition is good, but it's not clear and specific," says Pedro, who's shaved his beard and grown his sideburns. He is a man of many hairstyles.

During the transport period, DeRoche and Gerth sit in the back of their classroom area by the computers. Angela Hensley enters, laughing. "Oh, I just realized I'm wearing my nose ring!" she says. "None of my students said a thing." With or without the ring, she looks like a teenager to me, though she has no trouble maintaining order in class.

"That's not OK?" Gerth asks.

"I asked Greg, and he said no," she says.

"I guess it doesn't qualify as business casual," says Gerth. "Look at me: I'm wearing red and blue!"

Later, students study the Versailles Treaty in history, and write a treaty to solve the conflict between Ralph and Jack in *Lord of the Flies*. Then they're supposed to read *Fires in the Mirror*, which gives blacks' and Hasidic Jews' perspectives on the Crown Heights riots in Brooklyn, which started when a rabbi's speeding car ran a stop light and killed an eight-year-old black boy. Blacks charged a private Jewish ambulance company had failed to help the boy. In the subsequent violence, a Jewish rabbinical student was murdered.

Actually, the students read photocopied excerpts. DeRoche ordered the book, but it hasn't arrived.

Gerth asks what conflicts they've seen at DCP. Pedro brings up cursing, disrespect of teachers, vandalism, "gang-related," and not showing the *ganas* needed to go to college.

Two boys who are good friends admit they had a fistfight over a stupid comment one had made about the other.

"What are the underlying values?" Gerth asks the class. "Why did they fight instead of talking it out?"

Roger: It was a word exchange.
Gerth: So you believe that if someone is insulting you, you have to . . .
Roger: Bust 'em.
Gerth: Say or do something bad.
Roger: Revenge!
Gerth: Why were they able to make it up?
Roger: Friends are more important than enemies.
Gerth: What was the belief?
Pedro: Forgiveness, regret.
Gerth: Friendship and forgiveness are important. What's the source of values?
Jaime: Family, friendship networks.
Rico: Conscience, morals.
Gerth: What's the source of conscience?
Pedro: Teachers. Where and how you're raised. Religion.

I hear DeRoche asking: "Where do teachers get their values from?"

Gerth: Where do you think I as a teacher get my values from?
Pedro: School rules.
Amy: Your experience.
Rajiv: If we're human, we're hungry. We need to eat. We have a need to forgive.

Gerth asks them to consider a current redevelopment conflict in San Jose. Should downtown San Jose improve stores or create affordable housing? When the city upgrades the downtown area, "what happens to property values or your rent?" she asks.

Barbara: It goes up! (Her mother and stepfather are moving to a town an hour south of San Jose, where they can afford a house.)
Gerth: What are the beliefs of those who favor better retail?

Jerry: Money.

Barbara: High class, civilized.

Amy: Tourism.

Rajiv: The general beauty of the city.

Gerth: What are the beliefs of those who favor housing?

Barbara: Family.

Amy: Education, if they build it for teachers. (The mayor has proposed building teacher housing.)

Gerth: What's the source of the values?

Jerry: It's greed and capitalism versus housing; that comes from a sense of community.

Byron: We need teachers. We don't really need tourists.

Gerth: Should a person who steals to feed his family go to jail? Give me a show of hands. (Eight students say no; ten say yes.)

Amy: If they're on welfare, that's kind of stealing.

Armando: It's OK to steal food, not money, because stores make a lot of money they don't need.

Barbara: There's a lot of places that will help people who need food.

Amy: They're stealing not to live fancy, but to get by.

Jaime: They should ask and not just steal.

Pedro: Get a job!

Byron: It's against the law.

Roger: If they go to jail, they'll have a home and three meals a day.

Adam: Human life is the key value.

Gerth asks the class to think of conflict as a clash of values and look at factors that can be a source of values such as race/ethnicity, religion, socio-economic status, and personal experience. "You'll be talking about war with values conflict and reading a book about values conflict."

She hands out photos from *Fires in the Mirror*. Groups are supposed to decide what's going on in each photo; each student must write half a page predicting what they'll be reading about in the book.

Pedro, though looking at a coffin with a star of David, says it shows a Mexican killed by whites.

Meanwhile, DeRoche's class is turning quotes from the book into found poetry. But they have trouble with Jewish ritual and language. "We can't turn off electricity on Shabbos" is one of the quotes.

"What's Shabbos?" a girl asks.

"The Sabbath," DeRoche says. "It goes from Friday night to Saturday night. During the Sabbath, Orthodox Jews can't turn on or off a light because it's considered work."

"That's not cool," says a boy.

"That sucks," says another.

"What's a Satmar?" asks a girl. "What's a Lubavitcher?"

These are different kinds of Hasidic Jews, DeRoche explains.

Fires in the Mirror, with its multiple and conflicting points of view, is supposed to tie in to their unit on World War I propaganda. DeRoche and Gerth want students to understand they can't trust only one source to tell them the full truth. They need to question a speaker's biases and understand there can be many ways to interpret a set of events.

Groups of students design a propaganda poster with a pro-black or pro-Hasidic slogan, imitating World War I propaganda posters. DeRoche tells them that racist or anti-Semitic words or images are unacceptable. "Absolutely no swastikas allowed," she says.

She shows examples of 9/11 posters. One says, "Be independent. Join the Army" over diagonal blue and white stripes. Another shows Eminem dressed up as a marine.

As the groups get to work, DeRoche moves among the tables. After a few minutes, she makes an announcement: The use of *kill* is banned.

When the period is over, she looks at their work:

- Ambulance—for Jews Only
- Jews Speed, Blacks Bleed
- Jews Want Peace. What about Blacks?
- Hate Hitler. Not Blacks
- Accident/Not Accident
- Accidents Aren't Intentional
- Recklessness = death
- Justice 4 Jews (star of David graphic) the Guilt is Obvious
- Red Means Stop
- We Deserve Justice (cross and star graphic)
- Be Equal (ambulance graphic)

"I'm nervous about this assignment," she says. "If someone walked in they'd think we're teaching prejudice. Next time we'll use fiction like *Lord of the Flies.*"

Despite her concerns, DCP students seem to have few hang-ups about race, ethnicity, or religion. In a school that's 83 percent Hispanic, the five-member Student Council includes one white student, Byron, and one black student, Jack.

I asked several non-Hispanic students whether it was difficult not being Mexican-American at DCP. All said it was no big deal. In the neighborhoods where they live, most students are Hispanic at any school.

A high percentage of students are Catholic, but Amy, the only Jewish student, is one of the most popular girls in her class and doesn't feel singled out as different.

The real division is between students who speak only English, a group that includes assimilated Mexican Americans, and the immigrants who speak English with difficulty in class and chat with each other in Spanish during breaks. Still, most students speak both languages and socialize with both groups. It's common to hear students who are talking in one language switch seamlessly to the other to accommodate a friend who's just sat down at the lunch table.

The next step in the humanities curriculum is linking the Versailles Treaty and the Crown Heights Treaty Project: While discussing in history how Europe failed to resolve World War I conflicts, English students brainstorm ideas to prevent future black-Jewish violence in Brooklyn. Then they'll write topic sentences and outline a paragraph.

A good Student Council president, Byron is full of ideas for activities to bring blacks and Hasidic Jews together. He proposes Friday night bowling and a barbecue on Sunday.

DeRoche reminds them that the Jewish Sabbath starts on Friday night.

"OK, bowling on Thursday and a barbecue on Sunday," says Byron.

DeRoche explains that kosher rules might complicate the barbecue.

"OK, softball on Sunday," says Byron.

DeRoche isn't sure whether Orthodox Jewish women play softball.

Byron is losing patience. "They can watch!" he says.

Meanwhile, Pedro and Jerry are arguing about bulletproofing the rabbi's car so the rabbi won't need to speed and won't risk hitting black pedestrians.

Jerry defends the rabbi's speeding. "He has death threats against him," he says.

Pedro says that's no excuse. "The pope has death threats, and he doesn't speed," Pedro says.

"He has the popemobile," says Jerry.

"The rabbi has bodyguards," says Pedro. He suggests enforcing the speed limit and eliminating private ambulance services.

Jerry still is worried about the rabbi's safety. "What if you're bishop of San Jose and someone wants to kill you?" he says. "Wouldn't you have a bodyguard?"

"I wouldn't care," says Pedro with a dramatic shrug. "When you die, you die."

They keep going back and forth, while their third partner, a shy girl, says nothing. Jerry thinks the rabbi is justifiably defensive; Pedro thinks the rabbi is an egotist. Besides, a real man should never show fear. For a few minutes, it looks as if violence is going to break out at the table. It's a clash of values: Pedro's tough-talking street culture versus Jerry's middle-class prudence. The end of the period ends the argument.

The 20-minute transport period, which gives time for students to move between sites, gives Gerth and DeRoche a chance to talk with each other.

Jessica Rigby, the ninth-grade history teacher, joins them. She's in a good mood. She's found a teaching coach—someone working on an advanced degree—who will observe her teaching and give pointers. Rigby isn't afraid to admit she needs to improve. At DCP, it's socially acceptable.

"I need a coach!" says DeRoche. "I need a therapist!"

The teachers talk about what they've learned in their brief time as teachers.

"I've discovered they don't know what I think they know," says DeRoche. "I think because I'm talking and they're silent, they're listening to me."

"Sometimes they're listening more when they're noisy," says Gerth. "Half of them are talking about what you're saying. When they're quiet, that's bad."

Rigby nods. It's too easy for students simply to drift off.

The teachers worry that they're spoon-feeding the students, breaking assignments into little bits, leading them through every step of the process. In DCP lingo, they're "hand-holding." But most of their students aren't ready to learn independently.

"We'll be a good middle school for ninth and tenth graders and a good prep school for 11th and 12th grade," says Gerth. "That's a realistic goal."

After *Fires in the Mirror*, DeRoche teaches Ntozake Shange's *The Desert*, a series of monologues written as prose poems. She writes a phrase on the white board: "You don't know what you're taking if you don't know what's yours."

Gina takes a lead in the discussion. She's come alive as a student since the end of the first six-week grading period, when her mother, looking at a report card filled with D's and F's, said, "I've given up on you." Gina has decided to prove to her mother that she can succeed. She's crossed over from apathy to commitment. She's now earning a C in English.

Gina: It's a psychic sense of place.
DeRoche: What's the "it"?
Gina: Society?
Melissa: Identity.
DeRoche: What's she saying about identity?
Gina: It's psychic.
DeRoche: What's *psychic* mean?
Gina: Identity is not what you show to people. It's more in your mind.
Melissa: It's who you think you are or where you stand.
DeRoche: Pedro, what communities are you part of?
Pedro (buzz cut, goatee): Family, friends, young people, the beaner community.
DeRoche: Beaner?
Pedro: Yeah, Mexicans. Beaners.

The poem talks about identity as an anchor. DeRoche asks whether it's good to be anchored.

Byron: I have a long rope. It doesn't make sense to only have an anchor in one place.
Adam: Maybe she means you'll have one anchor but float to other places.
Byron: The anchor should be placed at your home. Everything else goes around it.
Pedro: The anchor could be bad. Like gangs: It restricts you.
Roger: Or the media. It just puts people in one category.
DeRoche: Is it better to mix or separate by race?
Nick: It's better to mix. When you go to work you might have to work with somebody you don't like. It doesn't matter. You have to get the job done.
Gina: What's an anchor?

To show World History students how to write an introductory paragraph, Shawn Gerth gave them a bad example, which they critiqued, and a better example. DCP students always get concrete examples.

Bad example:
Hello, my name is Ms. Gerth. This is my introduction paragraph. I am here today to talk with you about why people are evil. People are not good. First of all, they do bad things. In *Lord of the Flies* Piggy and Simon are treated bad. Like they get beat up on and stuff. Second, imperialism. White people treated other people unfair. Finally, terrorism shows people are evil. I hope you enjoy this essay.

Better example:
People are essentially evil for three reasons. First, as shown in *Lord of the Flies,* they destroy human life. Second, imperialism proves that people are evil because they destroy each other's self-respect. Finally, terrorism shows people are evil because they are willing to destroy each other's lives. For these three reasons, as well as many others, it is clear that people are essentially evil.

8

strike 67

When Hector disrupted his classes in the first months of the school year, he was told to step outside the room to calm down. He kept mouthing off. Detentions piled up for failure to do homework and obey class rules—and then for failure to make up detentions in early morning study hall. When Hector disrupted his classes in the first months of the school year, he was told to step outside the room to calm down. He kept mouthing off. Detentions piled up for failure to do homework and obey class rules—and then for failure to make up detentions in early morning study hall. Then came referrals to the principal's office, which are reserved for more serious offenses, such as disrespect, defiance, vandalism, and violence.

After five referrals in the fall semester, Hector must face the dreaded disciplinary committee, made up of administrators, teachers, and parents. The committee typically requires service hours, such as cleaning the school, and compliance with a behavior contract. Students who violate the contract must leave DCP.

Hector, who's up to seven referrals by the time the meeting is scheduled, sits with his father in DCP's largest classroom at St. Paul's.

Tonight, Lippman and Case, who always participate, are backed up by Aaron Srugis, Alicia Gallegos, and two DCP parents. A tall, handsome boy, Hector is normally cocky and talkative, but tonight he sits silently, looking straight down at the scarred classroom table. His father, a burly man with a jagged scar on his neck, listens quietly.

Lippman explains Hector's major sins: showing disrespect for his tutor, being rude to the teacher in Spanish class, throwing tomatoes at lunchtime, stealing the teacher's grade book. Nothing truly serious, but it's not a pattern that will be allowed to continue.

Srugis praises Hector's good nature and urges him to show more maturity.

Asked whether he wants to speak, Hector shakes his head "no" without lifting his gaze. He appears to be on the verge of tears.

His father promises Hector will do better. "I don't like to appear again here," he says. "Next time I bring my mask."

Everyone looks confused.

"Like in wrestling," he says. "On TV?"

The DCP staffers look nervous. It sounds as though the father is promising to beat Hector if he doesn't behave. Case says they hope Hector's family will help him improve.

The father goes on to say one of Lippman's magic words: "I don't like to be verguenza," he says. It means "ashamed."

"Verguenza is the right word," says Lippman enthusiastically. He believes shame and guilt are powerful motivators. Hector should feel *verguenza* for his behavior. Hector has brought shame to himself, to his family, to the DCP community. Hector is capable of doing better. If he works harder he can bring *orgullo*—pride—to his family.

Hector bows his head even lower.

Case says she'll work out a contract spelling out the service—usually cleaning the school—he'll do, and specific rules he'll have to promise to follow.

Still mute, Hector nods in agreement. As he leaves, he shakes hands with all the adults, looking as if he's faced the wrath of God and come away a new man. Lippman, Case, Gallegos, and Srugis exude the warmth of evangelists welcoming a penitent back into the fold. Hector manages a faint smile.

"I like him," says Srugis, once Hector and his father have left. "He's a mischievous kid, always talking, but he's not angry. He's just goofy."

"He's got very low academic skills," says Case. Hector can't afford to be goofy. He's got too much catching up to do.

Case also has worries about the family. Neither the father nor Hector could explain what happened to his older sister, who enrolled in DCP the week before, attended for one day, and never returned. The father doesn't seem to know where she is. Families who misplace teenage daughters for days at a time are not highly functional families. And she's still uneasy about the father's "mask" comment.

She likes Hector too. But can he make it?

In the first year, DCP let some discipline problems slide, says Richard Ruiz, who usually volunteers to fill one of the two parent slots on the committee. "This year we get on it right away." A marine veteran, Ruiz is a formidable presence who scares students just by looking at them. Because he plays the heavy, DCP staffers can take the "good cop" role.

Ruiz was disappointed when his two older sons decided against college. He sent his third son to the downtown parochial school, Saint Patrick's, but found there were 36 to 38 students in a class and little personal attention. "They'd call two days before the end of the term to say he had 11 homeworks missing! You're taking half my check. I want a call."

Ruiz forced his reluctant son to go to DCP. Now a sophomore, his son has made the honor roll, Ruiz says proudly.

Students accept rules that are enforced consistently, Lippman says. He's proud that DCP teachers can control their students because they know he'll back them up. But consistency has its price: Several students who might have turned around in time had to leave for violating their contracts. He hates to lose students, but he sees no alternative to setting and enforcing rules. Schools that tolerate disorder fail all their students.

While they wait for another student, Lippman and Case talk about Henry, who has a permanent case of the jitters. "I taught a class with Henry," says Lippman. "He was bouncing off the walls. That's why I like substitute teaching. I can appreciate what my teachers are facing."

An evaluation done at his middle school concluded that Henry doesn't have Attention Deficit Hyperactivity Disorder, a common diagnosis. The teachers are amazed: Henry seems to define hyperactivity. Case wants another evaluation. But San Jose Unified, which contracts to provide special ed services to the charter, doesn't have enough psychologists. There's a long backlog of requests for evaluation. Until a psychologist can talk to Henry, the DCP staff will have to figure out how to calm him down and teach him the rudiments of self-control.

The last student on the schedule never shows up. He'll be expelled for violating his behavior contract. "It's Strike 67," Lippman says. "It's critical that we sometimes say: 'You can't stay here.'"

Case will try to get him into The Foundry, the district's most effective alternative school for troubled teenagers, but spaces are hard to come by.

Lippman lightens the mood by reminding them of one of their worst students from the first year: "He had nine referrals by October last year. He was in here screaming and crying. His mom was crying. He's only had one referral since last December."

Every student who leaves takes $5,600 in state funding out the door. It's worth it to maintain a safe learning environment, Lippman says. "I'd rather take hits on dwindling enrollment than have kids who disrupt the DCP community."

A few weeks later, Henry is caught drinking malt liquor on campus. It's an automatic expulsion, but he can reapply the following year. To everyone's surprise, Henry vows to come back. Constantly in trouble and failing academically, Henry sees something at DCP that he wants: caring adults, stability, perhaps even hope.

At the Discipline Committee Meeting, Hector and his father got a written report explaining exactly what he'd done wrong and an evaluation of his overall performance at school.

Student: Hector A
Reason: more than 5 referrals
Description of Situation: Hector has received 7 referrals for disrupting the work of teachers and students at DCP.

- When told his teacher was absent, he stood up and cheered
- Getting involved in a food fight
- Ignoring a teacher's repeated request to stop talking
- Copying homework
- Saying to a teacher who asked him to stay after class "oh shit, no way am I going to stay"
- Stealing a detention sheet from a teacher
- Cutting school for a whole day after he knew that he was appearing before the discipline committee

Description of Student: Hector is a good young man. He takes responsibility for his actions when he is confronted with them, and he is honest and eager to be a part of the community here. However, he does not seem to feel that it is necessary to follow the rules, especially when he feels like he won't get caught. His last two referrals, stealing and cutting, come after a lot of long discussions with him about the vision of the school. Hector currently has a 0.78 GPA, not on track to graduate from high school, let alone college. I think he wants to do right, but he has not yet learned how.

9

outside the box

On a November day, Greg Lippman visits Academica Calmecac, a brand-new charter high school in East San Jose run by the Mexican-American Community Services Association (MACSA). He quickly bonds with Alfonso Reyes, a burly ex-teacher who's the principal.

Reyes sees Lippman as a grizzled veteran; DCP has made it to its second year. Calmecac has taken many ideas from DCP, including the summer program to orient new students, a mandatory tutorial every day, and parent classes. There's even a school clap like DCP's.

Calmecac has something DCP lacks: a building of its own. The school is housed in MACSA's new, well-designed Youth Services Center. It has real classrooms with walls, space for students to exercise, and even a rec room with pool and ping pong tables. Outside, students can play soccer or basketball.

Lippman is impressed by Calmecac students' ability to talk about their school and ask him questions about DCP. "They're crisp," he says. "I wish our kids were crisp."

The students—mostly, but not exclusively, Hispanic—seem no crisper than DCP students to me.

At Calmecac, students attend a daily advisory class to build school spirit and a sense of community. "We have a kid who was a loner," says Reyes. "He hated school. Now he loves to come here. He goes to his barber and recites the mission statement."

Lippman loves the story and wonders whether DCP, which holds advisory only once a week, should spend more time on the intangibles. On the other hand, Calmecac's stress on community and character building means less time for academics. As at DCP, most students are way behind in reading and math. Unlike DCP, Calmecac doesn't guarantee that graduates will be admitted to a four-year college or university.

DCP recruits students who were doing badly in school; Calmecac doesn't target D and F students, but that's who enrolls. "We have kids who were born here and they have a second-grade reading level," says Reyes, shaking his head in amazement. "They can't spell *play* or *boy*." Only 10 of 50 ninth graders tested as ready to learn algebra.

DCP students did well on San Jose Unified's writing test, outscoring nearby high schools. Reyes is impressed. Lippman tells him the test measures basic writing skills, which DCP students are mastering, thanks to the countless accordion paragraphs they write. He's concerned about their ability to get beyond the basics. In particular, Lippman is worried about their reading comprehension. Will they *really* be ready for college reading? "It's all come down to that," he says. "Reading, reading, reading."

Reyes nods. "We just have to be persistent and consistent, call them on little things, not give them enough breathing room to goof off," he says. "Tutorial is a sacred spot in the day: 90 minutes of doing work, no talking."

Lippman also wants DCP's tutorials to be "sacred." Too many students just aren't willing to do the work, he complains. This year's ninth graders pose more behavior problems than the first year's class. "We have 10 to 15 freshmen whose every second word is a curse. Their parents made them come. There's no buy-in."

Many parents at both schools are fighting the culture of the streets, looking for a safe environment above all else. "I made a promise to the parents," says Reyes. "I will not let gangs or drugs take over this school." Some of the parents are gang members like their parents before them, he says, but even they want better for their children.

Calmecac's attendance is an astounding 98 percent, Reyes says. "Kids want to be here." And, despite enormous challenges, some of the students are learning. "One of our girls was supposed to write an essay," he says. "She went to the library and copied from a book. The teacher was ecstatic: OK, the girl plagiarized—but she went to the library! She read a book! She found the topic!"

DCP doesn't belong to the state charter school group, founded as California Network of Educational Charters and renamed California Charter Schools Association. DCP isn't part of the Essential Schools movement or the Bay Area School Reform Collaborative. It's a stand-alone school. But Lippman and Andaluz work with other school reformers and charter founders to trade ideas and help each other along.

Some charter schools band together to share special education or business services, taking advantage of economies of scale without losing independence. While for-profit education management companies, such as Edison Schools, Inc., get most of the press, only a few are making money. Caroline Hoxby, a Harvard economics professor specializing in education, predicts that not-for-profit organizations such as Knowledge Is Power Program (KIPP) and Don Shalvey's Aspire Public Schools will dominate charter schools. "It's very hard for a mom-and-pop operation to start a school from scratch," she said in an interview. The not-for-profit networks can handle the finances, such as ordering supplies, processing payroll, or borrowing money to rent a decent facility from day one.

California-based Aspire centralizes school management expertise, letting principals concentrate on the educational challenges. KIPP, a nationwide network of middle schools with very strong results for minority students, concentrates on training principals, who will found new schools. The William and Melinda Gates Foundation, which is encouraging small high schools, has given millions of dollars to replicate promising charter models.

DCP has missed out on some grants because it's only one school with no plans for more. Lippman and Andaluz believe they need to concentrate on getting DCP right, then hope others will be inspired to start similar schools. They'd be delighted to see their teachers get experience and then go off and start schools of their own. Calmecac, though it doesn't have the college-or-bust mission, is DCP's first chance to spread its influence.

For years, as charter schools sprang up across the state, none opened in San Jose, the heart of Silicon Valley. The high-tech boom had made land and classroom space too expensive. Up the Peninsula, troubled East Palo Alto turned to charters: The for-profit Edison runs an elementary and middle school; the not-for-profit School Futures Research Foundation started East Palo Alto Charter, a K–8 school which later joined the Aspire network. All lease existing school buildings for one dollar a year.[1] On the other side of the Bay, low-scoring Oakland also tried charter alternatives.

San Jose lagged behind. The city didn't get its first charter till DCP and an elementary charter, Sherman Oaks, sponsored by the Campbell Union Elementary District, opened in 2000. In 2001, MACSA opened charter schools in East San Jose and Gilroy, and two reform-minded teachers started Silicon Valley Essential (SVE) Charter High in Mountain View. Just across the county line, Aspire, partnering with Stanford's School of Education, opened East Palo Alto (EPA) High.

All the charter high schools are small, aiming for a maximum of 400 students. Nationwide, median enrollment at charter schools is 252 students compared to 520 for the average public school, reports the Brown Center on Education Policy.[2]

EPA and SVE favored progressive teaching strategies, such as mingling subjects, assigning group projects, and providing hands-on learning opportunities; teachers tried to reach students with different learning styles. The MACSA schools focused heavily on building a sense of community and motivating students to care about school.

DCP also places great importance on building a learning community, and DCP teachers use some progressive strategies. But DCP is the most structured of the local charters in its teaching and rules. It is the most relentless in pursuit of a clear academic mission: Prepare all students for success at a four-year college or university.

Thanks to Andaluz's fund-raising skills and a savvy board of directors, DCP coped well with the financial and managerial problems that are common to charter schools. Other local charters struggled to keep going.

About 9 percent of charter schools have closed their doors, usually for financial reasons rather than academic failure, estimates the Center for Education Reform.[3]

Six weeks into its second year of operation, SVE in Mountain View closed. The school had failed to enroll enough students to meet its budget. The frustrated teachers walked out. Students had to transfer to their local high schools or find other alternatives.

MACSA's Gilroy high school lost two principals (one as a result of an auto accident) and most of its teachers in the first semester. When a group of DCP staffers visited, they were shocked to see MACSA students chewing gum in class and playing a violent video game during a break; a trash can was tipped over and nobody picked it up. None of that would have been tolerated at DCP. "I knew it's not my school and it's not my place to interfere, but I had to restrain myself from taking charge," Arreola said later, still distressed by the disorder. "There was trash just lying there! That's not right!"

The Gilroy school lacked strong academic leadership and a well-thought-out curriculum, the DCP visitors thought. But there was a promising sign: Students had gone on strike to demand a permanent math teacher. "The kids cared enough about learning math to do something," said Gallegos.

MACSA responded. It had been hiring through the Gilroy Unified School District, but now started doing its own hiring and found a permanent math teacher and a new principal, Reyes's wife. The school survived, though with poor test scores.

Five years after DCP opened, 17 charters were operating in the county, many serving poor and working-class immigrant neighborhoods on the East Side of San Jose. New charters include a KIPP middle school, an eleventh-twelfth-grade charter for Conservation Corps participants, a vocational school, and two high schools devoted to preparing disadvantaged minority students for college. DCP is not alone.

10

life dreams

"Did you see the *Simpsons* episode when Homer thought he was going to die from eating poison blowfish?" asks Alicia Gallegos. "He made a list of what he wanted to do in the 24 hours before he died." For example, Homer wanted to "teach Bart to share."

Each week, Gallegos meets with the 12 students in her advisory group in the only available space, the back hallway of Saint Paul's. I grab a folding chair and join the group, a mix of ninth and tenth graders.

Gallegos hands out a sample Life Dream list, allegedly made by a teenager 50 years ago. Many of the things he listed—a lasting marriage with children, a college education, a rewarding career—came true, she tells them. You're more likely to reach your goals if you have goals. She's following a lesson plan drawn up by the counselor, Steve Smith, who wants DCP students to plan for the future. Unlike middle-class teenagers, who can follow their parents' path to college without really thinking about it, DCP students will have to make their own way.

Students take turns reading the list aloud. "Keep a possible attitude," a boy misreads.

The listmaker wants to make a positive "community impact." Gallegos asks whether they know what that means. Everybody's heard of the movie *Sudden Impact.* Unfortunately, the students think *impact* means "collide." When Gallegos explains, the interest level falls.

The freshmen are content to plow through the list, but the sophomores challenge it.

"Staying in love with my spouse . . . some of this you can't control," says Amy. "Like staying in love . . . it depends on the other person."

Rajiv points out that one of the goals on what's supposed to be a 50-year-old list refers to video games. Closer reading reveals it's "inspired" by a real list compiled 50 years ago.

Byron disagrees with the idea of setting lofty goals. "When people say to shoot farther than you can go . . . you'll miss and be disappointed."

"Don't just live for future goals," says Rajiv. "Live life as it comes."

I'm surprised. Rajiv is one of DCP's most diligent students, to use a vocabulary word, one of the few who aren't living life as it comes. Maybe he thinks he's working too hard.

Rajiv's parents immigrated from India but don't fit Silicon Valley's Indian stereotype: They're not engineers or doctors; they sell windows. They're ambitious for their son, who's always done well in school, unlike most of his DCP classmates. Rajiv's father periodically threatens to transfer him to nearby Lincoln High, a performing arts magnet, which offers more advanced classes. But DCP's personal attention has prevailed. And Rajiv, who's small, is respected for his intelligence at DCP, not harassed.

One day I heard two girls talking in rapid-fire Spanish. All I could understand was "Rajiv" until one girl said, "Hecka smart." The other girl said something in Spanish with "Rajiv" in it and then nodded approvingly. "*Hecka* smart," she said.

In Gallegos's advisory class, students write their own list of life goals, and the goals they think their parents have for them. College is first on every list, but only the sophomores think to list the steps that will take them to college, such as earning good grades.

Byron wants to be a professional baseball player. DCP is not a good school for a talented athlete, but Byron can get some exposure playing Police Athletic League baseball in the summer. And going to DCP is not his choice. His grandparents, who are raising him, are determined that Byron get an education. In middle school, he was a slacker. Now he's got a shot at the honor roll.

I dubbed Byron "Fonzie," because he's organizing a car club. But that doesn't do justice to the letter-sweater side of his personality. Handsome, outgoing, and popular, Byron is a Big Man on Campus.

Byron has a backup plan, if baseball doesn't work. It is unexpectedly practical: He wants to be a realtor.

Amy writes that one of her parents' goals is for her to marry a Jewish man. "DCP isn't a great place to meet a Jewish guy," I say. Amy laughs. She fits in easily at DCP after attending a bilingual immersion school, which has made her fluent in Spanish. Not trusting public schools, Amy's parents tried to get her into a Catholic high school, but her grades weren't high enough. She is one of DCP's social butterflies, involved in everything.

A few months later, I'm back in advisory. Gallegos starts by asking students to evaluate their moods on a scale of 1 to 10, and say what they're happy and sad about, and what they did on the weekend.

Then they divide into three groups to discuss the options in a dilemma she's presented.

- You're defending an accused murderer who you think is guilty. You can get charges dropped on a technicality.
- You're a landlord who hasn't raised rent in years and business is doing badly. Your renter, a single mom with kids, is six months behind on rent. A new tenant wants the apartment and will pay higher rent.
- A 15-year-old girl needs a heart transplant. An 80-year-old woman has been hurt in a car accident. You can keep her alive but there's no chance of full recovery. Her heart is a perfect match. Her family leaves it to you, the heart surgeon.

The first group decides to raise the technicality and free the accused killer. "We don't know he's guilty," a student says. "It's the right thing to do."

The second group sides with the landlord: "Let the single mother pay half the back rent and then move somewhere cheaper."

"I'd kick them out," a boy says.

"What if it was your own family?" asks Gallegos, whose father works for Social Services.

"If it's your family, they still have to follow the rules," a girl answers. "Family is family. This is money!"

Gallegos is taken aback, knowing her advisees are growing up in families who are far more likely to be behind on rent than to be landlords.

On the other hand, DCP students know about moving to cheaper places. Even in a recession, San Jose rents are high. Some students share a parent's two-hour (one-way) commute from Merced or Modesto; others live with relatives during the week and join their parents in the Central Valley on weekends. Several have friends whose parents moved the family back to Mexico when jobs dried up in San Jose.

I've seen it before in other classes. Critical Thinking, which is really about social problems, is taught by Joe Albers, a Santa Clara graduate student in religious studies and Spanish, when Jill Case, the official teacher, is busy. A true-blue liberal, Albers struggles to get students to sympathize with the poor. Many of them *are* poor, and they're not very sympathetic.

Albers's sales job on the homeless was a flop. There are too many transients begging near the Y and in students' neighborhoods.

Albers: From your reading, what's a reason people become homeless?
Roberto: Domestic violence. But why don't they ask their families for
    help?
Gina: What if people don't want to be helped? Some people don't.
Ella: If you give them money they'll just spend it on alcohol, but if
    you offer them food, they reject it.
Albers: Maybe they've already eaten. Maybe they're offended. Is it as
    simple as black and white?
Martina: Give them flyers on where to go for food.

Most of San Jose's poor are working poor: janitors, warehouse workers, laborers, gardeners, fast-food cooks, retail clerks. DCP students believe everyone should work for a living. They'd like to get enough education to qualify for a decent job.

One boy told me that when his single mother moved the family up from Mexico, they lived with an aunt. His mother, who couldn't afford a car, bundled her eight-year-old son in two sets of clothes to ward off the morning chill, put him on the handlebars of an old bicycle, and rode him to school at 6:00 A.M. Then she bicycled across town to be on time for her first cleaning job. On the long walk home from school, the other boys would stop at a convenience store to buy snacks. He couldn't buy anything, because he never had any money. "Not a quarter," he said. His life goal was to go to college, get a job, and have a car, an apartment, and enough money for snacks.

Back in advisory, group three, struggling with the transplant question, is hoping for a high-tech solution. Gonzalo wants to put the old lady on an artificial heart and use her heart to save the girl. Rico wants to save the girl with an artificial heart. Forced to choose, they go for youth. "An 80-year-old with zero chance? It's obvious!" says Byron. "Let the old lady die and give the heart to the girl."

All the advisees seem to agree. Gallegos, a devout Catholic, looks troubled. Before she can say anything, the sound of chair shoving echoes from the real classrooms. She glances at her watch. Advisory is over.

Sample Life Dreams List

Family
1. Get married
2. Have 3 kids
3. Stay really in love with my spouse until we're old
4. Stay close with my parents
5. Be a good role model for my little brother
6. See my cousins at least once a week
7. Have family reunions in fun places

School/Learning
8. Graduate from high school and get into my first choice college
9. Graduate from college
10. Own a dog
11. Learn a foreign language I don't already know
12. Read the 10 best selling books ever written
13. Read the Bible

Career
14. Do something that helps other people
15. Teach a college course
16. Write a book

17. Be on TV
18. Become a millionaire
19. Travel to new places
20. Invent a new video game
21. Organize big social events
22. Start a company
23. Be a manager for at least 10 people
24. Interview people who are famous or have done amazing things
25. Do something with my interest in music and art

11

on trial

Sydney Price, leader of a college environmental group, opposed the expansion of a ski lodge. But did Syd start the fire that burned the lodge? A fellow student, Casey Ballard, says Syd hinted he (or she) started the fire; fire-bomb information downloaded from the Internet is found in Syd's home and a partial license plate seen at the scene matches the license plate on Syd's pickup. But Syd has explanations and an alibi of sorts. And Casey, who lied when first approached by the police, may be motivated by rivalry or guilt. There are witnesses on both sides, and questions about whether some evidence is admissible.

It's the 2001–2002 Mock Trial case. (Names are unisex so male or female students can play all roles.) Mock Trial is an activity that's become an alternative to debate team in some high schools. While learning legal procedures, students develop their ability to read, analyze, argue, listen, and speak in public. Students must learn law and logic to make and respond to objections; they must be able to keep cool under pressure.

In the fall, each team gets the facts of the year's case, usually "ripped from the headlines." The team splits into prosecution and defense sides, complete with lawyers and witnesses, which practice against each other. Then competitors "scrimmage" against other schools. A coin flip determines which school takes the prosecution and which the defense at any given competition. In February, teams compete in a county tournament, often judged by local judges, which leads to state and national tournaments. Since it's hard to make the facts of each case a perfect toss-up, teams aren't judged on whether the defendant is convicted or acquitted but on how well the judges think they've argued their side of the case and dealt with legal issues.

In English, history, College Readiness, math, and science, DCP students learn to develop a thesis and support it with logic and facts. Is Cortez or Montezuma responsible for the destruction of Tenochitlan? Why does $X =$ 6? Show your reasoning and your evidence. Make your case. Mock Trial extends that into another arena: Make the case that the defendant is guilty or innocent.

Lippman and Andaluz see it as a fun way to build critical thinking skills and help students improve their public speaking. In DCP's first year, all students took a Mock Trial class taught by Andaluz once a week. That year, students analyzed the case against a parent charged with causing a child's death: Was the memory of the key witness—the surviving sibling—trustworthy 15 years later?

My daughter did Mock Trial at Palo Alto High, one of the county's perennial contenders. She was timekeeper as a sophomore, a prosecutor her junior and senior years. In her last year, Paly won the county competition and placed fifth at the state tournament. I went to a lot of trials. As a veteran Mock Trial mom, I volunteered to help Andaluz with one of the classes in the school's first year. That's how I first met Amy and Barbara, now co-presidents of the team.

That first year, DCP fielded an all-frosh Mock Trial team against experienced teams, including the county's top teams: Leland, Lincoln, Lynbrook, and Palo Alto.

"We got killed," Lippman says.

Vicky Evans, the college counselor, remembers the cross-examination of a DCP witness at one scrimmage.

"Would you read the underlined passage for the court?" the opposing lawyer asked. The boy started to read, slowly. The cross-examination time—which is limited—ticked away as he worked his way through the sentence. The opposing team's lawyer stood there baffled; she'd never met a Mock Trial competitor who had trouble reading. By the time he finished, she had little time left to ask her questions.

"I thought he'd feel humiliated," says Evans. "But the next match was the one where we brought the wrong half of our team: We were supposed to be arguing the defense, but we brought our prosecution side by mistake. I said that he must feel relieved that he wouldn't have to go on, and he said, 'Oh no! I was really ready this time!' He wanted to try." What Evans had seen as humiliation, the student had experienced as a triumph of sorts: He'd made it through the sentence.

As it turned out, the boy did go on. When the DCP lawyers and witnesses realized the mistake, they refused to forfeit. With no preparation, the prosecutors switched sides and argued for the defense. It was the proudest moment of DCP's Mock Trial season, the moment they all remembered later. They hadn't won, of course. But they'd made their case.

Mock Trial wasn't a class in the second year. To their frustration, Andaluz and Lippman decided students weren't getting much out of a weekly class, and they didn't have space in the schedule to offer more.

But again DCP would field a Mock Trial team. Bob Weeks, a retired public defender and a former Mock Trial judge, volunteered as coach. Tall, bald, and impeccably dressed, Weeks insisted that students adopt a confident demeanor. As a backup, he recruited Ashu Kalra, a young public defender with experience as a Mock Trial competitor, coach, and scorer. Lippman, former coach of Gunderson High's Mock Trial team, served as assistant coach. For him, Mock Trial is a chance to build skills and character toward the distant future day when DCP can compete with the best.

Eager to observe DCP students in another setting and experienced as a Mock Trial booster, I volunteered to help out with the team. Fifteen students signed up initially. Most came from English-speaking homes, including brothers Adam and Bill, both excellent students; Rajiv, also a top student; Jerry, whose mother is a paralegal; and Amy. But some immigrant students signed up, too, undaunted by the challenge of speaking in English. I was impressed by Clara, who jumped into every activity with enthusiasm, despite her mother's complaints that she spent all her time at school.

Not all the Mock Trialers were successful students. Roger, an eager veteran of last year's team, had made it to tenth grade by the slimmest of margins. Lippman warned him he had to raise his grades, which had slipped alarmingly, to stay on the team. (DCP students who have less than a C average can't compete in extracurriculars. Lippman believes this policy helps send the message that academics come first and motivates students to try harder.) A freshman named Gonzalo caught on quickly, but he too had to raise his grades to remain eligible.

At the first meeting, Weeks starts by insisting that the students stand up straight when they speak, with their weight balanced on both feet, without hands stuffed in their pockets or eyes focused on the floor.

Bill—his hair gelled into Medusa shapes—talks about the burden of proof, rocking his shoulders, shifting from foot to foot, and starting with "OK." Weeks keeps making him start over. On his third try, Bill stands straight and speaks firmly. Casey, the main witness against the suspected arsonist, Syd, isn't credible, Bill says, because Casey first denied being a member of Syd's environmental group before admitting he (or she) was a member.

Weeks writes on the white board: Falsus en uno, falsus en omnibus (false in one thing, false in everything). He also gives them a concise definition of prejudice: "Believing is seeing."

Lippman takes over, asking for a volunteer to be cross-examined. Alan agrees.

> Lippman: What color is the sky?
> Alan: I don't know. It's different colors.
> Lippman: Have you ever seen the sky?
> Alan: Yes.
> Lippman: Are you color-blind?
> Alan: No.
> Lippman: So, what color is the sky?
> Alan: I don't know. People usually say it's blue.
> Lippman: Do you make your decisions based on what other people believe?
> Alan: No.
> Lippman: What color is the sky?
> Barbara: Objection, your honor! Asked and answered.
> Adam: Your honor, he's badgering the witness.
> Weeks: I'll sustain both objections.

The self-appointed lawyers are delighted to have won their objections. Lippman is pleased they had the nerve to speak up.

"My point is that testimony in court is different from what you'd say elsewhere," Lippman tells the team. "Words have precise meanings in court. Alan just would have said the sky is 'blue,' if he wasn't on the witness stand." He goes on: "What is the meaning of *trial?*"

"A case in court," says Roger.

"It can be a test," says Bill.

"Yes, or a struggle," says Lippman. "I want you to focus on the third meaning of trial as a push-pull struggle between two versions of truth."

After the students go home, Lippman tells Weeks that he doesn't care whether the team wins. He doesn't expect them to beat experienced teams like Lincoln, the nearest high school, which has gone to the state tournament many times. "Last year, they cleaned our clock," he says. "They will this year, too." That's not important, Lippman says. He wants DCP's Mock Trialers to show team spirit, to compete with class and dignity, to improve their skills.

At heart, Lippman is a very competitive person. He wants his kids to be the best. But he has to stay in touch with reality. So he talks about "glorious failure," which means trying something that's too hard, falling flat on your face, picking yourself up, and doing it better the next time. That kind of glory his students can achieve now. Winning will come later.

To remind students that they're striving to be the best, Lippman starts every Mock Trial meeting by asking each team member to say what he or she has done during the week to demonstrate "the spirit of the Mock Trial team." In what way have they tried to excel?

> Rajiv: I presented a math POW [Problem of the Week] as a judge. I
> used Roger's coat as a robe.
> Roger: I was bailiff for Rajiv when he did the POW. And I paid
> attention to Syd Price clues.
> Jerry: I worked on my good/evil outline [for humanities]. I chose good
> even though it was harder. I argued people will sacrifice their lives at
> times to save others.
> Adam: I did the closing in the history debate.
> Barbara: I used my Mock Trial skills in the history debate.
> Gonzalo: I studied hard for the math test. I got A-.
> Amy: I said "your honor" in the history debate.
> Bill: I did a quick counterargument in the debate.

Kalra, the young public defender, tells them to come up with a one-sentence theme for the prosecution and for the defense that explains their theory of the case. He provides students with an example to get them going:

"Consumed by jealous rage, O. J. murdered his ex-wife and a bystander."
Or, a countervailing theory, "O. J. was framed by cops for murder."

Converting that to the Mock Trial case, Rajiv, Jerry, and Barbara, playing prosecutors, decide on "Ambitious ecoterrorist burns down building to save trees."

Defenders Adam, Amy, and Gonzalo assert, "Syd Price, a responsible, hard-working student, is wrongfully accused based on unfair stereotyping and misleading evidence."

Then, they work on defining Syd Price.

To the prosecution, Syd is wild, young, student, hippie, tree hugger, angry, ecoterrorist, misled, militant, uncivilized, EGO leader, fanatic, arsonist, jealous, follower, extremist, drama king/queen, anarchist.

They discuss double meanings. *Leader* can be good, or it can mean Syd had the moxie to commit arson. *Immature* can be used to argue Syd talks big but wouldn't act, or that he's irresponsible enough to burn down the lodge.

The defense also gets to define Syd's character: model employee, hippie, exceptional student, gentle, nature lover, ecoactivist, innocent, young, helpful, good friend, responsible, intelligent, mature.

As the weeks go on, some students decide they don't have the time for Mock Trial, and one boy's family moves back to Mexico. The team may be too small to compete.

In November, Lippman recruits a new team member. "He's been arguing all his life," says the principal, introducing Warren, a stocky ninth grader with a light beard. "He's a natural."

Warren, one of the school's few white students, has been in trouble at every school he's attended. He can be surly, sullen, withdrawn—or quick-witted and analytical. Within minutes, Warren grasps the idea of Mock Trial and starts making intelligent suggestions about the case. He actually smiles.

Today, students who didn't audition last week try out for roles as prosecutor, defense attorney, or witness. To demonstrate their courtroom skills, they read an Atticus Finch speech from *To Kill a Mockingbird*.

Roger, rocking from side to side, reads in a halting voice, stumbling over *distaff, gravely, inferiority,* and *pauper,* but makes it to the end, seemingly undiscouraged.

By contrast, Bill stands tall and reads with understanding and expression. He's sure to be cast as a lawyer; he asks for defense.

Weeks offers to give Warren a week to prepare, but Warren doesn't want to wait. Standing with his hand stuck in his pocket, Warren reads forcefully, nearly as well as Bill. Warren also wants to be a defense lawyer. He really wants it.

Weeks and Kalra are ecstatic about Warren. But Lippman warns them that Warren may not be eligible to compete. With Mock Trial as a motivator, Lippman hopes Warren will fight his way to a C average by the end of the semester. He's got the intelligence and skills to be an A student someday, if he can learn to control his emotions. But Warren has a long way to go.

Lippman also tells them that Roger is off the team. Despite his promises, Roger isn't doing homework; his grades are in a tailspin. His parents will pull him out of DCP, a place he loves, at the end of the semester, unless he can pull off a miracle and pass his classes. He needs to work on the miracle.

The next week, Weeks and Kalra announce the roles. Bill will be the pretrial attorney, the most intellectually challenging job, for both the defense and prosecution teams. He'll try to exclude evidence as a defender, then argue for its inclusion as prosecutor. Warren will be his understudy. If Warren is academically eligible, he can take over one of the pretrial jobs; if not, Bill will be prepared to do both. Rajiv, Jerry, and Barbara are prosecution attorneys; Adam, Amy, and Gonzalo will argue for the defense. That leaves Clara as a witness for both sides, with the lawyers also doubling as witnesses. Normally, a Mock Trial team has eight lawyers, including two for pretrial; another eight witnesses; a timekeeper; and a bailiff. The team is down to nine people, and two of them may not be eligible when the tournament starts in February.

Gonzalo is confident he can raise his grades. Warren, with a sense of responsibility he's never shown before, is worried that he'll let down the team. "I don't know if I can do this," he tells his teammates.

"Talk to your teachers and ask them what you need to do," says Lippman.

Warren sighs. "I have a big job ahead."

He really is trying. In class, he's become more respectful of his teachers, more diligent about his work. He asks for extra-credit work. But he still has bad days when he's told to step outside the room to cool down. And he's trying to make up for zeros he earned at the start of the semester, when he was perpetually angry and defiant.

Trying to recruit new team members, Warren helps create a motto, which expresses his love of Mock Trial: "Why get in trouble for arguing with your teachers, when you can be rewarded for arguing with the judge?"

*

At the semester's end, Warren had raised his grades significantly, but still hadn't reached the minimum C average. Neither had Gonzalo. Furthermore, Amy's family was moving to Southern California. Roger's parents transferred him to their neighborhood high school, where the work would be easier.

At the start of Intersession in January, when the team should have been practicing intensely for the county tournament, Lippman and Weeks faced the sad truth: The team was too small to compete.

"It's good we can't compete this year," said Gonzalo, determined to find a bright side. "It will motivate us to do better next year."

As a farewell gesture, Weeks gave each student a copy of Anthony Lewis's book *Gideon's Trumpet,* on the landmark case that established the right to counsel.

Nearby Lincoln High won the county tournament, qualifying for the state competition. The day after spring break, Barbara rushed up to Andaluz. "Did you hear? Lincoln won state! We'll have to really work to beat them next year!" She dashed out.

"Yes, we'll have to work," Andaluz said.

Lippman asked team members, "What's your favorite objection?"

Barbara: Badgering the witness.
Gonzalo: Not responsive.
Jerry: Hearsay.
Clara: Lacks relevance.
Amy: Asked and answered.
Bill: Vague and ambiguous.
Rajiv: Calls for expert opinion.
Warren: I don't like objections.

12

the shortest basketball team in america

At the start of the year, with ninth graders still adjusting to the school's demands and tenth graders recovering from the summer slump, grades were low. At the end of the first six-week grading period, 40 percent of students had less than a C average. With so few students eligible for extracurriculars, the coed soccer team and the boys' basketball team folded. Four boys ran cross-country, but just for practice. DCP's last hope was girls' basketball. Lippman and Arreola went to every girl with a C average, begging her to join the basketball team, regardless of athletic skill. They knew the DCP girls would be outmatched on the courts. Competing was a point of pride: Real schools compete in sports. DCP needed to field at least one team. Lippman told girls they'd need extracurriculars on their college applications; Arreola appealed to school pride.

Clara signed up. Growing up in rural Mexico, she'd never seen a basketball. She didn't watch it on TV. But she had a C average. And she wanted to do everything DCP had to offer.

Selma signed up. Selma wasn't much of an athlete. She wasn't five feet tall. But she'd made huge gains academically since deciding to take school seriously. She had a C average.

Barbara already participated in Student Council and Mock Trial, but she signed up for basketball, too. She stood less than five feet two inches tall in her sneakers. But that was about average for the DCP team, possibly the shortest high school basketball team in America. Barbara knew how to hustle. And she was eligible.

School spirit motivated Selena and Emilia, both honor roll students. Like Clara, they'd given their full allegiance to DCP.

The star turned out to be a petite, graceful Cambodian girl named Neary, also an A student. Her sport was tennis, but she promised to give basketball a try.

One of the fathers volunteered to coach with Lippman. They drove the girls to the Washington Youth Center for daily practices after class. The parent coach's daughter, Andrea, was the only girl who really knew the game. Neary was the only talented athlete. But slowly, the team started to take shape. The girls learned to think ahead, to set up a defense, to set up a play, to work together.

DCP teams would be the Lobos, Spanish for "wolves." Lippman and Andaluz wanted a Spanish name that expressed determination. In the faith that someday there'd be boys' teams, the girls called themselves the Lady Lobos.

When the girls played teams from much larger schools, teams with juniors and seniors, the Lady Lobos lost by huge margins. Against Lippman's old school, Gunderson, DCP lost 36–6.

"Mr. Lippman said we played tough on defense, but we have to work on offense," said Barbara, showing up for Mock Trial in her basketball uniform. The size of the defeat didn't faze her.

The next week, the Lady Lobos lost by 38–10. "Our defense fell apart," Barbara said, echoing Lippman again. "We didn't play our best game. We have to do better next time."

The girls kept practicing, improving, and losing by 20-plus points. They never lost heart.

Finally, after a string of lopsided defeats, DCP traveled north to play another small charter school, East Palo Alto (EPA) High. The city of East Palo Alto—across the county line from affluent Palo Alto—is heavily Hispanic, black, and Tongan. Ironically, the charter high school is located in an old middle school in a quiet, leafy, very expensive Menlo Park neighborhood that 18 years earlier managed to secede from Ravenswood, East Palo Alto's low-scoring elementary district. (Neighbors successfully argued that secession wouldn't further segregation: All the white children in the neighborhood, and almost all of the blacks, attended private school.)[1]

As a first-year school, EPA has only 80 students, all ninth graders. But EPA has a gym to practice in, uniformed cheerleaders, and girls who tower over DCP defenders.

Seven players suit up for DCP; an eighth girl is unable to play because of a twisted ankle. Some of the Lady Lobos are playing against EPA girls who are six or seven inches taller. To their surprise, the DCP girls take a slim lead. Their aggressive defense confuses EPA. They out-hustle the taller girls, fighting for every rebound and stealing passes. But, except Neary, the Lobos can't shoot.

Lippman tries to persuade them to try for the basket. "Shoot anytime you're open," he says. "If you miss 100 shots, you won't be kicked off the team. Andrea, you took a couple of great shots. Try to move the ball quickly and get closer. You all go full speed."

They run back on the court at full speed, but the Lobos still are basket-shy. Clara eyes the net nervously, then passes to Selena. "Take a shot," yells Lippman. "I don't care if it goes in. Just shoot!" Selena heaves the ball up in the air; it goes two feet to the right of the backboard, where a surprised EPA girl catches it.

"Look at the rim when you shoot," says Lippman at the next huddle. "Work with the rim. The rim is your friend!"

Defense keeps it close. When time runs out, the score is tied.

"They can't get through our defense," Lippman says proudly.

But, in the overtime, EPA gets through and scores. In the last seconds, DCP wins a fight over a rebound at the EPA net. The shot goes wild. EPA wins 23–21.

The Lobos, who've never come within 20 points of winning, are elated. For the first time all season, they were in the ballgame every step of the way. They see a possibility never envisioned before. "Next time, we'll win," they say to each other.

A week later, DCP is back at EPA High for a rematch. In the pregame huddle, the Lobos shout a cheer that Neary has written:

We got the power.
We got the might.
We know we will win this fight.
'Cause you know and I know
There ain't no doubt:
Lobos girls are going to knock you out.

Once again, it's a close game, with DCP's defense baffling EPA's players. But the Lobos have spent the week working on their offense. They're aiming at the basket and taking their shots. The rim is now an acquaintance, if not a close friend. Neary is hitting nearly every shot, but she's not the only one scoring baskets.

Angela Hensley and Alicia Gallegos arrive to watch the last half of the game. Gallegos boasts that she recruited Neary, tipped off by a friend at Notre Dame High that a girl with DCP potential had been rejected for admission. "She was so shy. She never said a word," Gallegos says. "She was afraid to go to a big high school, so I got her to come to DCP."

The EPA players fight back, scoring three goals in a row. They take the lead, smiling with relief.

Then DCP catches fire. Neary steals the ball, streaks down the court, and executes an elegant layup. "Michael Jordan" whispers Andrea's father. Then Andrea steals the ball. Then Neary again. And again. EPA is rattled. The Lobos will not let their opponents get near the basket. Now all the DCP girls are intercepting passes, grabbing rebounds, dashing back and forth. The Lady Lobos have taken control of the court.

DCP wins 27–23.

Neary is in the center of a circle of screaming girls. Once again, they yell the team cheer. "We got the power. We got the might. We know we will win this fight!"

Lippman grins wildly. "It sounds like they've won the World's Cup," he says.

Neary leads a new cheer: "Pizza! We want pizza!"

By second semester, grades are up, and more students are eligible for extracurriculars. DCP is able to field a boys' baseball and a girls' softball team. Once again, the season opener is against a large high school.

At staff development day, teachers who missed the opening game ask about the score. Playing Los Altos High, the girls lost 24–0. The boys, with Roberto pitching, lost 34–0. But, amid the pain, there's hope.

"What's this I hear about Shakespeare?" asks Andaluz, who's running the school while Lippman spends time with his wife and new son, born six weeks early.

Jorge, who'd read *carousel* as "carrot salad" in ninth grade, who'd gone from F's to B's and C's, stood in the outfield quoting *Macbeth:* "Fair is foul, and foul is fair." The tenth graders on the team explained the reference to the ninth graders.

"Our kids were quoting Shakespeare," says Aaron Srugis, the coach. "That means we won."

"Are the kids really down about the scores?" a teacher asks.

"No, actually, they're OK," Jill Case says. "They know the story of the girls' basketball team. They kept talking about it, about how the girls lost big at the start of the season, but they kept at it, and they won in the end. The kids know they need practice now, but they believe they can get better. They believe they can win."

For a few seconds, the room falls silent. Then Andaluz speaks softly. "That's what DCP is all about," she says, almost whispering. "That's it. That's the whole thing."

DCP students enter the school as academic losers. They don't know how to play the game. By the standards of middle-class high schools, DCP students aren't really *in* the game. But if they keep working, they get better. If they stick with it, they'll win a college education.

A few weeks after their 34–0 defeat, the baseball team beat a San Francisco private school by 15–10. A week later, playing a San Jose private school, the softball team won, too.

Srugis predicted the Lobos' baseball team would win half their games in the third year, when DCP is scheduled to play in a league for small private schools. "I've never coached a team with more heart," he said. "And they keep getting better."

The following year, DCP fielded a boys' basketball team for the first time, entering a tournament with much larger schools. The *San Jose Mercury News* ran a brief story about the Lobos' attitude that set the school's phone ringing with calls from parents interested in enrolling their children.

UNCOMMON HOOP DREAMS
By Clay Lambert
San Jose Mercury News, Dec. 5, 2002
Sammy Garcia is one basketball player who can see progress in a 98–10 loss.

"What do you mean? This was much better than the first game," he said Thursday.

Downtown College Prep High School, where grade-point averages mean more than scoring averages, lost its opener the day before, 110–6.

The San Jose school, which serves students who traditionally haven't been encouraged to attend college, takes a different approach to sports. It is a place where the girls get the prime practice time in the gym and all the players—part of a largely Latino, senior-less student body of 300—focus more on academics than basketball strategy.

The sting of the laughable losses is tempered by the fact that this is the boys' first season. San Jose's first charter school lacked a bona fide campus.

"Half the kids haven't even played the game before," said Jose Arreola, athletic director at the school, which opened in 2000.

Jennifer Andaluz, the school's co-founder and executive director, doesn't worry that the routs will harm the psyches of her students.

"These kids have all lost before," she said.

13

last chance at first semester

George Patton would have admired Aaron Srugis's pep talk at the November 27 assembly. First, Srugis honors students who improved their grade on the Problem of the Week, a challenging math problem that may take hours to solve. Warren, trying to raise his grades so he can compete in Mock Trial, is up by 40 points out of 100; my tutee, Lisa, is up by 60.

Then Srugis tells the ninth graders to get ready for finals. "It's time to go to war," he says. "Your teachers have given you the weapons and ammunition. You have to hunker down."

Some of the teachers flinch or smile at the war metaphor, but Srugis has the students leaning forward.

"You have two weeks until finals," he says. "We talk about *ganas* here and *ganas* there. What impresses me are students who hunker down and do it."

They've gotten sloppy about doing the DCP clap, Srugis says. They're rushing through it without thinking. He wants them to do it right. "The pause between each clap represents pain," he says. "It takes time. Do a real DCP clap, slowly. You're going to war together. You have to clap together."

He starts the clap, slowly, solemnly, then picks up the pace.

To clap in unison, students have to tune in to what's going on around them. They stop fidgeting and concentrate on clapping together, louder and louder. At the end, they cheer.

Then, Case honors students who've improved their GPA by 0.3 point or more. Once again, Lisa's name is called.

The student with the lowest average went from 0.0 to 0.55—from all F's to a mix of D's and F's. The top improver climbed from 3.3 to 3.6.

Case announces the honor roll. "These are people who are on track for college," she says. Of 190 students, only 31 have a B average or better. At some schools, a majority of students make the honor roll. DCP teachers can't give out inflated, self-esteem grades without sabotaging students' chances to prepare for college work. Honor roll really is an honor, and students cheer for those whose names are called out. I notice Byron has made it, for the first time ever.

In the prefinals advisory group meeting, Laura DeRoche asks second-year students to offer advice to students who are taking their first DCP finals. "Finals are good," Lorenzo says. "It's fun to get out early and forget about it."

"How did you do on your finals last year?" DeRoche asks.

"Good," says Lorenzo.

Knowing he's repeating ninth grade, DeRoche is puzzled. "You got good grades on your finals?"

"No," Lorenzo says. "I passed some of them."

"So what's your advice on preparing for finals?"

Lorenzo smiles sweetly. "Someone once told me to do my homework. My advice is: Do your homework."

"So, do you do yours?" DeRoche asks.

"Um," Lorenzo smiles again, "sometimes."

The final counts for only 10 percent of the final semester grade. Students who have less than a C- in English or math take review classes during the two-week Intersession period, and then retake the final. Students who don't need a retake can sign up for three electives during Intersession.

Many ninth graders have never studied for a big test. The week before finals, all teachers work to prepare students. DeRoche assigns English students to write about finals, encouraging them to think about their preparation: "What are you feeling about the final exam? What are you most worried about? Which exam do you think you'll do best on? How are you going to prepare?"

Across the divider, Gerth's only class of ninth-grade history students is discussing which final will be their hardest, and how to cope with stress. Gerth reviews how to take coded notes and write a persuasive paragraph. She tells students to write two to three sentences: "How happy are you with your work this semester? How hard did you work? What are your grades? What can I do to help you succeed?"

In College Readiness, Gallegos reviews study methods. Students fold paper in threes—"like the Mexican flag"—to create a "Quiz Yourself triptych."

"What topics do you think will be on the exam?" Gallegos asks. The homework is to teach the topics to someone else—a parent or friend—who must sign the homework sheet.

Students write sample questions and answers. "What is a poem?" asks Art. In the answer space, he writes, "Something that rhymes." His exploratory question is "Why are poems sad sometimes?"

Emilio asks, "What's a simile? What does a poem mean?"

Then Gallegos gives her students time to study for any of their upcoming finals in other subjects.

Students look up definitions of vocabulary words: *motivated, determined, tenacious.* Lorenzo complains about Buddy's flirting with Lisa, using one of the students' favorite vocabulary words. "They're *hindering* me," he says with a smile.

Gallegos sits next to Teresa to help her with vocabulary. Teresa has let her tough-girl mask slip today. She seems younger, softer, and needier. She flips through her word list.

"What does *successful* mean?" she asks.

Lisa is reviewing science, her least favorite subject. The study question asks about dropping objects from a tower: Which will hit first, a bowling ball or a baseball? Why?

"Bowling ball," Lisa writes. "Because it's heavier."

I'm no science whiz, but I'm pretty sure this is wrong. "Did your teacher talk about Galileo's experiment?" I ask.

Lisa looks blank.

"Didn't Galileo throw objects—something heavy and something lighter—off the Leaning Tower of Pisa to see which would hit first?"

Dennis, who's kibitzing, gets it. "Oh yeah! They hit at the same time!" He smiles with genuine pleasure. I sense that there is an A student trapped inside Dennis. At the very least, he should be getting an A in science, one of his favorite subjects. But he's not.

"I think that's right," I say. "The weight doesn't matter. There's some law involved. Gravity?" I'm not playing dumb to get him to think through the question. I really don't know.

Carolina, competently cruising through her science questions at the next table, discusses the issue with Dennis. Lisa withdraws into stubborn incomprehension. Leaving "bowling ball" as her answer—an answer she knows must be wrong—she moves on to the next question.

At the back table, Lorenzo is copying the answers from Larissa's neatly completed study sheet.

"You're not helping him, Larissa, by letting him copy," says Gallegos. "Lorenzo needs to learn this."

Lorenzo smiles sheepishly. When Gallegos moves away, he copies Newton's second law of motion from Emilio, who's doing his study sheet in Spanish.

Felipe isn't working, but he has the study sheet in front of him, which is progress.

At the front table, Buddy is sitting alone looking peevish. "How can I study my notes?" he says. "I don't have any notes." He seems to think this is somebody else's fault. Buddy flutters through his notebook, looking to see whether elves might have taken science notes for him.

Lorenzo strokes Lisa's hair. "She's so good," he says. "She's not bothering anyone."

Gallegos asks Teresa to demonstrate a four-step summary on the board. Teresa mumbles to Gallegos, who tells her to face the class and speak up. Teresa can't do it. Gallegos coaxes her to speak, and finally Teresa says a few words to the floor and rushes back to her seat. It's a revelation: Without the protective armor of attitude, Teresa is painfully shy.

Remembering *chivalrous,* the vocabulary word, I think about Gallegos's students as armored knights. What would the mottoes be on their shields?

Teresa: Don't touch me.
Dennis: Just joking.
Felipe: I'm invisible.
Art: Help!
Buddy: It's not my fault.

Lisa: Good enough.

Larissa: No problemas.

Lorenzo: Take it easy.

Dennis is showing Art his "Horny" pills, a gag gift he's pulled out of his pocket.

I catch his eye and give him my "Cut it out" stare. I'm a mother; it comes naturally.

"It's just candy," Dennis says.

I shake my head.

Dennis puts the bottle back in his pocket.

"You will have to write a four-step summary on the final," Gallegos says. "Pay attention. This is exactly what's on the test."

Dennis takes a quick peek at his "Horny" pills, as if for inspiration, and turns to his vocabulary study sheet. *Motivated,* he writes.

Most ninth graders do very poorly in their first semester at DCP; as students get used to the school's demands, their grades start to rise.

Midyear Grade Point Averages, 2001–2

Ninth graders: 1.54

Tenth graders: 2.23

Honor roll: 35 students at or above a 3.0 (B) average

Academic probation: 44 who have less than a 1.0 (D) average

14

the zoot suiters

For two weeks in January, in the Intersession between semesters, DCP students try new things: hiking, guitar, Ultimate Frisbee, portrait drawing, karate, peer counseling. Staffers are trying new things, too: Laura DeRoche teaches a math review class to prepare students to retake the algebra final, while Itziar Aperribay, normally the advanced Spanish teacher, teaches English review to surly sophomores who need a second try to pass the English II final. Math teacher Aaron Srugis takes Shakespeare; biology teacher Omar Safie teaches poetry and mural painting; science teacher Jeff Fox shows students how to make vegan egg rolls.

I circulate, observing teachers and students in unfamiliar roles.

Jose Arreola, the burly activities director, teaches one of the most popular classes, called Zoot Suit History. Students read Luis Valdez's play about the wartime Zoot Suit Riots in Los Angeles and compare the Mexican gangs of the late 1930s and 1940s to the gangs they know all too well in twenty-first-century San Jose.

Students are fascinated by the rituals and language of the zoot-suit-wearing *pachucos*. How were they "jumped in" to the gang? they ask. What music did they like? What cars did they drive?

Arreola fills the board with *pachuco* slang. A girlfriend was a *ruca* or *laina*. A car was *ramfla*. *Labote* or *la pinta* meant police and jail. Gun was *fusea*.

Gil proves to be an expert on gang slang: *chota* for police, *cuete* for gun, *carnal* for friend or brother, *trucha* for watch out.

"Why are there so many Latino words for jail and gun?" Arreola asks. He wants students to understand Chicano history without glorifying the dead-end gang life that they see around them in San Jose. The Mexican Mafia, he says, "was founded by three guys who spent most of their lives in prison, so they had lots of time on their hands."

The class talks about gang nicknames: Payaso (Clown), ShyGirl, Joker, Shadow, Shoopy, TearDrop, Puppet.

Dopey, Sleepy, and Grumpy were popular, says Arreola. "They watched the Seven Dwarfs way too many times."

He tells students to write about their personal experiences with racism as perpetrator, victim, or observer.

The essays reflect San Jose's multiethnic character. Students describe witnessing hostility between Asians and blacks, blacks and Hispanics, Hispanics and whites. A pale girl with an Anglo first and last name writes about hearing new neighbors complain about "Mexicans" and wondering whether to tell them she's half Mexican herself.

Several essays deal with Hispanics hassling other Hispanics. Roberto writes about being harassed by Mexican American gang members because he's an immigrant. The Norteños tend to be American-born, while immigrants who join a gang usually become Sureños. Roberto was playing soccer in a park with friends when younger boys started squirting them with water pistols. He knew the boys were trying to pick a fight, so their Norteño brothers would have an excuse to beat up the immigrants. Being a prudent person, Roberto gave up the soccer game and went home.

In a stylish new haircut, Roberto no longer looks like a newcomer, and his English is improving steadily, along with his grades. In Zoot Suit History, he can excel. When Arreola wants to make sure he's using accurate Spanish grammar and spelling, he turns to Roberto.

Students at the level Roberto was last year take English as a Second Language (ESL) during Intersession. Gallegos teaches the small class, which meets in the hallway at the church. With so many extra classes running at once, there's no other space available.

Gallegos leads a half-dozen students through tongue twisters to help them improve their pronunciation. "Peter Piper picked a peck of peekled peppers," they chant, struggling to nail the vowel sounds.

"Let's try it again," she says.

Behind her on the mobile white board, she's taped a card with a quote from her students: "Our teacher makes us suffer." She knows learning English is very hard work for students who came to America as teenagers. If students can't enjoy it, at least they can take pride in being tough enough to suffer and survive.

Two sisters, newly arrived from Mexico before the start of school, show it's possible to succeed: Both made honor roll in their first semester. Now they're laughing at their own mistakes as they try to perfect "Peter Piper picked . . ."

Larissa goes from ESL to Dan Greene's algebra review class, where she's the star, eagerly volunteering to work problems at the board. During her pregnancy, Larissa was uncharacteristically subdued. Now she's glowing, animated, exuberant. She also makes DCP's uniform look stylish: She's wearing a thin black cardigan over a black DCP shirt; the belt in her khaki pants has a silver belt buckle with her initial on it. As she explains $1/4x + 6 = 12$ in Spanish, her silver loop earrings jiggle.

Greene translates her explanation to English; only one boy, Eli, says he doesn't know Spanish.

Larissa volunteers to do the next problem, but Greene wants to involve others. He asks the class: "How do you do 9 x 4/3?"

"Get a calculator," Eli says.

"You need practice on fractions," says Greene. "You guys are challenged by fractions."

He picks a boy to present the problem. I notice that *timesing* is the DCP argot for multiplication.

Then the eager Larissa gets another turn. She tackles $8-2x = 2$, but adds instead of subtracting.

"Is it 2 or negative 2?" asks Greene.

Larissa sees the errors, laughs at her foolishness, and fixes the mistake.

She appears to understand English perfectly but is reluctant to speak it. Her only English occurs after her third appearance at the board, when she exits with a precise, nearly British "Thank you" and a smile. Larissa appears to be enjoying herself immensely.

Over at the Y, Mock Trial is meeting in the entryway at the bottom of the stairs. Although the team won't be in the tournament, they plan to perform part of the trial before fellow students at the assembly that concludes Intersession. Mock Trialers have dressed as lawyers, to the best of their ability. Barbara is sharp in a black and white striped skirt, white top, and black sweater.

Bob Weeks tells them not to inject personal opinion. Say, "The evidence shows. . . ." Take out personal pronouns.

Warren, wearing a gray shirt and blue-striped tie with his hand tucked behind his back starts out in a low, gravelly voice: "The facts will show. . . ."

Rajiv neatly summarizes the evidence and tells which witness will testify to what. Syd had time, motive, and opportunity to commit the crime, he says, speaking with real conviction.

Gonzalo—gray pants, white shirt, red tie—summarizes for the defense: "The police officer will testify he followed a liar's advice . . ."

Weeks tells them the prosecutor doesn't use the defendant's name; it might humanize him. For the same reason, the defense counsel never talks about "the defendant." If you're defending, always use the name. "He's good, old personalized Syd."

As they rehearse, people go in and out the door and up the stairs, walking through the group at the foot of the stairs. The students barely notice. They're used to it.

Safie's poetry class is popular, and not just with girls. In many ways, rap has changed poetry's image. The class attracts boys who like the spotlight: Pedro, the rapper, and James and Jack, who are both on Student Council.

Students break into pairs to write poems about each other. Told to reveal two things about themselves to their partner, Jack says, "I'm black."

"No kidding?" I say. He is the only black male student in the school.

Jack thinks. "One time a rat ate my shoe," he says.

It sounds like a poem just by itself.

Safie also asked students to bring in something they consider poetry.

Pedro says he's brought a rap by EasyE, which he proudly announces is "perverted."

Safie tells Pedro he can't read or play the rap in class because the lyrics "dis" women.

"That's OK," says Pedro, who's having a tough-guy day.

"Even your mother?" asks Safie.

"It's everyone, even my grandmother," says Pedro. "That's what I write."

"It's poetry because it deals with what you're feeling," says Safie.

"Early rap, like '94, was poetry," says James. "Now it's crap."

James has the Bible. "There are some verses that sound like poetry," he says. He's also got the Rolling Stones' "Sympathy for the Devil."

Jack has seeds. "Because they're emotions," he says. "You can nurture them and make them grow."

Safie nods.

In middle school, Jack just escaped being sent to a special class for troubled students. At DCP, he's a leader, an honor student, and one of the least troubled kids around, as far as I can see. OK, he's fidgety. He reminds me of Gumby because he's always twisting his long arms and legs in anatomically unlikely positions. But, so what? He's a teenage boy. I wonder whether he was singled out in middle school because he's a black male, or whether something changed in his family situation, or whether all he needed was a fresh start.

In the second week of Intersession, I slip through the curtain that separates poetry from "Zoot Suit." Students are writing letters using the *pachucho* vocabulary. For once, Gil has done his homework. I've never seen him so engaged in a class. Roberto writes in English about how he learned about *pachucos* from his brothers and from watching *American Me*. His letter concludes, "Now there are too many *cholos*, too many drugs and alcohol."

Other students write letters pretending they're living in the zoot suit era. Some pretend they're *cholos* in jail or that they're writing to someone in jail.

Arreola is a good teacher. But it's eerie to see how quickly students connect to the material.

For a homework assignment, students write about a personal experience with gangs. Nobody raises a hand to say, "What if I don't have an experience?" Everyone has an idea.

During tutorial that day, Lisa springs to work immediately on her gang experience story. She starts by describing her aunt's birthday party. Guests were listening to music, dancing, eating, and talking. Then the phone rang. It was a call for her cousin. He talked for a minute, then conferred with Lisa's brother. The two of them spoke to their "crew," telling them to send their girlfriends home. The boys left, too, refusing to say where they were going.

Lisa's mother was frantic. Finally, she reached the brother's girlfriend on the phone and found out the phone call was a challenge from a Vietnamese gang.

It all sounds very *West Side Story.*

Lisa and her mother drove to the fast-food restaurant where the confrontation was set, but arrived after the police. Her brother and cousin had gotten away; some of their friends were arrested.

"My brother was really stupid," Lisa writes.

I beam at her rejection of gang violence, but I've got it wrong.

"The Vietnamese had a gun," Lisa writes. "It was stupid for the Mexicans to go because they didn't have a gun. They were not prepared."

I try to suggest tactfully that going to the fight in the first place was stupid, and that it could have gone even worse if both sides had been armed.

Lisa doesn't seem persuaded. She explains that the Vietnamese were selling drugs in a mostly Mexican neighborhood. Naturally, Mexican drug vendors objected.

I ask whether she knew Vietnamese students in middle school. "Oh, they're cool," Lisa says. "But the ones in gangs shouldn't do that, because they're stealing our identity. It's not their culture. Gangs are a Mexican thing or a black thing."

Of course, I make a pitch for Mexican culture. It doesn't have to mean gangs and drugs, I say. There are lots of ways to be Mexican American. Lisa can choose a way that will take her away from violence and gangs, a path that will take her to college.

Lisa says she's not going to be a *chola,* a gang girl. "They just sit around and let the guys tell them what to do," she says, dismissively. She's seen the life, and it's not what she wants.

Lisa admires her parents, who want her to go to college. She doesn't admire her brother. She sees gang life as boring. Good signs. But she thinks gang culture is *her* culture. For all DCP does to promote Mexican art, music, dance, and literature, Lisa clings to a narrow barrio definition of what it means to be Mexican American.

Tutorial is ending. Rather than firm up her conclusion, Lisa packs her things away a few minutes early. She is reverting to her usual policy of doing no more work than necessary. But the scene setting at the beginning, the flow of action, her analysis of the underlying drug disputes—it's very well done. I conjure a vision of Lisa in college, writing a competent college essay. She has three and a half years to get there. It is possible.

All the classes participate in the end-of-Intersession exhibition, which lets them share what they've learned with other students, parents, and visitors. Gallegos decided her ten ESL students should make short speeches about themselves to conquer their fear of speaking English in public.

The ESL students line up across the stage. The acoustics of the room are terrible, and none of the students speaks loudly enough to be heard—except Larissa. Always eager to talk, she gives her speech in lightly accented, surprisingly confident English.

"I like to dance," she says. "I'm from Guadalajara. Algebra is my favorite subject because I can understand it. For the future, I will study more and get better grades. I want to become a lawyer to help people. Even though it's difficult, I want to continue dreaming."

The room erupts into applause. DCP students cheer each other on with genuine enthusiasm. They all want to continue dreaming.

Then all the ESL students recite "Peter Piper picked a peck of pickled peppers," getting a very good hand.

Next in the exhibition, the Mock Trialers put on a very abbreviated trial of Syd Price. Barbara closes strongly for the prosecution, refuting the claim that the chief prosecution witness was motivated by jealousy of Syd's power. "Joseph and his brothers led to jealousy, but Syd is no Joseph," she says, with a sneer. "Ladies and gentlemen of the school, Syd Price is guilty."

The Digital Collage class, which has learned to use Photoshop, demonstrates their art. Evolution is the theme. Roberto does "The Evolution of Life." Byron does "Evolution of Corvette."

The performance of two scenes from *Zoot Suit* is the highlight of the exhibition. Arreola has come up with huge pictures of red-shirted zoot suiters to flank the stage, and he's found an authentic zoot suit for the narrator, Pachuco.

Lisa plays the kid sister. Gil is a police officer. The star of the show is Roberto, playing Pachuco. He sweeps onto the stage, resplendent in a shiny white suit and tie with a black shirt and a black hat. Usually amiable and quiet, Roberto transforms himself into the sneering, profane, dynamic Pachuco. Talking in English and chanting poetry in Spanish, Roberto dominates every scene. Other students muff their lines here or there; Roberto is word perfect and never breaks character.

The students laugh when Pachuco says, "Don't tell them shit" to the defendant, and "If that isn't bullshit, I don't know what is." They love to hear forbidden words spoken in school.

When the exhibition is over, Andaluz asks Roberto to pose for a photo in the hallway. He tilts the black hat, leans insolently against the wall, and exchanges his pleasant smile for a wolfish grin. He is still glowing with the heat of his performance. In the dim light of the corridor, the white suit gleams.

Gil struggled with written work, but he eagerly wrote about his involvement with gang life, which started when he visited the Virginia Street youth center.

Racism Assignment
Zuet Zoot Story
Gil

When I came involved into gangs. I did not wanted to join in because I thought it was cool or because my friends. For me it was all for the respect I was going to get. It all started when I when't to see if their was work at Virginia's youth center. To get the job their I had to work for a year their, so next year I would get the job. I whent their everyday. on the first week their was some nortenos by the park. I was wearing all blue. In that time I did not know or cared about gangs. They called me a srap. They told me if I bang and I said no, they told me why was I warring blue. I responded back, because I wan't to were it. They told me to get out of her and not come back, and the next day I came back. The reason I came back was because of my job, not because I wanted to back because of the nortenos. when I came out from work, I saw them again where we saw last time siting on the picnic bench. They told me: (didn't I told you to get out of here and not come back) I past by and said fuck you. One of them got of the bench and push me to the ground, but I got up quickly and started runing because I knew they were going to jump me. From that they on they got hate on me. I always got punk by nortenos. That made me grow hate in side me. One day I saw my friends at washigthon, I have not seen them from a long time. I look at them they were in blue and gang related. I told them are you guys nortenos, they said no why you are a chapete. I told them I wasn't gang related. They told me they were surenos from SSP. It was little cholo and tortuga. I meet their barrio and they all were nice to me, nicer than the nortenos. I grew up nowing them and kept my hate with nortenos. I was not in no gang, because hanging around with SSP made me bee in it. One day I was walking with them and I saw the nortenos that punk me. I told my friends to go jump them. Whe did and from their on on I got problems with nortenos. even though I left gangs behind me I have people coming up to me and causing trouble. It was hard for me to leave gangs behind.

15

red flag

By midyear, most sophomores and some freshmen were working hard and making progress. Still, there were plenty of ninth graders sleepwalking through school, apparently unaware they couldn't get to tenth grade, much less to college, with a D- average.

At a faculty meeting, DCP staffers analyzed the effectiveness of Intersession and looked for ways to wake up the "red flag" kids, the ones at risk of failing ninth grade.

Students aren't taking Intersession review classes seriously, Srugis complains. Here they had a chance to turn an F into a passing grade, and they didn't seem to care.

"There is no red alert this year," Lippman says, recalling last year's campaign to get students to pass their finals on the second try. "Kids know the material but they don't do it."

While the successful students were enjoying their enrichment classes, the students who'd failed their finals were sulking in review classes. "They were supposed to write four accordion paragraphs [in English review], and 80 percent did none of them," says DeRoche.

"My huge error was making Intersession three long periods instead of four shorter periods," Lippman says. "We have a different crew of freshmen. They're not as eager to please." With more review time and less chance to try enrichment classes, red flag students had reached the limits of their attention span.

English teachers want to put red flag students with teachers who know them and their needs, instead of mixing up teaching assignments. Lippman and Andaluz disagree, saying it's good training for students to learn how to learn from different instructors.

"It's not remedial education," says Andaluz. "Call it 'intensive.' We may be doing fractions, but we're still on the college track."

They're awfully far back on the college track, says Rigby. Her students need to be taught capitalization; they don't know the difference between *there* and *their*.

Case argues for returning to the system in last year's Intersession, when students were tracked into Math A, B, or C, depending on their achievement level. "You're surrounded by kids at the same level, so you can experience success."

"We need a class called Work Ethic, in addition to the basic skills classes," Srugis says. He does a deft imitation of student fidgeting styles, tapping on the table, knocking and flipping his hand while maintaining an expression of cherubic innocence. It brings down the house.

"Our motto is culture before curriculum," Lippman says. "When we say 'school culture' there are people who think we mean celebrating Cinco de Mayo." He means creating an academic culture that encourages students to be serious about schoolwork.

Andaluz agrees that the "intensive" Intersession classes need better curricula. If students aren't improving, DCP will have to come up with something else.

What's clear is that students love the electives offered during the two-week period; they don't get much of a break from straight academics during the rest of the year. Andaluz is afraid students are burning out on the workload.

"Next year if Oscar needs more English and math, he doesn't get to take art," says Aperribay, talking about a well-liked sophomore who's just barely passing. "That would kill Oscar."

Andaluz agrees. "For me the Gong Show gong at Intersession was art," she says. "We need to make art part of every class, make it a way of seeing."

Teachers complain of burnout too. Those who've been teaching nothing but remedial classes want a chance to teach at least one elective.

Lippman acknowledges the problem and promises that next year everyone will get a chance to teach an Intersession elective. He's also planning to redesign the curriculum to ease the pressure on ninth graders.

What impresses me is the willingness of DCP staff to talk about problems without defensiveness and to try new ideas. Surrounded by failing students, they don't fear failure. Their attitude frees everyone's energy to look for solutions.

Most of the students repeating ninth grade were still doing poorly—but better.

Gil had started ninth grade with a perfect 0.0 and finished with a 0.55 GPA. On his second try, he started strong. "He's got a shot at a C average," Lippman said after the first grading period. "He's a hero." Gil finished the semester with a 1.73, an enormous improvement.

Larissa, also on her second year in ninth grade, was trying to learn English, while taking care of her baby daughter and holding down a part-time job. Teachers were impressed when she returned from a short maternity leave with all her homework neatly done. She raised her grades, but only to a 1.18.

Some who barely made it to tenth grade were showing signs of progress.

Pedro raised his GPA above a D average for the first time. He's capable of much more: When Lippman talks about "the Pedros of this world," he means smart students who don't do the work.

Roberto, who'd finished ninth grade with a 1.52 GPA, moved up to a 2.73 by the end of fall semester. Hard workers are known as "the Robertos of this world." He vows to make honor roll by the end of the year.

Barbara had earned C's and D's in ninth grade and finished the year on suspension. She was closing in on a B average by the end of the fall term.

Some "red flag" students were coping with serious learning disabilities, but most just weren't working hard enough to succeed. At another faculty meeting, Lippman hectors teachers about keeping their homework charts updated. "This isn't the Rosetta stone," he says. "Keep it simple and easy to read."

Some teachers are offering homework rewards. In photography, if everyone does the homework for five days, the class gets a pizza party.

Lippman is all for it. "We are willing to do almost anything legal in the state of California to get them to do their homework," he says.

In English and history, students who haven't done homework must update the chart themselves. "We all call it the Walk of Shame," says Gerth.

Lippman tells teachers they need to do a better job of keeping parents informed. Rigo's parents didn't realize their son still wasn't doing his work— why not?

Srugis gets angry. Teachers work very hard at DCP, he tells Lippman. They call parents again and again, and it often makes no difference: Some students just aren't doing their work.

DeRoche points out that teachers were promised help in contacting Spanish-speaking parents and never got it.

Lippman apologizes for the implied criticism, admitting he never got the Spanish support system organized. "You're right," he says. "I'll make that a priority." The tension eases.

"If they refuse to do homework, they fail," says Lippman. "We should be comfortable with that if we've given them a platform for success."

Working from two sites, Lippman and his teachers frequently communicated via e-mail:

Dear Staff,
I hope you have all had a great holiday. Before I go on to all the info contained in this e-mail, I want to share something with all of you that gives a visceral sense of the progress we are making. Last year, at the end of the first semester, we had 38 9th graders below a 1.0. This year is much the same—37 9th graders below a 1.0. But among our returning sophomores, we have 7 under a 1.0. There are three times as many sophomores on the honor roll as under a 1.0. Bizarre. And extremely encouraging. . . .
Thanks,
Greg

Dear Teachers,
. . . to reiterate what Jill said yesterday, there is simply no excuse for not giving homework in every class. Not giving homework undermines the ability of Tutorial teachers to do their work, and sends the absolutely wrong message. I expect that I will not hear again from any staff member that a student did not have homework. No class is exempted from this.
Take care,
Greg

16

the efficiency expert

Lisa, a petite girl with a heart-shaped face, is an efficient student: She exerts the minimum effort needed to get by, with no energy wasted on trying for a grade higher than C. And she'll settle for a D, which is what she's getting in most of her classes. But, at the end of the first six-week grading period, when Lisa realized she was flunking algebra, she asked for a tutor.

I'd volunteered to tutor, specifying that my strengths are English and history. "Anything but math," I said. Naturally, I got Lisa.

At first, I pulled Lisa out of her Monday math class to go over her assignments one on one. Sensibly, she said she'd rather stay in class.

For several weeks, I sat next to Lisa in math class and enjoyed it. Srugis, her math teacher, is a natural showman with a dry sense of humor. He doesn't let his classes drift into dreamland. Algebra started to come back to me. But there wasn't much I could do to help Lisa without disrupting Srugis's class.

It made more sense to me to help Lisa during the tutorial period from 3:45 to 5:00.

Students get a short break and a snack, before settling down to do their work in rooms supervised by a teacher. The tutors—most are Santa Clara University students or AmeriCorps volunteers—work with the neediest ninth graders in a separate room.

None of the Monday tutors was any good at math, which is the weakest subject for many of the students. I found myself helping other tutors. At the start of ninth grade, Lisa, her classmates, and many of the tutors couldn't add or multiply reliably in their head. To multiply 3 x 9, Lisa reached for her calculator, a bulky, obsolete model that had been donated to the school. Other students did the same. They had no sense of how numbers work or what answers made sense.

I soon realized that Lisa, with her flair for efficiency, had decided that understanding math was too much trouble. She memorized the rules for adding and multiplying fractions but didn't know how to apply them. She zipped through problems, applying algorithms randomly.

When I was able to slow her down and get her to think, Lisa proved to have a decent mathematical brain. She had the ability to think logically; she just needed to make it a habit.

Throughout the fall semester, Lisa improved. She got a B- on an algebra test, which she proudly showed to all her friends. She aced the graphing unit. I had the thrill of seeing her volunteer to present problems in class. At an assembly, when students were honored for improvement in algebra, Lisa's name was called. She stood up to receive her classmates' applause. I nearly cried. Still, her progress was erratic. Lisa pulled her algebra grade up in the second grading period and then flunked the final. She shrugged it off.

Furthermore, her other grades remained low. At the end of the fall semester, she'd barely managed a C in Spanish, her native language, even though she'd been placed in Spanish I. Lisa admitted she could earn an A, if she worked on her grammar and vocabulary, but she wasn't willing to put forth the effort.

Science was her weakest subject. I wasn't much help, so she turned to friends, all of whom seemed to have much better notes and a much clearer understanding of what had happened in class.

In English and history, Lisa had trouble understanding what she read because her vocabulary was limited. To understand the reading on New Spain's economy for History of the Americas, she had to ask me the meaning of *legal tender, customs, duties, contraband, black market, merchandise, stifled, ambushed,* and more.

One of the agricultural products of New Spain—*henequen*—was in italics. Since it was a Spanish word, I asked Lisa whether she knew what that was.

"Oh, it's beer," she said.

Several hours later, back at home, I sat up with a jolt. "Heineken's!" I said to myself. I googled *henequen*. It's a plant found in the Yucatan whose fiber is used to make rope and coarse fabric.

Lisa was born in San Jose and picked up English from her older brother, but the family moved back to Mexico when she was three. She started school there. When she was six, the family returned to San Jose.

San Jose Unified School District settled a desegregation suit by promising bilingual education for all Spanish-speaking students with limited English proficiency.[1] When Lisa was in elementary school, Spanish-speaking kindergartners and first graders were taught in Spanish 90 percent of the time; one period a day was spent learning English. In second grade, English was added gradually, starting with physical education, art and music, then math.

In theory, students will learn concepts in their native language and achieve proficiency in reading, then transfer their knowledge and skills to English, perhaps by the middle of third grade. By the end of elementary school, they'll be bilingual and biliterate. In theory.

In reality, students like Lisa usually become semiliterate in two languages. They can carry on a conversation in Spanish or English, but they don't have the vocabulary or grammar to read or write well in either language.

"Bilingual ed?" Jill Case, DCP's dean of students, sighed when I asked her opinion. "The intentions were noble. The teachers were committed. But, it didn't work."

In addition to the delay in teaching English reading and writing, the academic content often is watered down in bilingual classes, so students fall behind in all their subjects. Along with other California districts, San Jose Unified couldn't find enough bilingual teachers, so Spanish-speaking aides—typically with a high school education—often took charge of teaching reading to the neediest students, a policy that bilingual education advocates condemned in vain.[2] DCP is filled with the victims of bad bilingual education, Case said.

Nearly half of ninth graders are considered "English learners," meaning they've tested below the thirty-fifth percentile in English, their second language. Most were born in San Jose or arrived as young children. They speak conversational English, often effortlessly, but reading in English is a challenge.

Again and again, I tried to slow Lisa down, to force her to think about what she was reading, to get her to expect things to make sense. Instead of letting her memorize vocabulary definitions, I explained the words. Sometimes, I acted them out. When she understood, her eyes would light up. Lisa enjoyed learning.

When she wrote, I'd tell her to read the sentences out loud to hear whether they sounded right. Unfortunately, she'd heard so much ungrammatical English that she couldn't always pick up the errors. But she started catching some of the mistakes, and her writing became more fluid.

In the end, I wasn't much help with algebra. Lisa's midyear spurt sputtered out. She ended the year with a D- in algebra, not good enough to meet college requirements.

Srugis and the other math teachers believed that students learn something from taking algebra and failing that they can use to pass it eventually. Some DCP students take algebra four times before they pass: ninth grade, summer school, tenth grade, and summer school again.

Lisa did it on the second try, earning a C in summer school. She passed on to tenth grade, and I returned as her tutor. Both of us disliked geometry, but Lisa managed to squeak through. English became her favorite subject; she completely got the story of *Macbeth* and accorded Shakespeare her highest praise: "Cool!" But she did poorly in Spanish, annoyed that the teacher insisted students learn grammar. She didn't resent doing the work in English; she felt Spanish should be an automatic pass.

I don't know whether my tutoring helped Lisa. We had moments when she recognized her intelligence and competence and her ability to enjoy learning. But they were just moments. Lisa never fully committed to DCP.

17

patience

What does it take to teach at DCP? Bill Triant, a Stanford M.B.A. student, asked the question in a survey he gave to DCP staffers. All of them gave pretty much the same answer: Patience, patience, patience, dedication, and hard work.

I wouldn't have the patience to be a DCP teacher. I've sat in Alicia Gallegos's class and fantasized about whacking inattentive students on the head with a rolled-up magazine. "Wake up! This is your chance!" I'd say. "How many years do you want to spend in ninth grade? Look how hard the teacher is working. If you worked half that hard, you'd be getting an A."

DCP teachers handle their students without assaulting them, or even yelling at them. In staff meetings, DCP teachers laugh about their problems. As a group, they are relentlessly cheerful.

But, by the end of the first semester, one teacher looked increasingly sad and tired. Francisco Lopez was frustrated, exhausted, and unwilling to go on. The strain of teaching Spanish I and ESL and the unruly Verbal Reasoning class was too much. Lopez called Lippman during the Christmas break and told him he wouldn't be back in January.

Finding a good teacher in the middle of the year wouldn't be easy. Lippman posted the job on computer bulletin boards and job sites and turned up three applicants worth interviewing. None had teaching experience or spoke Spanish as a native language. But they were bright, energetic people: worth a look.

Lippman invited the three candidates to teach a sample lesson to a panel made up of Lippman, Andaluz, teachers, students, and parents. I sat in, too.

The first candidate is an accountant who's traveled widely. Nobody can envision him coping with the unruly reading class, or even with ESL.

Candidate number two is a tiny, peppy young woman who's worked for Anderson Consulting and taught technology as a volunteer at a heavily Hispanic elementary school. She hands out props—a hat, a pencil, a book—teaches the words in Spanish, and makes us practice. It feels like elementary school.

During the question period of the interview, the woman asks, "What would I need to do to do well as a teacher here?"

Be patient, says Byron.

High expectations, says Aperribay.

Be calm, know your mistakes, acknowledge them, and do better next time, says Gallegos.

Andaluz recalls Gallegos's note in the Intersession ESL class: "The teacher makes us suffer." She says, "You have to be hard on the ESL kids or they'll never make it to college."

After the candidate leaves, the committee talks about her chances of "surviving" the remedial reading class. Can she take the pressure?

"She'll get beaten up for the first two weeks," predicts Itziar Aperribay, the lead Spanish teacher. "But she won't crumble."

"If she lasts 18 weeks, we can hire a better teacher for next year," says Andaluz, who hopes to fill the job before the start of the second semester.

The third candidate is a laid-off programmer whom Jesse Robinson met playing Frisbee in San Francisco.

He presents a well-organized Spanish lesson. It turns out that both his parents are teachers. He'd always thought about teaching, and now that he's out of work, he's interested in giving it a try.

He asks the students on the interview panel what they think of DCP.

"Middle school was a lot bigger," says Byron. "There wasn't much attention so I got to slide. I came here and tried to do the same thing. I couldn't get away with it."

"In middle school, they just paid attention to good students," says Selena. "Kids said, 'You're a schoolgirl,' because I tried. Here they congratulate you if you do something good."

"I wasn't doing that good in school," Debra says. "I went to Bridge [the summer tutoring program] and I hated it. I didn't think it was real school. Now I like it, even though I'm not working to my ability. Teachers are more responsive. It's cool we can do this, interview teachers we might have."

The programmer's Spanish is good, but what really impresses Lippman and Andaluz is a nine-month bicycle trip he took through Mexico and Central America after graduating from college. They think he's tough enough for Verbal Reasoning.

"If it were first semester I'd be concerned," says Lippman, "but the Lukes are on the run by now," referring to a boy notorious for wild behavior.

Something in the next room crashes against the wall. Lippman opens the door. "Luke!" he yells. "What are you doing?"

Everyone on the committee roars with laughter.

"Go to tutorial!" Lippman yells.

The programmer gets the job. "I'm not totally confident he'll work out," says Lippman. "But we could leave students without a teacher for three weeks and not get anyone better."

The night before regular classes resume, the new teacher calls to say he's changed his mind. He's had a nibble at a programming job and second thoughts about teaching. And, if he does want to teach, he can find an opening at a school closer to his home in San Francisco.

In the first weeks of the second semester, Lopez's classes are taught by Lippman, Andaluz, and Adam Zapala, a law school graduate who is subbing for DCP while studying for his bar exam. Zapala can't stay, though. He's got an internship lined up in a senator's office in Washington.

Finally, Lippman finds a teacher, Justin Tomola, who takes the job. Tomola is young, energetic, and, I notice, cheerful. Compared to his past teaching jobs, DCP students aren't all that tough.

Many principals and teachers see their schools as castles under constant attack by barbarian taxpayers and savage journalists. In short, they're defensive. And they're not about to discuss what's wrong with the drawbridge or admit that the moat has run dry.

At DCP, all the energy that usually goes into self-defense and self-pity is channeled into figuring out how to improve. It's OK to make mistakes. It's OK to fail. The only thing that isn't OK is to quit trying.

Here's Laura DeRoche talking to Shawn Gerth during transport period:

"I didn't prep my students well enough for the good versus evil debate," says DeRoche. "They are going to be so bad. . . . The tenth graders said to me—and I could hear Greg in their voices—'why didn't you give us a sample presentation as a model?' Next time, I'll spend more time on that. I guess it'll count as one of Greg's 'glorious failures.'"

It's good for students to get out there and try something bold, even if they can't pull it off, Gerth says.

"I think glorious failure applies to teachers too," says DeRoche.

Failure is a dirty word at most schools. Better to pretend that the students are doing fine, or that their deficiencies are balanced by unnamed excellences in some other field. Better to blame parents or taxpayers or the media or society. In most schools, principals and teachers can't learn from their mistakes because nobody's willing to admit to any.

Greg Lippman cheerfully critiques his own mistakes, liberating his staff to do likewise.

For example, in the weekly meeting, Lippman asks for ideas about how to improve students' speaking skills at assembly. Most students, even those in Leadership Club, which runs the weekly assembly, are hesitant, shy, and inaudible.

"We've been very focused on literacy, but I haven't paid enough attention to speaking skills," Lippman says. "That's my fault. We need to do more on oral presentations in class."

When a teacher worries about students being embarrassed about speaking in public, Lippman replies: "I disagree that it's more humiliating to be told what you're doing is crappy than to have people tittering in the audience. . . . Bombing out, and coming back from bombing, is a big part of what we do here. It's just like those PSAT scores. They were crap, garbage. OK, let's go and get better."

Since it's OK to admit problems, it's possible to fix them.

Gallegos told a prospective teacher how DCP coped with problems in the discipline process. "What should we do as the infractions get more serious? When do we give referrals? We talked about it at staff meetings and with each other. We try something, see if it works. If it doesn't, we figure out why not and do something else. Now we have a definite process based on a lot of mistakes from last year."

In midyear, the math teachers faced up to the fact that students lacked very basic skills, even those students who'd passed algebra and moved on to geometry. Srugis e-mailed Robinson and Greene: "Our kids don't know fractions!"

The math teachers met to talk about it. What don't students know about fractions, decimals, percents? What do they need to know?

The math teachers halted algebra and geometry for a campaign they called "Give Piece a Chance." It hurt to lose all that time to teach elementary and middle school skills. But they'd decided it was a mistake to teach advanced math before nailing down the basics.

In staff development, when teachers talk about what they're proud of, many are proud of their ability to cope with failure and frustration.

Rigby remembers a truly horrible class. "I said, 'Greg, I'm not going back in there. . . . ' We sat down and figured out a way to deal with it."

"I'm proud of the failure of Student Council," says Arreola, who's suspended Student Council meetings for poor attendance. "Because they're finally seeing it's their responsibility, not mine."

It's OK if students fail to meet high expectations, argues Aperribay, who prides herself on setting clear, consistent rules. "It creates discipline in students' lives." Every day, she asks Lorenzo for his homework folder. He never has it, but she always asks. "If a student gets an F, at least he's learned that there are clear consequences," says Aperribay.

The teachers also see success. Robinson has two students who are "hyper and crazy as ever. But now they're crazy about math."

After studying World War I propaganda posters, Gerth's students began to notice other forms of persuasion, including DCP's campaign to sell students on working to prepare for college. She was delighted when a student pointed to a classroom sign, "Work HARD. You're going to college," and exclaimed, "That's propaganda!"

Twice, Gallegos took the girls' basketball team to see a game at Santa Clara University. The first time, they sat quietly. "The second time, they acted like we belong here too," Gallegos says. "They were cheering, shooting free throws at half-time, waving a 'We Want Pizza' sign to get a free pizza. They're comfortable on a college campus."

DeRoche says she's proud of DCP's use of student performance data to "change or sustain what we're doing" and asks for more help for teachers to learn to use statistics.

In my years covering education, I talked to many teachers who had no respect for administrators. They didn't trust their principals to know good teaching from bad, to evaluate curriculum, or to enforce rules consistently. These teachers felt alone in a hostile world.

DCP teachers face enormous challenges, but they don't do it alone. The shared sense of mission and effective support from administrators give them strength:

> Srugis: Everyone on staff cares about every kid and takes responsibility.
> Arreola: Every adult who sees kids in the hall asks why they're there.
> Longosz: We all have a sense of humor and can laugh together. Teachers and administrators back each other up.
> Andaluz: The administration team is really a team. Everyone has authority, and the kids know it.
> Srugis: It really helps the freshmen to see certain behavior isn't tolerated.
> Rigby: I'm proud of being part of this school and the charter school movement.
> Robinson: I'm proud we're all doing this, even though we're not sure it's going to work.

Though Greene says, "Sophomores have internalized how to be students," Aperribay worries that DCP isn't demanding enough responsibility from older students. "I'm worried that we're treating them like little kids. When do we stop holding their hands?"

It's the great challenge for DCP. Hand-holding—leading students step by step through the skills they need to learn—has proved very effective. But, at some point, students have to learn to learn independently.

Earlier in the year, I'd heard one of Robinson's geometry students complain indignantly about an assignment that forced her to think. "If she doesn't spend time to explain it to me why should I take time to explain it to myself?" Melissa said to a classmate.

By spring, her attitude had changed. At the staff meeting, Robinson told colleagues about a recent conversation with Melissa. "Next year they won't hold our hands anymore," Melissa had said. "We have to learn on our own."

Bill Triant, a Stanford Business School student, surveyed DCP teachers' attitudes and compiled their comments. He found very high satisfaction with the "autonomy you have in determining how to carry out your job," the "recognition and acknowledgment you receive from DCP administrators and teachers for your individual contributions," and "your understanding of how your work contributes to the success of the school and students." Two-thirds of teachers were very satisfied with the "fairness and consistency with which the school administers policy." Most teachers were very or somewhat satisfied with communication among teachers and training opportunities.

Teachers, each assigned a number to protect anonymity, answered the question, "What traits should the ideal DCP teacher have?"

1. The belief that all students should have access to a higher education, patience, enthusiasm, content knowledge, creativity, energy.
2. Integrity, dedication, and good communications skills.
3. Belief that all students can go to and succeed in college, persistence in working with students who don't always "get it" the first time, teamwork attitude, and commitment to the school community.
4. A DCP teacher should be patient, dedicated, hardworking, and passionate. They should understand our students and the community our students live in. They should be willing and able to work with students outside of the classroom. They should be willing to work outside of their technical job description if necessary.
5. Smart, hardworking, relational, excellent with young people, passionate about subject matter and mission of school.
6. Patience, hard work, willingness to change, willingness to receive criticism, flexibility, subject matter knowledge, interest in students.
7. Bilingual, collaborative, strong classroom management skills, flexibility, desire to be a part of the community.
8. The ability to have high expectations and give students opportunities to consistently build toward those expectations. The DCP teacher needs to be optimistic, but refuse to accept mediocrity or apathy. And the DCP teacher has to want to be part of the whole school community and reach out from the classroom into the world around them.
9. Dedication to the mission and ability to go the extra mile. Also, a genuine care and concern for the students to motivate them to do well.
10. A DCP teacher must be patient; must be committed to the idea that all students can succeed, despite their circumstances or attitudes; must be willing to put in long hours; must hold all students to high standards and yet be able to scaffold learning for them to reach these standards.

11. Compassion, fairness, hard work, and dedication to the success of the students in all aspects of life.

12. They should be dedicated to teaching underserved students. In other words, they should understand and enjoy the challenges that come with teaching students who can't yet read or compute. Teachers should be self-reflective, willing to get feedback and criticism. They should be excited about what they do and willing to put in more than their job description requires. They should be dedicated to the mission and believe that it is possible. They need to believe that every child can learn and be successful.

13. Dedicated, skills-based, patient, good curriculum designer, able to enforce rules and policy of the school, collaborative, willing to work longer than the average teacher.

14. Patience, patience, and more patience.

18

carrying the torch

Inside San Jose's Civic Auditorium, more than 400 students tinker with their devices made of wood, metal, plastic, and Legos. This year's Tech Challenge is "Design, build and operate a device that will pick up, move and set down a make-believe torch. The torch has to be moved from one pedestal to another one 11 feet away. For success, your invention will place the torch firmly in the second pedestal within 3 minutes."

Last year, DCP's entry, inexplicably named Big Chicken Dinner, finished fourth in the high school division, an impressive performance for a team made up of ninth graders.

This year, the school is fielding three teams. Big Chicken Dinner II, designed by Rajiv, Bill, and Esteban, is the favorite. During the demonstration in assembly that morning, it actually worked. Made of copper pipe and held together by duct tape, the device is controlled by two remotes, one for backward and forward motion, the other for lifting the torch up and placing it down again at the end.

Realizing that only boys had signed up for Tech Challenge, Andaluz persuaded five ninth-grade girls to form a team. The Lady Lobos have an underpowered motor that's not strong enough to lift the torch. They've incorporated string to provide the needed lift.

Team D*Fens—Rico and Adam—is struggling. They started with a wood base and used Legos for the gears. But the plastic in the Legos stretched during testing. While waiting for journal judging—teams must document the design process to prove they built the device themselves—Rico and Adam realize a key gear is slipping. The machine has lost its lifting power.

Around them are more than 100 teams with kids ranging from fifth graders to high school seniors. Some are in costume: One middle school group is in clean room suits; two teams are wearing togas, one with laurels, the other with—who knows why?—plastic Viking helmets. Palo Alto's Gunn High is dressed in Hawaiian shirts and straw hats. Pinewood School, a private school in Los Altos, has sent a team of boys dressed as knights with round shields and hobbyhorses.

DCP's high school competitors are more conventionally dressed, with T-shirts bearing their team name and symbols. Esteban seems to be echoing the torch theme with his hair, gelled into huge spikes like the Statue of Liberty, but that's his normal style.

The Lady Lobos go first. Their device makes a clean grab of the torch and starts down the platform. But the battery—bought that morning by their coach, science teacher Jeff Fox—is feeble. It seems to die in midjourney. The impatient judge nudges the device with his pencil. Finally, the girls give it another shove and safely deposit the torch inside the pedestal.

Harker, a San Jose private school, has sent Pyrrhic Victory, which wheels out a giant arm powered by gravity. It lifts the torch, the counterweight spills out of the open jar, and the arm flips over the top and deposits the torch in its hole. It is very fast and accurate.

Almost all the entries are bigger than the three DCP models. Many of the teams are from private schools or upper-middle-class public schools. Many have larger budgets to buy parts and parents who are Silicon Valley engineers to help as coaches. The DCP students designed and built their models themselves on very small budgets, working without a parent coach.

Big Chicken Dinner II gets into trouble at the very start. The pincers grab the torch and yank it so energetically it flies out of the device's grip. Rajiv quickly puts the torch back in the holder. On the second try, their device grabs, lifts, and speeds to the other holder, wavering a bit over the hole and then easing it down till it rings the bell. With the time lost in the restart, are they fast enough for a prize?

That leaves Rico and Adam. But they've arrived late, reluctant to miss DCP classes. Now they're stuck in an endless, unmoving line to present their journal documenting the development of their project to judges, who will score it and verify that they did the work themselves. They're worried about their device. They haven't made it work yet in testing. The competition will be its first run.

The teams wait. Fox buys nachos at the snack bar and offers them to the students. Esteban gives Adam a dollar to buy a Coke; Adam returns with the dollar. A small soda costs $2.50. Esteban shakes his head. He can't afford it.

In front of their seats, middle schoolers and parents are frantically trying to repair a giant device made of plastic toy parts, Connex. All the king's horses and all the king's men can't save it. No sooner do they replace one link then five others break.

Finally, Rico and Adam complete Journal Judging. For the next hour, they frantically try to repair their device. A plastic gear has loosened. A tread keeps popping off. The pincers aren't gripping properly. The torch doesn't hang straight. The wheels don't turn well, making steering a nightmare.

Rico tries welding with a pocket spot welder, gluing it with Super Glue, tightening the frame. His father, a technician, and older brother offer suggestions. So do Fox and last year's coach, Dan Greene. As DCP's long school day ends, classmates walk over to see the contest.

Bombarded with useless advice, Rico displays a saintly patience. "I've tried that," he says, respectfully, to his father's suggestions. "That won't work; it can't get any traction," he tells his brother, without the hint of a snarl. If he blames Adam, sitting in silent pain, Rico doesn't show it. He keeps fiddling. Nothing works.

Finally, Byron, who's there to watch, warns that the last entry is about to be called. Time is up. Rico borrows string from the Lady Lobos and ties it to the weight. But the weight isn't heavy enough. Rico's dad hooks on his car keys. Two string men are needed to control the lifting, so Byron volunteers to help Adam while Rico steers with the remote.

Even as they start, Rico is wincing at the clunkiness of their machine. But the device lifts the torch, backs up, goes forward, backs up, goes forward. Slowly, very slowly, Rico turns the device. His three minutes are ticking away. Then one wheel goes off the platform. He's stuck. Adam shrugs and lifts the device back on, disqualifying the team. Rico gets to the second pedestal, but the torch is so slanted in its holder that it can't possibly get in the hole. And time has run out. They're already disqualified. Adam picks up the torch and dunks it in the hole, ringing the bell. It's over.

Minutes later, the award ceremony starts. "You are all champions," says the presenter. Adam and Rico look dubious. They don't want anyone saying this was their best effort, because it wasn't. They can do better.

At least they avoid winning Most Spectacular Failure, which goes to Peterson Middle School's disintegrating plastic arm. The knights take Best Costume. In the Best Overall category, Harker's Pyrrhic Victory wins. Once again, DCP takes fourth with Chicken Dinner II.

The Lady Lobos also aren't satisfied with their performance. They glare at their yellow ribbons, given for participating. Their machine didn't work, and they're not going to pretend it did.

The Lady Lobos aren't techies. They're there because Andaluz didn't want DCP students to think robotics is for boys only. But now the girls seem hooked. They stop fuming about the battery and start planning for the future.

"Next year," says Heather.

"If we get an earlier start," Carolina says.

19

principal's day

Following Greg Lippman for a few hours is like running with a hard-working sheepdog. First, he's barking about enforcing detention. Then he's dashing off to round up a student.

At a Wednesday faculty meeting, he announces the inauguration of Saturday detention. To work off detention hours, students are supposed to arrive an hour early, at 8:00 A.M., but many never show up. So they get more detention. Felipe owes 62 hours. "We haven't done a good job on detention," says Lippman. Students shouldn't believe they can get away with ignoring the rules. Next year, he's considering making Friday a short, no-tutorial day—except for students in detention. Once they're already at school, it's easier to make sure they put in the time.

I ask Lippman about Felipe, whom I now think of as The Detention King. "He'll be working off detention till he's 42," says Lippman, gleefully. "I'll call him up and say, 'Come over here and sweep the auditorium. You owe me hours!'"

Andaluz, Lippman, and their staff discuss the difficult search for a site with space for 400 students, the target size with all four classes. The church and the Y are stretched to capacity: If Andaluz can't find a larger site, DCP won't be able to add a new class of students in the fall. There's empty office space downtown, because of the recession, but landlords aren't eager to rent to a school of rowdy teenagers.

DCP is losing three students. A ninth-grade girl is pregnant and will go on a home-study program. Two other students are leaving because their families are moving: One family is bound for the Central Valley; the other is going back to Mexico. As the economy worsens, DCP families are leaving San Jose, which still has high rents and no longer has high-wage jobs for low-skilled workers. Still, half a dozen students are commuting to DCP from new homes hours away.

With satisfaction, Lippman reports that Clara is not leaving. She'd made plans to live with a classmate's family and continue at DCP, if her mother moved to the Central Valley. Her mother decided to stay, at least for now.

To replace students who leave the school, DCP has decided to accept ninth-grade transfers—many are kids who've been kicked out of their previous school—and a few tenth graders able to do the work. But it's difficult to integrate new students into the culture midyear, and most of the ninth-grade transfers are expected to repeat the year.

However, Lippman is delighted by a new phenomenon: Students who've left DCP, complaining it's too hard or too strict, are asking to return. After a semester or two at a large high school, they miss being nagged about their homework. One boy left DCP in the fall and returned after six weeks with a new sense of commitment. His grades have soared.

Lippman tells Andaluz he's heard from Wendy, last year's Queen of Referrals, a girl who seemed to hate DCP with a passion. Wendy is flunking everything at her new school, and, as far as she can tell, nobody cares. "She wants to come back here next year," Lippman says. "She'll have to repeat tenth grade, but she says that's OK. Wendy! I can't believe it."

Lippman decides to skip the assembly, which is run by Arreola. He craves the chance to work in peace for 30 minutes.

The outside office doubles as the faculty lounge, though there's barely room for the office staff—Irene Zuniga and Maria Figueroa—and the photocopier. So teachers also use the inner office, which is Lippman's, in their free period to read papers or eat lunch.

Lippman's domain consists of a cheap metal desk, four chairs, a table, a file cabinet, a three-shelf black metal bookcase, a bulletin board, and framed newspaper stories about the school's opening.

"The lunch lady quit yesterday," he says. Zuniga is out with pneumonia. And he has to leave at 11:30 to take his very pregnant wife for an ultrasound.

A student sticks his head in. He needs to put his skateboard away. Lippman grabs the key from Zuniga's desk and unlocks the storage closet. As soon as he sits down, another student asks to store his skateboard.

Lippman taps at his laptop. "I dream of spending eight hours cranking out documents," he says. "The tutorial rotation has errors. The daily script—who goes with the kids on the bus—needs to be done."

He reads his e-mail and checks education stories in the *Mercury News*. The latest says half of Hispanic high school seniors in San Jose Unified aren't on track for graduation. The district now requires all students to pass college-prep courses, though, unlike at DCP, a D- is considered a passing grade. One-quarter of Hispanic seniors are way behind in credits they'll need for graduation, the story says. And these are the survivors: At least a third of Hispanics who started as ninth graders have dropped out or switched to alternative programs.[1]

Lippman believes in setting high expectations but suspects district students won't get the intensive help they need actually to master college-prep courses. Instead, teachers will lower standards, especially in summer school, to qualify students for graduation.

Zapala, who's working as a substitute, sits down at the table in Lippman's office to go over the Verbal Reasoning lessons. He offers to teach for a half-day before he has to leave on a family trip. Lippman gratefully accepts.

Robinson comes in to ask for another van for DCP's new Ultimate Frisbee team. They have a field trip on Saturday to a regional tournament. She's recruited 15 students for the team. A local philanthropy has donated two vans, so DCP no longer has to charter a bus to take students from the church to the Y and back again. Lippman agrees she can have the second van.

Rigby asks for one minute to share a concern. "Some kids get special treatment from the staff," she says. "For example, some kids are allowed to have food in tutorial; others get in trouble. We need to be consistent."

Lippman knows who it is she's talking about, evidently a support staffer who helps out with tutorials. "I've spoken to her about it," he says.

Support staffers go way beyond their job descriptions at DCP, he says. "They try to see gaps and fill them. Irene and Maria, if a chair needs to be scrubbed, they'll do it. But this business of giving kids love, of being a friend to students . . ."

"We're nice. Teachers are mean," says Rigby.

"Ah! Evil teachers!" Lippman says.

Arreola pops in to say the Kiwanis are looking for a four-weekend volunteer project; he'll work with Andaluz to find something for the Kiwanis to do to help the school.

"The dance team canceled its performance," Arreola says. "We only got seven kids at the softball meeting, but we've got others interested, so we still look OK."

He's scheduled a field trip to a small Catholic college in the area, talked to parents about the Parent Council elections, and firmed up the Student Council's plans for a "black light dance." Using black light "is a way not to decorate," he explains.

"Can we make it an unwritten codicil of my job that I never go to dances?" asks Lippman, who's made his loathing of school dances a running joke.

Arreola also is trying to get a grant to fund sports and field trips for Summer Bridge, the mandatory orientation program for incoming ninth graders.

"That reminds me," says Lippman. "I should call San Jose State to get classrooms for Summer Bridge. I'm going to spend the summer being the academic dean, working with teachers on the academic structure. Your role will be heavily Summer Bridge. Is that OK with you?"

"I'm looking forward to it," says Arreola.

Lippman plans to name a "ninth-grade principal" who will run Summer Bridge, with Arreola as activities director. "Bridge becomes a place for your Leadership Club kids to participate," he says. He asks Arreola to think about how next year's juniors can work with freshmen.

Arreola agrees to cover Saint Paul's, till Smith can come over from the Y. That frees Lippman to get his teacher evaluations written and go to the ultrasound. The principal asks Arreola to get Figueroa to call Jacob's and Senta's Spanish-speaking parents to set up a meeting. "They're not speaking English, and they need to."

"We should send two nuns to their home like Richard Rodriguez's school did," says Arreola. In Rodriguez's book about his quest for education, *Hunger of Memory,* he credits his Irish Catholic teachers with persuading his immigrant parents to make him speak English.

Hired as a PE teacher, Arreola became a key staffer "in ten seconds," says Lippman. DCP has no time in the schedule for PE this year, and Lippman needs to find out whether state graduation requirements, which call for two years of physical education, apply to charter schools. "We may have to give PE credit for walking between Saint Paul's and the Y," he says.

With Arreola in charge of the office, Lippman moves to a shabbily furnished room called the Penthouse (for no apparent reason) by DCP and the Oxford Room by the church. Once, Lippman dreamed it would be the faculty lounge, but the pastor of Saint Paul's isn't willing to give up control of the room.

Andaluz calls to say she's going home with the flu.

His wife calls to remind him of the appointment.

Ines Trevino, the lead support staffer at the Y, calls to say she's hired a new lunch lady. "You're a genius!" he says.

As he writes up his classroom observation notes, Lippman can hear the College Readiness class next door. Gallegos is teaching synonyms and antonyms.

"*Valiant*," she says.

"*Brave*," says a student.

"*Courageous*," says another.

Zapala comes in to confer. "What do these numbers mean for the VR kids?" he asks, showing Lippman the information he's been given on each student.

"It's a rough measure of their ability to read individual words, not their comprehension," says Lippman.

Figueroa pops in to say she's driving the ESL students to the Y. Their schedule doesn't fit with the normal transport period.

Lippman goes to the ultrasound, then returns to the Penthouse. Students, still on their lunch break, are standing in the hall outside the room. One shouts, "FUCK." Lippman steps out. "I don't want to hear that."

The student apologizes.

Lippman goes back to work. Outside, on the narrow stretch of pitted asphalt that serves as lunch area and playing field, kids are throwing a Frisbee and kicking a soccer ball. Back in the hallway, there are shrieks, thumps, and a scream: "Noooo!"

Lippman pops out. "No, no, no, no," he says. He turns it into a rap rhythm. "No, n', no, no, no, n', no."

"Sorry," says the screamer.

Lippman gets back to work. Minutes later, there's an enormous thwack, as though a bulldozer has hit the wall. Lippman runs to the door, where a bunch of boys are standing, trying to look as if they haven't rammed the wall. His good humor is gone. "Who's doing it?" he asks Jacob, who looks guilty. "Don't lie to me. Do you have *valores* [values]? Do you? We're in a partnership with the church. If we destroy the building . . ."

Jacob mumbles a confession. Lippman takes him to the office, and asks Figueroa to call Jacob's parents. He was planning on meeting with them anyhow.

On his way back to the Penthouse, a new girl asks to speak to him. According to the new girl, she accidentally jerked Larissa's backpack and now Larissa is furious and on the verge of a fight.

"You go to class and let me deal with it," says Lippman. "That's why they pay me hundreds of thousands of dollars to do this job."

He cuts Larissa out of the milling herd of students, who are heading for their next class, and takes her into the Penthouse. Larissa sits on the mercifully faded lime green couch. Lippman rolls over a chair.

He tells her the other girl is upset.

Larissa gestures impatiently, flailing her arms, and complains in Spanish that it's all the other girl's fault.

"This is what you did last year," says Lippman, windmilling his arms in imitation. "Relax. Think how you come across to others. There are times when you want people to be patient with you."

Larissa replies in Spanish, but without flapping her arms.

"This is nothing, a misunderstanding," says Lippman. "You're acting like it's very important—*muy grande*." He spreads his arms. "And it's—how do you say small?—*poco, muy, muy, muy poco*." He brings his hands together. "You can't let people push you off the path so quickly. Your Spanish is excellent, by the way."

Larissa laughs.

As he speaks softly, and she responds, her large eyes fasten on him.

"You have had experiences with your mother, coming from Mexico, now with your baby. You are a serious person. You have made a serious commitment. When I see the old Larissa"—he does the windmill—"I get worried. Don't forget where you're going."

Larissa nods, gravely.

"Now you're missing class, and you're upset."

I can't tell whether Larissa is about to cry or laugh. At any rate, the anger is gone. She shakes Lippman's hand.

"Good luck," he says.

Larissa smiles and goes off to class.

Lippman shakes his head. "They have a 50-minute lunch today. I hate long lunch periods. It gives kids time to get into trouble."

Once again, Gallegos's vocabulary words come through the thin wall. *Valiant* means brave or courageous. "The antonym is . . ."

"*Scared*," says a boy.

"*Afraid*," says a girl.

"*Cowardly*," says Gallegos.

"Some school reformers want kids to be activists, critics of society and the media," says Lippman. "I want students to be respectful, dignified people. . . . If we have students well prepared for college and sometimes unhappy, that's OK."

"*Capable*," says Gallegos.

"In previous jobs, I felt working harder was futile because there was so little return on the investment," says Lippman. "Here, we're all pulling on the same rope."

"If you are *capable* of finishing your homework . . ." says Gallegos.

"It's OK to fail," says Lippman. "It's OK for teachers to think I'm a prick. I'm a good teacher. I know how to do school. In one or two more years, I'll be a better administrator than I am now. We're finding out some of our ideas don't work, but we can pivot quickly. . . . That's what I like about Silicon Valley. It's OK to fail."

Next door, the search for the meaning of *capable* goes on.

The staff was meeting on a Saturday, when a mother came in to drop off the permission slip for the weekend field trip to Sacramento. There was no field trip. Her daughter, who'd created the phony permission slip, was located hanging out at the mall with a girlfriend. Lippman vowed eternal detention, even as he admired her ability to mimic DCP's forms.

Field Trip Permission Slip
Last weekend, Saturday the 25, only 2 of the 5 students that were selected could attend the field trip to Sacramento, so we rescheduled to see the trials and Bill Clinton. students need to meet at SJSU college at 9:00 am sharp. We will still be transporting the students by means of the DCP vans. Please take

note of this and make sure that your child is prepared. We will be arriving back at Saint Pauls at 5:00 to 5:30 on Sunday the 2nd of May. We need to know if your student will be attending this field trip on May 1st and 2nd so please sign this permission slip below and send it back with your child tomorrow.

Sincerely,
Mr. Lippman and Ms. Andaluz
Field Trip Supervisor

I give my student _____ permission to attend all DCP field trips. I hereby release all liability from Downtown College Prep and the Across the Bridge Foundation, and all personnel employed by these agencies, from any and all harm and wrongdoing.

   I give permission to administer services in case of an emergency.

20

the knife

On a gray January day, Buddy sits glumly on a chair in the outer office at the Saint Paul's site.

"Why are you here?" asks Irene Zuniga, the office manager.

"Ms. DeRoche wants to take my pager because it went off in class," says Buddy. "But it didn't go off. She's lying!"

Zuniga reminds Buddy that pagers are banned.

"My mom gave it to me for emergencies," Buddy says.

Parents often want their children to carry a pager or cell phone, and DCP may lift the ban. At the moment, however, it's still in effect, and defying a teacher compounds the offense. Zuniga hands him the contract all students sign at the beginning of the year. She points out the section saying that contraband pagers and phones will be confiscated.

"Till the end of the school year?" Buddy is indignant. "Are you guys going to pay for it?"

"You made a bad decision," says Zuniga in a level tone that discourages argument. She is the mother of three boys, one of them a DCP student, and she is no pushover.

Maria Figueroa, who also works in the office, enters and asks why Buddy's there. "My pager went off in class and I wouldn't give it to Ms. DeRoche," he says. "My mom paid for that pager!"

"It was your decision," says Figueroa, also the mother of a DCP student. Her coordination with Zuniga is like tag-team wrestling.

Lippman rushes in, hears the story, and asks whether Ms. DeRoche has written a referral. Not yet, says Zuniga. She's still teaching the class. "If he gets a defiance referral, call his probation officer," says Lippman, on the way to his office door.

"I'll give it to you!" says Buddy, thrusting the pager at the principal. "Here it is!"

"He wouldn't give it to Ms. DeRoche," says Zuniga.

"That's defiance. Call his probation officer," says Lippman.

"Why are you doing that?" asks Buddy in a wail.

"Because I said I would, and I do what I say," Lippman answers. He goes into his office.

"You're going to get me in trouble," cries Buddy, though Lippman is gone. "I'll go to Juvenile Hall. I just came from there. They'll make me take out my eyebrow ring! I just got it." Buddy is on house arrest; he's supposed to go directly home after school and stay there. He spent a weekend in Juvenile Hall because he wasn't home when his probation officer visited.

Zuniga suggests he write an apology to the teacher. Maybe she won't write a referral.

Buddy borrows a piece of paper. "How do you spell *referral?*" he asks.

Figueroa tells him.

"How do you spell *apology?*" he asks.

Zuniga writes the word on a piece of paper. Then, with a sigh, she adds a few sentences of apology and gives the paper to Buddy, who copies it eagerly. "Thank you, Ms. Zuniga," Buddy says pleasantly. He settles back to wait for Ms. DeRoche to decide his fate.

A month later, with Lippman off at a conference, Andaluz takes over for the day at Saint Paul's. By midafternoon, she's expelled three students, a DCP record for a single day.

Joshua, readmitted after being expelled the previous year for marijuana possession, is caught smoking marijuana in the bathroom. He's out.

Another boy, on a strict behavior contract for previous misdeeds, gets a referral for calling his math teacher an "asshole." It's one referral too many. He's out.

And then there's Buddy. His mother had called his counselor to say she took a knife away from Buddy in the car on the way to school. He said it wasn't for use at DCP; she assumes he feared a gang fight on the way home. Buddy was "jumped into" a gang before he entered DCP; his former friends and rivals aren't convinced he's left that behind him.

Taking a knife to school violates the zero tolerance policy, even if he didn't get it in the door. It violates DCP's promise to its students, parents, and staff: You will be safe at this school. Buddy is expelled.

When Lippman returns, he jokes with Andaluz about her "reign of terror" expelling three students. But he would have done the same if he'd been there.

In the neighborhoods where DCP students grow up, gangs offer status, power, and a sense of belonging. On the East Side, which has its own school districts, Independence High School adopted red, white, and blue as school colors when it opened in 1976, the bicentennial year. Later, Independence banned its own school colors, fearing students were using school loyalty as a pretext for flaunting gang colors.

Parents often feel powerless to protect their children.

Tomas told me his parents warned him to stay away from gangs, but he paid no attention till a summer day when he was ten years old. He was hanging out with his best friend. A Norteño hit a pregnant girl with a baseball bat. Her Sureño boyfriend, his friend's big brother, pulled out a gun and shot the attacker. More Norteños drove up and shot the older brother, killing him on the street in front of the two ten-year-old boys. Tomas decided that maybe his parents were right about gangs.

Some kids don't have that revelation. Others try to avoid gangs but can't find a school, church group, community center, or club that can provide a haven from gang violence.

DCP promises to be that haven.

Buddy's mother appeals the expulsion. The appeal is heard by Lippman and two DCP board members: Tamara Alvarado, wearing a sweatshirt, is program director at Washington United Youth Center; James Gibbons-Shapiro, in a sharp suit, is an assistant district attorney.

Buddy comes to the evening meeting wearing a hooded gray sweatshirt over his khakis. It's an ominous sign: He knows DCP considers hooded sweatshirts gang clothing. His new ring gleams in his eyebrow. Next to him sits his mother, looking very small by comparison. She works as a staffer at a program for troubled adolescents, which is located at a continuation school for students who've been kicked out of mainstream schools.

Buddy lived with his father after his parents divorced; he repeated a grade in school and got into minor trouble. When his father, who's in the navy, was transferred to Japan two years ago, Buddy came to live with his mother in San Jose. In his freshman year at Silver Creek High, Buddy flunked all but one class, mostly because he rarely attended. He was attacked by rival gang members at high school for wearing red, his gang color. "He broke his arm in the fight," she says, "and he got a red cast." He was expelled.

Buddy ended up on probation, in drug rehab, and—his last chance—a freshman at DCP.

His mother was driving him to school and saw a bulge in his pocket, she tells the board members. She asked what it was and discovered he'd taken an eight-inch knife from his 14-year-old brother's knife collection.

At the phrase "knife collection," a look of distress flashes across the faces of Lippman, Gibbons-Shapiro, and Alvarado.

Buddy still refuses to say why he was carrying the knife, except that he had nothing against anyone at DCP. His mother's theory that he feared being jumped by gang members on the way home seems plausible.

His mother called his counselor to say that Buddy "was in a bad space," not thinking a knife that never made it to school would cause his expulsion. Now she's faced with a horrible irony: Because she did the responsible thing, her son is losing his chance to stay at DCP, the only school that's ever worked for him.

"I really feel good about this school," she says. "Buddy has a close relationship with his counselor."

Buddy has tested clean for drugs since he went on probation, she says. His probation officer doesn't think the knife is "that big a deal."

Gibbons-Shapiro looks surprised at that but says nothing.

"Since he started at DCP, he's been doing a lot better at school and with family," she says. In the fall semester, he earned five D's and one F for a 0.93 GPA. "But he's starting to do more work."

Buddy wants to be the class clown, his mother says. "He's still thinking D's are OK. I don't think he fully understands this is college prep, not just high school."

His last week at DCP was his best. "He was doing better than he ever had," said his mother. "I told him he was going to get A's and B's this semester. I believed that."

Buddy's mother says Child Advocates told her a knife in a student's possession "en route" to school isn't a zero tolerance offense. She wants her son to get another chance at DCP.

Lippman reviews Buddy's discipline record. He's had several referrals for showing disrespect to teachers, plus a few run-ins involving a girlfriend, whom he eventually agreed not to see, at her parents' request. Lippman says Buddy's behavior has improved; his academic work started to pick up in the weeks before he was expelled.

"Buddy is one of the most intelligent people at DCP—emotionally intelligent too," says Lippman. "He can speak in a very adult way with a complicated, subtle sense of humor, very perceptive. I've had some excellent conversations with him. He's a very smart young man. But that hasn't translated into academic success."

I think of Buddy as a giant Saint Bernard puppy, eager and clumsy and good-natured. I haven't seen emotional intelligence or a subtle sense of humor. I've seen only the face he shows to his classmates. Lippman has spent hours talking to Buddy, one on one, and he genuinely likes him.

"At the beginning of the school year, Buddy was spending a lot of time locating the source of the problem outside himself," says Lippman. "It was Mr. or Ms. X's fault. Never his own. That's changed."

"He told doctors in his drug program he felt smarter because he's not smoking marijuana," the mother says.

"Buddy was getting acclimated to being watched, and becoming less rude to teachers," Lippman says. "He's a strong-minded, strong-willed individual. We were able to agree to disagree in a civil, respectful way. He was able to see his situation was the result of his actions. Referrals decreased in frequency."

"I searched high and low for a school that fit him," says his mother. "At Silver Creek, there was too much freedom, too much else going on. He would go to the bathroom and never go back to class. They'd let him do that. They never called me till he was on the verge of being expelled."

Though Silver Creek High serves an ethnic and economic mix of students, it's basically a middle-class school. However, it's big enough to include stoners and gang kids along with honor students, skaters, band geeks, and jocks. It's big enough to lose track of a student like Buddy.

"I recommend DCP to people who are having problems with their children," his mother says.

Buddy has been sitting silently, but now he speaks. "I really enjoy going to this school," he says. "I made a lot of friends here, and it's keeping me on track. I've only missed three or four days of school. Last year, I never went. I didn't care about school."

He made his mother sad when he was expelled from Silver Creek, Buddy says. "I wanted to make her happy. I was hoping I would do well this semester so I could graduate from ninth grade."

"Last year, I made a lot of mistakes. This year, they're still in me." Buddy sighs. "Some of the things I've done here aren't very intelligent," he says.

Alvarado, Gibbons-Shapiro, and Lippman step outside the room—Rigby's History of the Americas class—for ten minutes to confer. Buddy goes down to feed the parking meter.

His mother tells me that Buddy's father is serving on the *Kitty Hawk*, now in the Persian Gulf supporting U.S. troops in Afghanistan. He wants Buddy to go to military school if he's kicked out of DCP. She only knows she doesn't want Buddy at continuation school, where he would have been sent if DCP hadn't taken him. Many students there have gang ties. It's exactly what he doesn't need.

The two board members and Lippman return. They offer a shred of mercy: Buddy's expulsion is changed to an involuntary transfer. But he must leave DCP, and, unlike most students who are asked to leave, he won't be allowed to return the following year.

"We do have the authority to expel for an 'en route' violation," says Gibbons-Shapiro, "but we don't want another expulsion on his record." Even with no intention to use the knife at DCP, Buddy might have gotten into a fight and used it. DCP was his second chance, says the deputy district attorney. "Transfer" is a third chance. "Pay attention to the great job your mom did in protecting the school and you from what might have happened," he tells Buddy.

"I'm afraid two weeks of good work don't cancel out the willingness to carry a knife," says Alvarado. "This is another chance you're getting." She reminds him that he's already 16. He needs to get his act together now. Time is running out.

It's clear that working in a youth center has left Alvarado with no tolerance for teenagers with weapons.

Lippman says he'll recommend a new school, Mount Pleasant High's multimedia magnet. "He needs a place that won't let him drift," he says.

"That's a backward step, back to a district school," says Buddy's mother. "I really feel transfer and expulsion are the same thing. You're not letting him come back. I'm not saying DCP is the only school for him, but right now it is. If I'd never made a phone call, trusting the school would find out why Buddy felt unsafe, this never would have happened."

No one contradicts her. We all sit for a moment like mourners in a funeral parlor. Then Buddy gets up and shakes hands with Lippman once more. He asks me to tell Lisa "hello" when I see her at school. Mother and son leave DCP for the last time.

"Buddy's not going to make it," I say to Lippman.

Lippman says he made a promise to his teachers, and he has to keep it. "I told them DCP would be a safe school."

Buddy returned to Silver Creek High, his old school, but didn't last long. He was expelled again and sent to continuation school. From there, he went to Juvenile Hall, where he earned a high school equivalency certificate, and to the Boys' Ranch, the county's juvenile detention facility. After Buddy's release, his father got him a job at a navy post exchange in Southern California.

21

f no es fabuloso

DCP's parent educator, Elena Mendez, was discussing grades in English and Spanish at an evening meeting for parents of the school's pioneer class. When Mendez explained the meaning of F, Lorenzo's mother looked puzzled. She turned to Jennifer Andaluz, who was sitting next to her. "F no es fabuloso?" she said. F doesn't mean fabulous?

"No," said Andaluz. "F no es fabuloso."

Nearly half of DCP parents don't speak English well enough to communicate with teachers in English. They come from rural Mexico, where schooling usually ends before high school. They don't understand the ABCs of the American education system, much less the edubabble that baffles even middle-class American-born parents. For example, an "emergent reader" in San Jose Unified is a student who can't read.

For poorly educated immigrant parents, their children are their interpreters. If Lorenzo says he's earning all *fabulosos* and he goes home with a "student of the month" certificate and gets promoted at the end of the year, how's his mother supposed to know he's failing?

The annual parent survey conducted by California schools finds more than 60 percent of DCP parents have an elementary or high school education; only 19 percent have earned a college degree. Even those who know what an F means may not know when their kids are getting inflated grades: A for being a good kid, B for making a halfhearted effort, C for getting too big to hold back.

As a result of language barriers, an unfamiliar education system, and a habit of deference to authority, immigrant parents often don't know their children are doing poorly in school until they're way behind. Looking back, many DCP parents regret not being more aggressive in demanding answers from their children's teachers. "I thought those people at the school are the authorities; they must know best," one mother said.

Despite being identified as gifted in elementary school, Pedro had been a problem student from the start. In middle school, he stopped going to class for half a year. Nobody called to tell his parents. He was passed on to high school but rarely attended more than one or two classes a day. His parents didn't know till Pedro flunked ninth grade. DCP, recommended by a friend at church, would be a fresh start, they thought. Someone would pay attention.

"At DCP, all of us are family," his mother told me several years later, speaking through a translator. "Teachers don't look down on us because we don't speak English."

She got a phone call every time Pedro stepped out of line. "If I was ten minutes late to school, they'd call her and she'd go World War III on me," Pedro recalled.

She appreciated the attention paid to her son at DCP and felt she could talk to teachers about her concerns. Pedro didn't turn into a model student, but at least she knew what was going on, unlike at his previous schools. Pedro "needs someone outside his parents to motivate him so he doesn't have to work like we do," his mother said. She cleans houses; her husband is a baker. Their own education ended in middle school.

Some parents believe that learning happens only in school; at the end of the school day, it's over. I heard this most clearly from a Mexican American mother—raised in San Jose since she was a toddler—whose four children were going to the same elementary school she had attended. The mom had completed a parent education class. "I learned that homework is important," she said. "I always thought it was just busywork. I thought children learned in school, not at home. Now that I know it's important, I make sure my children do their homework right after school, before they play or watch TV."

"Has it helped them do better in school?" I asked.

"Oh, they're doing really well now," she said.

This was a nice lady, reasonably intelligent, clearly a devoted mother, *educated in the United States from kindergarten through high school!* Yet she'd never realized that homework matters. When she was persuaded it did, she changed her rules. Her dreams for her children—doctor, lawyer, architect, teacher—no longer were impossible.

DCP asks ninth graders' parents to attend a monthly class on how to help their children succeed in school. Mendez warns parents their children's grades will be terrible at first. Don't let your child give up, she says.

That message does get through. Virtually all the DCP students I talked to told me they hated DCP at first because the work was so hard and the day was so long. They wanted to quit. All said pretty much the same thing: "My mother told me to keep trying, so I stayed and I got used to it."

The main message: homework, homework, homework. It's not optional. Parents aren't asked to help with homework, but they're asked to make sure their children make time to do their work and have a place, such as the kitchen table, to do it. Parents sign the daily homework log, and they're told not to believe a child who claims there's no homework on a school night. There's always homework.

DCP's long hours force changes in parents' expectations. Many of the parents I spoke with expect a responsible teenage girl to take care of her younger siblings. A responsible teenage boy takes a job so he can help with the rent and the food bill. Many DCP students do have part-time jobs, but their hours are limited because DCP doesn't get out until 5:00. Some parents complain their children are spending too much time at school—not just the eight hours of class and tutorial but even more time to play basketball or rehearse for the dance team or volunteer for Key Club. And then they get home and say they can't cook or clean or keep the younger kids busy; they have to do homework. In parent classes and conferences, DCP staffers work to persuade parents that the long school day capped with more hours of homework is essential to realizing their children's college ambitions.

Many parents are accustomed to taking long vacations in Mexico at Christmastime to visit with family. Lippman begs parents to let their children finish taking finals before leaving and then return in two weeks so their children can attend review and enrichment classes during the two-week Intersession.

Emilia, one of the school's best students, missed her finals freshman year and got B's instead of A's when she returned from Mexico and took makeup exams. In tenth grade, her father talked to Case before scheduling the family trip. He asked whether missing finals would hurt her grade. "She has the chance to earn scholarships to pay for college," Case told him. "She could go to UCLA. Don't risk that." Emilia aced her finals and then left for Mexico.

For parents, DCP's demands can seem to be a threat to their traditional values. They're being asked to spend less time with their parents, brothers, sisters, and cousins so their child can get ahead—and leave the family behind. Which is more important, family or education? Staying connected or getting ahead?

DCP parents want their children to go to college, and they've taken the initiative to enroll them in a charter school. But by the second year, the school is getting more passive parents who've gone along with what a counselor recommended or let a child follow a friend to DCP. Beyond the core of committed parents who helped found the school, there's a much larger group who aren't used to playing an active part in their children's education. They want college to happen to their kids. They don't know what they or their children should be doing to turn the dream into reality.

In addition to parent classes, DCP invites parents to a series of school events showcasing their children's achievements: There are Talent Night; Open House; the midyear Exhibition; Mystery Night for geometry students; the College Readiness "Dinner Party," at which students show off their celebrity "guest" and plate design; and the Architects' Fair, at which Math Readiness students display proposed designs for a DCP building.

Parents who have the time also help judge demonstrations of students' skills, such as the humanities debates on industrialization, nationalism, and colonialism. They serve on the disciplinary committee and help interview prospective teachers.

Still, only nine parents show up to elect new officers of the Parent Council. The meeting is conducted in Spanish, with Eugenio Ramirez translating for my benefit. Byron's grandmother, who speaks only English, usually attends, and Ramirez is used to translating for her.

It highlights a problem: It's hard to unite the parents when about half speak little or no English, and about a fifth speak little or no Spanish.

Ramirez is devoted to his children's education. If a parent speaker is needed at a school-sponsored event, he volunteers. Aaron Resendez, the new president of the Parent Council, served on the English as a Second Language committee at his children's middle school. He's also willing and able to speak out.

But they're the minority, frustrated by the Parent Council's weakness. Organizing a "thank you" lunch for teachers isn't difficult. Getting DCP parents to play an active role in shaping school policy is the challenge.

One of DCP's goals is to educate the Mexican immigrant community in downtown San Jose, says Andaluz. She wants aunts, uncles, and cousins to learn what students need to be doing to prepare for college. "Maybe this sounds arrogant, but we want to influence the community. Our parents can spread the word to other parents."

DCP's college counseling program starts in ninth grade with field trips to Stanford and UC-Santa Cruz and expands in tenth grade with a series of parent classes on college requirements, financial aid, and testing. There are field trips to Southern California and Bay Area colleges, and an East Coast swing funded by donors for honor roll students such as Emilia, Selena, Adam, Bill, and Rajiv.

At a college class for sophomore parents, Vicky Evans promises DCP will set up a free SAT prep course, teach students how to write an admissions essay, and help them apply for financial aid. All tenth graders will meet with Evans and Jill Case to discuss whether they're on track for college.

Because DCP's mission is to send all students to four-year colleges, the A through G requirements set by the state universities govern the DCP curriculum: To be eligible for the University of California or the California State University system, students need four years of English and three of math (algebra, geometry, advanced algebra, and trigonometry) for college. They need three years of lab science, two of history/social studies, two of foreign language, one of visual or performing arts, and an academic elective. The minimum acceptable grade is a C-.

She hits that point again and again. Many DCP parents have seen their children earn D's and F's and move on to the next grade. Lippman and Andaluz plan to drop the D in the school's third year so parents and students will understand that students must earn a C or better in every academic class to be eligible for college.

Evans, an M.B.A. who worked at the Defense Language Institute in Monterey, volunteered with other highly educated mothers in the college center at her children's high school. Then she read about DCP in the newspaper and decided it was a place where she could make a difference. She's worked on several management projects and now concentrates on college counseling.

Many parents don't know the difference between two-year community colleges and four-year colleges. Evans starts by telling parents what a bachelor's degree is.

Students with a B (3.0) average in academic courses are guaranteed admission to most California State Universities, such as San Jose State, whatever their SAT scores; a 2.4 and average (980) combined SAT score also will qualify.

The elite UCs—Berkeley, UCLA, and San Diego—require very high grades and test scores, but nearby UC-Santa Cruz takes students with a 3.2 GPA and average SATs.

"If your student's GPA is 2 to 3, look at CSU," she says. "If it's 3 or better, look at UC." For Santa Clara University, which appeals to students because it's close to home and not as large as the public universities, a 3.0 is the effective minimum. But don't give up hope, she says. Private colleges have more flexibility than the public system. "Even with poor test scores, if you have a 2.0 (C) or above, there is a four-year college for you." In junior year, Evans will meet with students and parents to go over specific college options.

Admissions officers are impressed by students who show improvement and by students who take more than the minimum courses, Evans says. They also give an advantage to students who'll be the first in the family to go to college and those who've grown up in low-income or otherwise disadvantaged families. Most DCP graduates will hit one of those categories; many will hit all three. Students also will be judged on their extracurricular activities and volunteer work and on their ability to contribute to campus life. She doesn't mention race and ethnicity; in theory, California's public universities no longer take these factors into account.

Parents will be told about SAT dates and helped to apply for waivers of SAT fees. Evans tells parents not to pay for a test prep course. Instead they can encourage their student to read to improve vocabulary or study flash cards; they can find free practice tests online and find test prep books in the library.

DCP gives students the PSAT as a practice test annually, so they can learn how to handle a high-pressure exam. Kaplan Test Prep & Admissions has agreed to donate an SAT prep course that normally costs $1,200; for DCP students, it will be free.

Only 12 to 14 students in the sophomore class have a shot at selective colleges, such as the UC campuses, Santa Clara University, or Cal Poly. For them, SAT scores will matter a great deal. For C students, respectable SATs will boost their chance of getting into CSU schools, which are the cheapest option.

Evans hopes DCP graduates will choose CSU–Monterey Bay over San Jose State. "My fear is that parents won't let their children, especially their daughters, leave home to go to college," she says. At best, stay-at-home students will miss out on the college experience. At worst, they'll join the majority of San Jose State students, who work, study, but never graduate. CSU–Monterey Bay is about 90 minutes away, a distance that gets students away from their old neighborhood but lets them go home to visit without much expense. The campus, converted from Fort Ord, is new, is still small by CSU standards, and has dorm space for freshmen. Unlike at some popular CSUs, which have raised admissions standards, getting accepted at Monterey Bay isn't hard.

Evans also wants DCP students to consider private options in the Bay Area, such as Menlo College, Notre Dame de Namur, Dominican, Holy Name, Mills, University of San Francisco, and University of the Pacific.

Tuition ranges from $400 a year for community college to $24,000 for private college. With room, board, and books, parents can expect CSU to cost $10,000 a year. "You *will* qualify for financial aid," says Evans. With scholarships, even the private colleges are not out of reach.

In theory, students can do their first two years at a community college then transfer to a CSU or UC school. But few community college students go on to earn a four-year degree. Most have a full- or part-time job: After a while, they tend to make work the priority and take fewer classes; eventually, finishing a degree seems impossible. To increase the chance students will earn a degree, DCP wants to send all graduates directly to four-year colleges.

"What books will they need for college?" a mother asks.

"It depends on the professor of each class they take," says Evans.

Rajiv's mother asks, "Do they have to stay in the dorm?"

Evans explains it depends on the college. Her antennae are up. Rajiv is one of the school's top students. His parents should be looking at UC-Davis or the equivalent, not planning to keep him close to home.

A few months later, half the sophomore parents show up to hear Shawn Gerth talk about testing and listen to Evans walk them through their children's PSAT scores, which are low for most students.

Gerth is writing a "sophomore exit exam," which will test content knowledge, skills, and critical thinking: Can students make and support an argument? She's incorporating questions from CSU's math readiness and English exams, which students must pass to avoid remedial college classes. She's also including analytical questions of the kind found on Advanced Placement tests: Can students analyze a historical document? Solve a complex math problem?

This year's version won't count, Gerth says. "We'll talk to students about the results. We want to tell whether they're on track for college." In the future, DCP is thinking of using CSU's algebra, geometry, and trig tests as semester finals.

More than half of CSU freshmen—students who are supposed to be in the top third of the graduating class statewide—have to take remedial English or remedial math or both, because they can't pass CSU's placement exams. Two-thirds of Mexican American CSU students must take remedial English, and more than half must take remedial math.[1] It's a shock for students who've made A's and B's in high school to find out they're not ready for college-level English or math. Gerth wants DCP students to get real about college demands, even if doing so means passing tests in high school that many CSU students fail.

In addition, DCP students will have to pass California's new graduation exam, Gerth tells parents. "The high school exit exam is a watered-down test that doesn't measure much. However, it's an important part of DCP culture to be serious about preparation for college. Students who need to take the exit exam again are getting extra work to prepare for it."

DCP students did surprisingly well in their first try at the exam: Sixty-four percent passed as ninth graders, equaling the state average and surpassing most San Jose high schools. On the second try, with only those who failed retaking the test, DCP had the highest pass rate in San Jose.

DCP students also take San Jose Unified's writing test. Again, their scores were much better than expected: The pass rate for sophomores was 100 percent.

It's good for students to learn to take tests, says Evans. "The worst thing is to be at college, away from home and floundering."

Mendez translates into Spanish.

Evans is honest with parents about the low PSATs, explaining that almost all DCP sophomores have scored below the median; even the best students are barely average. But they're also ahead of schedule: The PSAT is geared to juniors, not sophomores. DCP's students have time to improve. With the help of the SAT class, which they'll take in spring of sophomore year, students can build the vocabulary, math, and test-taking skills they'll need to do better.

Ninth, tenth, and eleventh graders who score in the top 10 percent of their class on the state's STAR exam earn a $1,000 college scholarship, Evans says. Students who do well on the Golden State Exam get an honors notation on their transcript that impresses colleges. Several DCP students have won Golden State honors in Spanish, and a few have earned algebra honors.

Finally, Evans warns parents not to plan a family vacation between June 24 and August 1, the dates of DCP's summer school. "If your child is between a C and a D average, he might need to take summer school," she says. Students who have a D or F in English or algebra must raise the grade to a C in summer school. To raise grades in other subjects, they can take San Jose Unified summer classes. Students will not be allowed to move on to 11th grade if they're not on track for college.

Mendez repeats all this in Spanish, and I see Pedro's mother nodding. In the fall, it looked as though Pedro had become a serious student. But now he's mouthing off to teachers; his grades are sliding. If he fails tenth grade, he'll be two years behind in school.

At Open House, Dominga Ramirez, one of the founding DCP parents, gave a short speech:

"I chose DCP because DCP gave me opportunity of better education for my son to go to university. He will be the first. . . . [She breaks down in tears. Her husband walks up to the stage and puts his arm around her shoulder.] I vow to you he is going to university and to the best university. He didn't show *ganas* at the beginning. Now he has *ganas* and he is on the honor roll. It's my responsibility and the responsibility of all parents to come in, to ask questions, to ask for help—that's why they're here. They have knowledge to help our kids. We have to work together to help our kids get to university. Come to meetings, talk to teachers, shake their hands. [She starts crying again.] I have no words to say how proud I am to be here."

Parents' Education

Not a high school graduate   34 percent
High school graduate   27 percent
Some college   20 percent
College graduate   14 percent
Graduate school   5 percent
* A total of 83 percent of parents responded.

From: Laura DeRoche
To: Greg Lippman
Subject: pre-vacation vacations

Greg,
What's the plan for students who are leaving early for vacation? Some students are beginning to tell me they aren't going to be here for the end of the semester and I'm not sure what to tell them. I think we need a uniform policy for this. Please let me know.
Laura

From: Greg Lippman
To: Laura DeRoche
cc: Staff
Subject: Re: pre-vacation vacations

Dear Laura (and Staff),
Students, despite our warnings, are deciding that finals period is a time for vacation. They must take the final when they return, and they will get no extra help. We have to make this as painful as possible if we want students to stop bailing before Christmas.
Take care,
Greg

22

class of '06

"Give me your tired, your poor": It could be the motto of DCP's recruitment campaign. In spring 2002, DCP staffers begin recruiting a third class of students. The goal is to enroll a ninth-grade class of 120 students, which attrition is expected to cut to 100 by sophomore or junior year.

Ads on Spanish-language radio stations and in a Spanish-language weekly promote the school. Jill Case, Jennifer Andaluz, Alicia Gallegos, Irene Zuniga, and others go to community events to pitch the school. Parents talk to other parents at church; students recruit their friends and cousins.

One of the largest sources of students is Case's network of middle-school counselors, who urge low-achieving eighth graders—the "wretched refuse" of middle school—to consider DCP. In theory, DCP prospects should want to go to college. In practice, many don't really know what they want; they're attracted by a small school with small classes. Mostly, they want someone to pay attention to them.

At a few middle schools, where Case has no personal connections, counselors and administrators are uncooperative. Apparently, they see the charter school as a threat or an annoyance. But counselors at Case's old school, Hoover Middle School, set up three recruitment sessions, pulling DCP prospects out of phys ed class. Case takes along Lisa and Armando, a crew-cut tenth grader, both Hoover grads.

"Our school was built for kids who'd be first in their family to go to college and for kids not doing as well as they could, maybe below a C average," Case tells the prospects. She doesn't emphasize that these students have been chosen because they're not expected to make it at a regular high school.

Lincoln High, the nearest conventional high school, has 1,700 students; DCP will max out at 400. Classes at Lincoln average 30 students; at DCP, there are 16 to 22 students in a class. "You get a lot more attention," Case says. "It's hard to get away with stuff. If you're chewing gum, if you have your hood up, if you're not doing homework, someone will call you on that."

DCP has a longer school day, 9:00 to 5:00 versus 8:30 to 3:00 for Lincoln. DCP students wear uniforms. She also warns that DCP doesn't offer as many clubs and sports as a larger school.

So far, the middle school students are most turned off by the prospect of wearing uniforms. Case's warning that they'll be closely supervised doesn't seem to bother them.

Armando takes over. "At first, I came to DCP because one of my friends was going," he says. "It turned out he didn't go, but I did anyhow. My mom said you sacrifice now and get it back later. What I like is the whole vision is going to college. At Hoover, I didn't do homework. I got C's and D's. Now I'm on the honor roll. I do my homework, pay attention, shut up in class."

It was hard, at first, says Armando. "My first semester I had C's, D's, and an F, but then I got used to it."

When Armando's mother moved to the Central Valley for cheaper housing, he stayed in San Jose, living with relatives during the week and commuting on weekends to his mother's home or to his father's place, also in the Central Valley.

Now firmly on the college track, Armando is active in the Leadership Club. The "Armandos of this world," in DCP parlance, are students who have the potential, if pushed, to go to Santa Clara University and other competitive schools.

After nearly two years at DCP, Armando is convinced of the importance of earning good grades and the benefits of doing homework. I'm not sure he's connecting with the eighth graders, who have that zombie stare. Grades? Homework?

I'm surprised Case asked Lisa, who has a D+ to C- average, to come along, but Lisa is a great choice.

"My parents tried to go to college, but they couldn't do it," Lisa says. "They didn't have the tools and information." She is the youngest in her family, she says, the last hope to fulfill her parents' college dreams.

"At DCP, they torture you," Lisa says, quite cheerfully. "It's really hard. But you get the feeling for what college is like. At first, I hated everything. I'd go home and complain." Her mother talked her into sticking with it. Now Lisa tells them it's better to be tortured in high school than in college. "When you go to college, if you're not prepared for it, you'll think: 'This is hard. I'm going to quit.' College being hard won't matter to me. I'm used to being tortured!"

I hope the prospective students understand that Lisa is speaking metaphorically. I suspect she's thinking of her brother, who scraped through high school, enrolled in community college, and promptly dropped out.

Lisa finally drops the torture theme. "The teachers help you at DCP, and everybody knows everybody. The classes are good: They know how to teach. I learned to do algebra. Before I had straight F's in math. Now I know it. I do my homework by myself."

Case invites the students to shadow a DCP student for a day and hands out a flyer in Spanish and English to give their parents.

In the second session, only half the students raise their hands to say they want to go to college. As in the first group, the kids are mostly Hispanic with a handful of black, white, or Asian students.

"I wanted to go to college, but it wasn't the main thing for me," Armando says. He wanted a good school. "They do ask you to do a lot but it will pay off."

After presenting her torture thesis, Lisa says, "I was doing really bad in middle school and I wanted to do good. Everybody in my family messed up on education. I'm the youngest, so it's all on me."

She's caught the students' attention. They know about messing up on education and wanting to do better.

DCP is a lot harder than Lincoln, but teachers will help you, Lisa says. "Once you get used to it, you're going to be proud of yourself. If you really want to go to college, go to DCP!"

All the students take a DCP flyer; they pay attention to Case's invitation to visit the school. They look hopeful.

In the third session, a student asks whether DCP is a continuation school for problem students.

"No! Not at all," says Case. "It's for kids who can succeed."

When the Hoover students file out, Case asks Armando and Lisa to pick a restaurant for the lunch she's promised as their reward for serving as recruiters. "Not McDonald's," she says, knowing that DCP students don't eat out much. "We can do better than that."

In addition to school visits, Case schedules bilingual evening events for parents and students. Sometimes, the parents of an A student attend, misled by "college prep." Case makes sure they understand most students enter with less than a C average; they usually vanish immediately. A surprising number of parents think DCP is a private school and ask about the tuition.

Eugenio Ramirez, president of the Parent Council, speaks to about 50 new DCP parents and students, telling them that family support is crucial. "Before my son came here, I only went to school if there was a problem," he says. "Even if they have the best teachers, if they don't have support from parents, children won't achieve anything."

He'd tried to get his son into a Catholic high school, looking for higher standards and safety from violence. His son couldn't pass the entrance exam.

Ramirez echoes Lisa's themes. "It's better to have hard times now than in university," he tells students. "You could get A's and B's now and go to university and not be qualified, and have to come home. The goal of DCP is not only for students to go to university but to graduate from university."

Ramirez says his son got A's and B's in middle school. When he started at DCP, he got D's and F's. "What happened? His A's and B's were fake."

DCP is hard, says Ramirez. New students will be scared by the workload, and they will want to give up. It's up to parents to make them stick with it. "When they go to university, they will thank you," he says.

Case warns parents that incoming sophomores must take reading and math in summer school to see whether they're ready for tenth grade. "We have many families who decide to have their student repeat ninth grade," she says.

A girl who arrived from Mexico a few months before the start of ninth grade speaks. "On the first day at DCP, I found out everything is English, and I cried," she says, in English and then in Spanish. "I was very scared."

But not too scared to make honor roll, Case tells parents.

Later, parents meet with Case while the prospective students mingle with DCP students.

"My fear is that it's not a normal school," a boy says. "If there was football, I'd have no problem."

Byron talks up DCP's baseball team and his creation, the car club.

A girl says she lives near Santa Teresa, a middle-class high school in East San Jose.

"Santa Teresa is no good," says a sophomore whose brother goes there. "Teachers don't care unless you're in the top class. You get away with too much." The sophomore pauses to consider what she's just said. "You think it's cool, but it's not," she says.

DCP students admit the school is hard. Again and again, they say, "Teachers care about us. If you need help, they'll help you."

While the conversation centers on homework, uniforms, and clubs, the girls are checking out the boys. One tall, good-looking boy seems to be a recruiting asset, just by declaring that he's decided to enroll at DCP. Byron also is a draw.

But Case still is short of her goal. Recruitment is hampered by the fact that DCP has no building for 2002–2003. Parents can see the cramped quarters of Saint Paul's and visit the Y, but it's obvious there's no room for another 120 students. Case can't tell them where DCP will hold classes in the fall. Andaluz is still looking for a new site.

Lippman is hiring teachers to staff a school with 120 freshmen. Yet, by the end of the school year, only 75 applications are in, with 10 to 15 students expected to repeat ninth grade. Fourteen students have applied for tenth grade; most will be told they'll have to repeat ninth.

Some former DCP students are straggling back. Ada was a gang member when she started at DCP. She got the strength to leave the gang, but after finishing ninth grade, she was tired of DCP's demands and transferred to her local high school. Now she wants to return. She told Andaluz, "Out there, nobody knows who you are."

Hitting the target number of students is critical to balancing DCP's budget. If the incoming class is small, it will trigger staff cuts or require the school to take out a loan.

Case keeps at it, and applications keep arriving over the summer. By July, DCP can announce it's rented a building with space for all its students and good transit access. Incoming ninth graders are signing up friends and relatives, motivated by the promise of free tickets to Great America amusement park. By fall, DCP enrolls 125 ninth graders—it's expected some will quit in the first few weeks or months—and starts its first waiting list.

DCP's third class is its most disadvantaged yet: More students are from low-income immigrant families; the average parent has less than a fifth-grade education. The new ninth graders also have weaker reading and math skills than earlier classes.

"These students are very needy," says Alicia Gallegos. That's OK. They are the students DCP set out to educate.

23

awake

By spring, most of the ninth graders are starting to act like real students. It's no longer possible to tell at a glance who's a freshman and who's a sophomore. They may not read or write or calculate like college-bound students, but they know how to sit down, focus their attention, take notes, do homework. They're awake.

One day, tutoring Lisa, I realize she's brought a pencil. For months I'd told her that nobody should try to do math with a pen. I gave her a pencil, choosing a sparkly purple so as to avoid the school ban on red and blue. It vanished. Today she has a sharpened pencil.

But she doesn't know what she's supposed to do for the science homework, so she asks Art. He tells her. Then she asks Art for the Spanish assignment. He shows her what he's written on his homework log. Then he gets back to work with his tutor, earnestly listening and writing and—

Art? Art is the go-to guy for homework? In the fall, Art never knew the homework because he had no intention of doing it. Now he's working on reading and writing skills he should have mastered in elementary school. It's as if he's an invalid with atrophied muscles trying to walk. Hell, he's trying to climb a mountain. But he's on the move.

In English, the ninth graders read scenes from *Romeo and Juliet*, mentally transforming Capulets and Montagues to Norteños and Sureños. Angela Hensley leads them through slowly, making sure they understand the meaning. They'll go on a field trip to the Oregon Shakespeare Festival; she wants them to be prepared.

Tenth graders read *Macbeth*. In history, they're studying the common elements in Plato, Aristotle, Machiavelli, Rousseau, and Descartes. For all the progress they've made, the reading is very challenging for the sophomores. But they take a certain joy in moving beyond the simple texts they're used to seeing. They know what they're studying is supposed to be hard.

DeRoche assigns groups of students to act out scenes from *Macbeth*. Speaking in a slight Spanish accent, Clara is a strong Lady Macbeth, capturing her passionate desire for power. Adam, as Macbeth, can't help sounding like an upright young man.

Barbara is a flamboyant Lady M. James, always happy to be the center of attention, is an enthusiastic Macbeth.

The highlight is Pedro's group. Although there's a girl in his group, Pedro insists on playing Lady Macbeth. "I'm the chick," he tells the class. Pedro makes no concessions to femininity in his portrayal: His Lady Macbeth is a stocky Mexican American boy with a marine-style crew cut. He gets to the critical line: "I have given suck, and know / How tender 'tis to love the babe that milks me: I would, while it was smiling in my face, / Have pluck'd my nipple. . . ." Pedro gets through "suck," grinning hugely, starts to crack up at "milks me," and completely loses it at "nipple."

I've never seen anyone enjoy Shakespeare more.

Meanwhile, in History of the Americas, Rigby is teaching ninth graders to analyze a document saying Cortez was "the greatest captain of his time."

"It's just the author's opinion so it's not true," a girl says.

Maybe, maybe not, Rigby replies. "We've decided we can't trust all of this article. Can we trust some of it? How do we decide what to trust?"

"SOAPS," students call out:

- Subject (big picture)
- Occasion (time and place)
- Audience (whom it's written for)
- Purpose (why written)
- Speaker (whose voice)

The class is not the shuffling, daydreaming crowd I saw at the start of the school year. With a few exceptions, they're focused on the discussion, confident that SOAPS will carry them through.

In May, Gallegos's College Readiness students—the entire ninth grade—hold their Dinner Party. Each student researches a famous person, writes a report on the biographee, writes a letter about the dinner party, produces a poster with the report, and designs an appropriate plate and place setting. Parents are invited to see the display of dinner plates and posters. (Other than the usual chips, salsa, and cookies, the Dinner Party involves no dinner.)

Rosita, who's flunking most of her courses, comes alive to do a respectable job on Frida Kahlo.

Lisa is assigned Nellie Bly as her subject. Later, my father sends me a series of stamps honoring women journalists, with a note saying, "Why aren't *you* here?" I give Lisa a Nellie Bly stamp. *"Cool!"* she says.

Only Felipe sits out the project. He has a perfect 0.0 grade point. Yet even Felipe is perking up. A flicker of the eyelid, a hint of a smile: Someone is alive underneath the mask of indifference.

In English, DCP students finish the year reading high school classics: *To Kill a Mockingbird* for ninth graders and *Animal Farm* for tenth graders.

Ninth graders draw characters and scenes from *Mockingbird,* giving students with artistic skills a chance to shine. I see an excellent cartoon by a boy who's flunking ninth grade for the second time.

Larissa chatted in rapid-fire Spanish when she was seated beside bilingual students in history. Gerth moved her to Jack's table. Larissa had to speak to him in English or not at all. Now she's gossiping with Jack in rapid-fire English.

Vocabulary words for the week are *contemporary, era, consistently, baffled, archaic, omnipresent, colloquialism.*

In algebra, Srugis and Greene are trying to push students through quadratic equations. As they'd feared, Give Piece a Chance, their review unit on fractions and decimals, ate up too much time. "They're going to flunk," Greene says. "We had to do the review. They can't go on without the basics. But now they're all going to flunk quadratic equations. We just don't have enough time to get through the curriculum."

Some will be able to earn a C in summer school. The rest will repeat algebra as sophomores.

Seventeen students in Robinson's geometry class have volunteered to take advanced algebra and trig over the summer: They'll be in classes seven hours a day, five days a week, for six weeks to complete the whole year's curriculum. Those who pass will take precalculus as juniors and AP Calculus as seniors.

Math Reasoning students design a new school for DCP, practicing perimeter and area measurements. Each team produces a poster showing and explaining their school design for the Architects' Fair, where they show off their work to parents and visitors.

Andaluz tells students she's looking for a new building for DCP, one big enough for three classes of students. "I like your design!" she tells one group. "I'll take it!"

I tell Greg Lippman that Lisa is now doing math with a pencil, that Art is keeping track of the homework, that I no longer can tell ninth graders from tenth graders by the way they walk into a classroom.

"They've changed since fall, haven't they?" he says. "I'm not crazy to think so?"

"You're not crazy."

On a humanities (English and history) test, sophomores were asked to "compare and contrast the French Revolution and the revolution in Animal Farm." Selena received 67 of 70 possible points for her essay. Expert is the highest level, followed by apprentice, worker and novice. She got "expert" marks for organization and evidence; her thesis statement was marked at the "apprentice" level.

Despite the fact that the revolution in Animal Farm and the revolution in France occurred in two different time periods they still share similar characteristics such as their economic problems, class structure, and the strategies/tactics of the revolters.

First, Animal Farm and the French Revolution had a variety of economic problems. For instance, before the animals in Animal Farm rebelled, Old Major, a wise pig, asked everyone in the farm, "What have you ever had except your bare rations and a stall?" (pg 29) Old Major and everyone else began to realize how hard they were working for so little recognition or pay. In addition, a cause of the French Revolution was bad harvest, where there was not enough bread produced and thereby paving the way for tax increase. The peasant and working class (3rd estate) were also recognizing that they were working hard and still their taxes were getting raised dramatically. Both revolutions are foreseeing the almost insurmountable amount of work and it is obvious that the pay will not be satisfying.

Therefore the idea of revolting begins in ernest. Because of these economic problems in both scenarios, the idea of a revolution spreads like wildfire.

Secondly, in both revolutions there is a social structure created to differentiate the classes. For example, in Animal Farm, there is Mr. Jones as the government, the pigs as leaders and the rest of the animals as the working class. Orwell, the author, shows that humans are the authority figure in this world and that the pigs are superior from the rest. Furthermore the French also had a differiation of social classes such as the first estate which consisted of the clergy, the second estate of nobles and finally the rest of the population (peasents) were the third estate. France had a monarchy type of government which meant that everyone was under one class structure. Both rebellions had a type of classification for everyone. Regardless of who you were, you always had a social class to identify with.

Finally, the revolters in each setting had strategies/tactics. For instance, in Animal Farm, Snowball was in charge of the defensive operation (pg 51). Snowball had tactics to defend Animal Farm during battle with humans. Snowball used the abilities of all the animals to be triumphant in the Battle of the Cowshed. Moreover, the French revolution also crated a Committee of Public Safety "to deal with threats to France . . . It prepared France for all-out war ordering all citizens to join the war effort" (pg 75 packet). The Committee of Public Safety inspired and pushed citizens to join the Revolution movement. Each revolutionary had tactics/strategies in order to have follower and advocates towards the revolutions. Despite your ranking or life style you can still be part of the new way.

In conclusion, even though these revolutions occurred in two different time periods they are revolutions therefore there are highly noticed similarities in both cases.

24

altius, fortius

Flexibility is the strength of charter schools. If something's not working, charter school leaders can change it, instead of defending the status quo. When Lippman and Andaluz started DCP, they thought students could handle advanced work, if they were motivated and pushed. It was all about the *ganas*. Motivation is all very well, they've realized. But it's not enough: They need a solid foundation of reading, writing, and math skills.

"Our big mistake?" Lippman says. "When students come here, they can't read. We didn't realize that when we started."

Lippman designs a new plan for the school's third year. He revamps the ninth-grade curriculum to focus intensely on getting students caught up in reading, writing, and math.

DCP's ninth graders have been taking six solids: English, History of the Americas, Algebra I, Integrated Science, Spanish, and College Readiness. "We're giving kids too much," Lippman tells teachers in a meeting. "They have six homework assignments on Monday." Students are overwhelmed.

After studying the UC/CSU requirements, he says, "It's amazing how little you need to get into San Jose State." Students don't need four years of history, science, or a foreign language. So next year's plan is to require only English I (or English as a Second Language), Algebra I, and College Readiness for ninth graders. That will free time for students to take remedial reading and math and sanity-saving electives such as physical education, drama, art, and photography.

In the first year, DCP offered no remedial classes. In the second year, 20 students are in Verbal Reasoning (VR), in addition to English, and 35 are taking Math Reasoning (MR), in addition to algebra. In the third year, Lippman expects most ninth graders to need remedial classes. "We need to work on how we assess where kids are at," he says. "We've got 35 kids in MR. Of the other 65, how many are really algebra ready? Arguably, none. In VR, we took the 20 lowest students. We should put every student who reads at sixth grade or below in VR."

Telling students they can't read is liberating, he argues. It identifies the problem that's holding them back and offers them a chance to improve.

In the future, DCP will make sure students learn the basics in ninth grade, instead of passing them on with huge gaps in their knowledge, he says. "It's not OK for sophomore teachers to say: 'Oh, they don't know fractions. Give Piece A Chance.' It's about getting kids out of their tunnel of F's."

We need to keep our promises to our students, Lippman says. "Can we prepare ninth graders so by tenth grade they don't need step-by-step, boot-camp skills? So they can handle open-ended questions?"

He's also planning to revamp the administration: The new "ninth-grade principal" will concentrate on the discipline and academic problems of new students.

"Now, 80 percent of my work is ninth-grade discipline and outreach. It's sitting for 45 minutes after school with Jacob's parents. I want my attention to go to whether Armando gets into Santa Clara."

The ninth-grade principal will make sure new students convert to DCP's culture. Getting families on board will be another big part of the job.

"We'd get a very low grade this year on parent outreach," Lippman says. "It's hurt our ability to do our job effectively. Last year we were so desperate to get parents committed to the mission. This year, we've let that slide."

He and Andaluz also want to hire a community liaison to connect with families, work on improving tutorial, and build closer ties to community organizations. "DCP can't be effective if we don't have families on board," says Andaluz. "We envision meeting with parents 40 percent on campus, 60 percent home visits."

Jill Case will concentrate on students who are on academic probation, the so-called red flag kids. One of the ninth-grade repeaters has been "drifting," Lippman says. Warned that he might fail ninth grade for the second time, his mother asked whether he could return for a third try. Lippman shakes his head. "We don't kick out students for academic reasons. But . . ."

"If a kid makes no effort, that's not academic. That's behavior," Andaluz says. "We can't have 20-year-olds in ninth grade."

Lippman will concentrate on getting students to college: He wants Santa Clara to promise to take seven DCP students a year; so far, the university hasn't committed itself to anything.

DCP also needs to help families legalize their immigration status, if possible, so students aren't frozen out of scholarships. About 15 percent of students are undocumented immigrants. If they're not legal residents by the time they apply to college, they'll be considered international students; they won't be eligible for federal or state aid, or for most privately funded scholarships.

Students are starting to be more realistic about their college plans, Case says. "Our students felt very entitled last year. They'd say: 'I'm going to Stanford.' Now they realize they have to do their part."

The last three months of the school year are filled with teacher interviews. DCP is adding another 120 students for its third year, and some teachers are not returning for various reasons, including the fatigue of a long commute (Rigby), a sick father (Safie), and pregnancy (Longosz). To make time for most ninth graders to take remedial reading and math, Fox's science class will be dropped, so he's leaving, too, and Rigby's History of the Americas class will be turned into an upper-class elective. Integrated Science hasn't worked well, and Lippman and Andaluz feel there's little point studying history when a majority of students can't read middle school or high school texts.

Interviewing teacher candidates is time-consuming for everyone. Ad hoc committees of teachers, students, and parents interview every finalist.

Eric Beck, an old friend of Lippman's from prep school days, flies in from Beijing, where he is teaching advanced students at an English-language school, to interview for a job teaching U.S. history at DCP.

Beck's sample lesson is ambitious. He asks, To what extent was ideology the main cause of the Cold War?

Faces go blank. Beck defines *ideology* and *Cold War,* and it isn't clear all the students get it.

"What are the values behind the ideas?" Beck asks. To help students answer, he asks them to analyze a "primary source," a Cultural Revolution statuette of a worker with his foot on a kneeling man. A woman in uniform waves a horn. A placard on the statue says, "Rebel against education."

The students and parents still look befuddled. Beck tries to lead them through the exercise, pointing out each element of the statue. He meets heavy resistance: DCP parents and students are trying to get out of the "peasant-worker-soldier" class Beck is discussing. They believe in education. They think the Cultural Revolutionists are nuts to reject it.

After Beck leaves, the students jump on his lesson, complaining he'd confused them. "It was too broad," Tanya says. "I got lost trying to follow."

"He relied on knowledge you didn't have," Lippman says.

"He didn't break it down for us," Martina says. "We need that."

"We're often confused at first but then we get used to it," says Esther. "What I want to know is, how is he going to relate history to English? Will we do paragraphs or essays? What about debates?"

"I can't believe it," says Andaluz, after the panel has disbanded. "They were wondering about his ability to integrate history with English! They questioned his scaffolding!"

Andaluz and Lippman are elated by the students' ability to critique Beck's lesson.

Byron had explained that DCP is a community and asked Beck what he'd add to the community. "They see it as a community," says Andaluz. "That's what we wanted to create, and . . . they get it."

Beck gets the job: Lippman and Andaluz have faith he can learn to tailor lessons to DCP students. And they want to give their best juniors a chance to take AP U.S. history.

In addition to the new teacher interviews, Lippman schedules evaluations with all his teachers.

Gallegos is finishing her second year as College Readiness teacher and thinking about her future. She let me sit in on her evaluation session.

> Lippman: I can't imagine your class being more high-functioning. Last
> year, you would do activities for 52 minutes. It was like a big ship
> changing direction; the transitions weren't very tight. Now, it's click,
> click, click. When you explained about the glass being half full, it
> was so in context of the lesson some kids were taking notes. Also I

was pleased to see you break down for them how to do a crossword puzzle.

You're doing more diverse activities: note taking and book reports and SAT stuff. It can be an awkward fit between Who's your hero? and organize your binder. You're doing better at integrating it, but it could be even better. You don't always need to drill down to the skill. SAT can also be organizing the binder; they can write on what they think the SAT test will be like.

The Achilles' heel of your curriculum is implementation of assessments. It's not clear what the stakes were for group work. The minute they started doing group work the energy level dropped. Your weaker students peeled off. There was no clear outcome for what they had to create, what their individual responsibility was. Your kids are ready to focus on peer review.

Even kids who are poor homework achievers do a ton of work in your class. How many kids are doing work that isn't reflected in their grade?

As for your learning environment, if I had the president coming to DCP, I'd take him to your class. Discipline is precisely pitched. It's not grim, not too loose. You don't let kids sleaze away with "I don't know." Kids feel responded to. . . . When I need to make a decision about DCP, you're one of the people I check with. You're not hermetically sealed in DCP.

As far as next steps go, I want you to do a presentation to the staff. You've impacted the school community by talking to me, but once you're not there in my ear or Jen's ear, these things evaporate. Take a day or two off to do a one-page philosophy of what ninth-grade teachers should be doing: We show up at dances, we pick up garbage in the halls, we call kids on things. What are the three words from the Olympics? *Altius, Fortius.* . . . Put in there that the principal never goes to school dances. Never, never.

Gallegos: The assessment part I knew would be there. I'm not so worried about the curriculum. The problem is organization or lack thereof. Where papers are. When it's OK for kids to assess themselves in class. Doing more at the end of the semester. Kids know there's some kind of credit, but maybe not for what.

Lippman: You never ask for time to set your ducks in a row, just to set up folders. Take time to talk to other teachers, see how they do it. Let a sub take over for a few days.

A lot of people have gotten a lot of curriculum planning time. I've constantly begged teachers to get their butts off the campus. Today is one of the proudest days in my young life: I have two substitutes working! I haven't done a good job of creating a sub structure so teachers can take time off.

In meetings, you tell classroom stories that are metaphors, homilies. We're going to institutionalize these stories to help new teachers understand the school culture.

I want to be the bad cop with teachers more than I have. Teachers need to be more nervous about not following DCP policy. I'm writing down rules: Do the homework chart like Laura, SSR [Sustained Silent Reading] like you and Angela, tutorial like Jessica. If a class raises the grade point average by 5 percent, they get a pizza. I want you to contribute to this. Write four bullet points about what you do that I can institutionalize as policy.

We need to think about next year's curriculum. We may have 80 freshmen in VR [remedial reading].

We need to talk about how to move our students to the next level. Our sophomores can write an accordion paragraph, but they can't land on an unfamiliar planet and find a water source. They can't think in unfamiliar circumstances.

Gallegos: I think I don't want to be teaching next year. I've been thinking about the two new administrative positions. I was talking to my mom about the community liaison position. She said, "You should do this."

Lippman: That job is for someone like your mom. Actually, we should offer her the job. You should think about applying for ninth-grade principal.

Later, the community liaison job is eliminated. Andaluz decides DCP can't afford a full-time staffer to work with parents and community groups. Instead, the responsibilities are folded into Arreola's job and into the new post of ninth-grade principal. Gallegos applies for the job.

At first, Lippman and Andaluz aren't sure she's ready for it. In essence, they fear she won't be able to stand up to them and challenge their ideas, tell them when they're off base, shake up their comfortable consensus. Her entire professional life—two years—has been spent building DCP. Can she introduce something new to the school?

Gallegos submits her ideas for how to structure the ninth-grade principal's job. Lippman and Andaluz, who've interviewed other prospects, are sold: Gallegos is the one they need.

To replace her as College Readiness teacher, they snag a Mexican American teacher who has five years of experience with AVID, a support program for minority students who enter high school with a C average or better.

It's a sign of DCP's future: After two years with a mostly white and mostly inexperienced staff, DCP is getting a flood of resumes, including applications from good Mexican American prospects. Students will see teachers who've gone from the barrio to college: The new art teacher is the youngest of ten children and the first in his family to go to college. Lippman is especially pleased that teachers who could find a job anywhere are applying to DCP.

However, he's resigned to high turnover. DCP attracts smart, young, restless people who aren't sure they want to be career teachers. Some will leave because the job is too hard or is not a good fit for their talents; others will seek new challenges. People willing to take a chance on a start-up charter school aren't the sort who work at the same job for 25 years.

At a Saturday meeting in June, Lippman writes the basic principles of DCP on a white board for teachers, including some of the new hires who'll start in the fall: Do homework every day, self-discipline, take responsibility for success, work ethic, know what you need to do, desire success.

While catching up the ninth graders, DCP must challenge the older students. They need to learn without "hand-holding," to write more than accordion paragraphs. "We've trained good soldiers," Lippman tells teachers. "We need warriors."

25

building for the future

At the start of the 2001–2002 school year, with nearly 200 students jammed into the church and the Y, Andaluz was thinking big: San Jose State would donate land near the university for a 400-student charter high school that could serve as a training school for future teachers and a showcase for DCP's strategy for educating working-class Hispanic students. Andaluz would raise $22 million from DCP's high-tech backers to build the school.

For a while, her dream seemed to be coming true. San Jose State University's president, Robert Caret, was enthusiastic. He joined the board of the Across the Bridge Foundation, DCP's fund-raising arm; the university identified parcels of land it owned or could buy to create a compact urban campus. DCP's architect designed a model school. Andaluz began lining up donors.

But by the end of 2001, the Silicon Valley economy had hit the skids. Multimillionaires were losing their multi. A board member took Andaluz aside and told her raising $22 million would be impossible. It wasn't going to happen.

In addition, the law had changed. Democrats, who wanted to pass school bond issues with a 55 percent majority instead of two-thirds, reached out to conservative voters by adding help for charter schools to the ballot initiative. Under the new law, any district that passed a school bond would have to provide or pay for classroom space for charter schools serving students who'd otherwise be taking up space in district-run schools. Eventually, all districts would have to provide facilities for charter schools. The law was so vague that nobody knew how to implement it, but it gave charters a bargaining chip.[1]

San Jose Unified was hoping to pass a $423 million bond issue; Superintendent Linda Murray and the board offered to write in $4 million for DCP to buy a building.[2] Under the district's plan, DCP would raise the rest, working with the city to get a match for the district funds. Andaluz calculated she could leverage $12 million for a permanent site. That would be enough.

Many charters are in a constant state of undeclared war with their local school district, but San Jose Unified had embraced DCP. Murray had been up-front, honest, and helpful.

Despite that, having the district own the school building would mean a closer relationship than Andaluz and Lippman really wanted. "We have to make a deal with the devil," Andaluz finally decided.

With her usual cheerfulness, Andaluz decided that losing the model building was for the best: The dream of the "boutique school," as she now called it, had been leading DCP away from its goal. How could DCP be a model for other schools if it had fundraising ability that others didn't? Succeeding with a bare-bones building would enhance DCP's ability to influence other schools.

Across the country, two of the greatest problems facing charter schools are getting classroom space and figuring out how to pay for it. In most states, charter schools get less money per student than the local district schools and then have to pay for classroom space from operating funds or raise private donations.

"I think of DCP as a launching pad for school developers," Andaluz told teachers at a staff meeting. "We hope people will work here and then go out and start their own schools. We have to try to make our model easily replicable."

Besides, DCP didn't really have a choice: The school would have a basic building with district assistance or no building at all. "Whether we're making a deal with the devil or one of the devil's more incompetent assistants, it's worth doing," she concluded.

DCP went to the San Jose Unified board in January to make its midyear report. Andaluz took along some teachers and let them do the talking. Their honesty and specificity impressed the board members. But Andaluz realized she'd need to work with the board on the site plan instead of going it alone. "We need to be less cocky and more of a supplicant," she said.

By the February 13 staff meeting, she'd found the perfect permanent site. San Jose Christian College wanted to sell its eight-acre campus next to the freeway and move to a larger site. All the classrooms were there, along with a gym and space for soccer fields.

"We have a lot of karmic energy," said Andaluz. "People in the DCP network know Christian College people." Andaluz and her allies were working on convincing college officials that DCP's values and community service were compatible with the college's mission. The relationship blossomed.

The catch was that San Jose Christian didn't have the permits needed to turn their new site, a faltering Catholic hospital in nearby Morgan Hill, into a college. Morgan Hill was fighting the plan, hoping to save the hospital. If San Jose Christian couldn't move, they couldn't sell their campus.

Meanwhile, DCP needed space for 300 students in DCP's third year. Once again, as she had when the school was getting started, Andaluz began driving around the area looking at empty buildings. Costs were astronomical: $2.75 a square foot—nearly double what DCP was paying—for space on the ninth floor of a building across from the airport.

Finally, she found the perfect short-term site. But was it available? A few blocks from Saint Paul's, a large Baptist church had 22 classrooms, enough for DCP's eventual enrollment of 400. It even had a gym. The church had lost so much of its membership that its classroom space was barely used.

Andaluz began wooing the Baptists. The church elders were willing to consider renting classrooms, but not all their classrooms. And the Baptists were nervous about hosting a bunch of rowdy teenagers. The negotiations wore on through the spring.

"If this doesn't work, we won't accept a third class," Andaluz told teachers. "We will not go to three sites. We've made a commitment to our families."

Finally, the Baptists sent a committee—all white, all middle-aged to elderly—to tour DCP's two existing campuses. The delegation started with a long talk with the minister of Saint Paul's, who had to admit that the church's aging restrooms had fared badly under the onslaught of DCP students.

Dennis and Lisa were going over a Spanish assignment at one of the picnic tables in the asphalt lunch area. I pointed out the Baptist delegation and told them the visitors had come to see whether DCP students would trash their building.

A few days earlier, Lippman had praised a sophomore—one of Galle-gos's cousins—in assembly for introducing himself to a prospective teacher; the student's friendliness had persuaded the teacher to accept a job at DCP. The story impressed students.

During the break, Dennis walked up to the visitors, smiled, welcomed them to the school, introduced himself, and shook everyone's hand. The Baptists were wowed by his social polish. Even Lippman looked surprised. Who knew Dennis ever listened?

Lippman told the Baptists about *ganas.* They could serve the commu-nity by providing a place for DCP students to transform themselves into se-rious students. But he was alarmingly candid. He also told them about the stink bomb set off in assembly, a product of spring fever.

It seemed to work. Since he'd been honest about students' propensity for mischief, the Baptists assumed everything else he said was gospel truth.

When the group moved to the Y, I tipped off Ines Trevino, who imme-diately grabbed her son and told him to check out the boys' restroom, mak-ing sure there was nothing there the visitors shouldn't see.

Andaluz took over the tour at the Y. She didn't mention stink bombs. But when a woman asked whether any DCP families were Baptists, or might be interested in joining the church, Andaluz responded honestly. "No," she said. "Almost all our families are Catholic. Most belong to Sacred Heart."

Clearly, the church elders were hoping to create a relationship that would boost their sagging membership. DCP's chances were slipping.

But then, during another change of classes, a ninth-grade girl intro-duced herself to the group, shook hands, answered a few questions, then ex-cused herself to go to class.

The Baptists glowed with goodwill. A church visitor told me how won-derful it was to see young people with good manners, how inspiring the school was.

It looked as if the Baptists were convinced. But the church needed more time to decide, so Andaluz kept looking.

In May, she found a failed fitness center across from Adobe Systems, one of DCP's high-tech donors, and beside the Guadalupe River, which was being turned from an eyesore into a nature trail. The Fitness 101 site was three blocks from a light rail station; it was a short walk from The Tech museum and the San Jose Art Museum. Inside there was space for 400 students, if the racquetball courts were turned into classrooms. There was a gymnasium.

Andaluz and Lippman toured the building in May with DCP's architect. Superintendent Murray, whose bond issue had passed, went along to admire its potential.

Of course, there was a catch. The owner of the building, Lew Wolff, didn't want to sell, and DCP's share of the bond—$4 million—couldn't be used for rent.

Andaluz talked to all her contacts and their contacts. She met with the city's planning director, who favored a downtown school, and Councilwoman Cindy Chavez, a DCP ally who represented downtown. Greg Jamison, a DCP trustee and president of the San Jose Sharks hockey team, turned out to be a friend of Wolff's partner.

At the same time, Andaluz kept talking to her contacts at San Jose Christian College. The college had lost its bid to convert the hospital and was now looking elsewhere. One of DCP's board members, a real estate agent, began faxing the college information on possible sites. In two or three years, college officials hoped their San Jose campus would go on the market, and DCP would be a favored bidder.

Months later, in June, DCP's board, chaired by Bob Grimm, a retired high-tech executive, talked about DCP's third year. With only a few months to go, DCP still had no site big enough for three classes of students.

Grace Baptist had offered DCP only five classrooms, instead of the nine rooms requested. It was just barely enough space, if DCP also rented the Y and Saint Paul's. Running the school in three separate locations would be a nightmare.

Andaluz had talked to Superintendent Murray about locating DCP in portable classrooms—basically, trailers—on a school site somewhere. It was a long shot: Thanks to the bond money, San Jose Unified was remodeling. Students from schools under reconstruction already filled the district's stock of portables and previously unused classrooms.

Fitness 101 was the only possible site that would house all of DCP's students, and it was still a possibility, Andaluz told the board. The developer eventually wanted to tear down the building and put up a high-rise, but the sour economy had pushed that project several years into the future.

Could the building be a school by September?

"It will take three months to get a use permit," Andaluz said. "Or maybe if it's the same use we won't need a permit. We could say it's still a fitness club. Mental fitness."

The market cost of rental was about $1.40 a square foot. Andaluz was hoping for a goodwill subsidy from the developer and help from the Redevelopment Agency and San Jose Unified, which technically was supposed to provide classroom space for all its students.

The cost would be high, said Andaluz. But the benefits of a building big enough for all students would be enormous.

Meanwhile, plans for the third year went on. "It's completely and totally about the ninth grade, about getting them hooked into DCP," she told the board. "Greg spends 60 to 70 percent of his time on ninth graders, especially on discipline. As a result, he neglects the sophomores." They all knew this structural problem needed to be fixed. With the new ninth-grade principal focusing on new students, the principal would be able to work more with teachers, helping them find ways to move tenth and eleventh graders beyond basic skills.

In the third year, Gallegos and Case would work on personal learning plans for all high-risk ninth graders, Andaluz told the board. All students testing below the sixth-grade level would take Verbal Reasoning and English, Math Reasoning, and algebra, plus College Readiness and an elective. Remedial classes would average 15 students, with 20 students in regular ninth- and tenth-grade classes and up to 25 students in 11th grade.

Thirteen of 16 new teachers had been hired, she reported. In addition, DCP would pay a stipend to the college counselor, Vicky Evans, who'd been working without pay.

Andaluz handed out a breakdown of DCP's expenses. Essentially, 70 percent of the budget went for salaries and benefits. She'd broken out the special costs of being a charter: $480,945. Most of this covered capital costs—classroom space and equipment—that other public schools don't have to take from the operating budget. In addition, DCP's mission—providing extra help for failing students—cost an extra $577,811 for smaller classes, tutorials, summer school, and counseling. The school's urban location added $17,640 in parking costs.[3] Fitness 101, she pointed out, has a parking lot.

"We should break even for the year, which, given the economy, is amazing," said Jamie Wang, the budget committee chair. In fact, DCP was showing a $40,000 surplus and had a $150,000 line of credit that hadn't been touched.

Like a shark, Andaluz would keep going forward, raising more money. She hoped to recruit an Adobe executive to the board, strengthening the school's ties to the largest high-tech company headquartered in San Jose. Adobe, she reminded the board, is across the street from Fitness 101.

Finally, in mid-July, Andaluz, backed up by Councilwoman Chavez and Jamison, met to negotiate a rental deal with Wolff. The building had been empty a long time. Plans to rent it to a day care center for $1.40 a square foot had fallen through; the slump had left day-care centers with openings.

Andaluz had gone to the meeting prepared to pitch charter schools, but it wasn't necessary. As it turned out, Wolff was a friend of Don Fisher, who'd given millions of dollars to charter schools. Fisher already had sold Wolff on the charter idea: freedom in exchange for accountability.

"That's the way schools should be," Wolff told Andaluz. He promised to help and told her he'd call the next day. Instead, he called a few hours later. He'd talked to his investors and persuaded them to forgo a profit. "How about 63 cents a square foot?" he said. Wolff offered a two-year lease.[4]

Andaluz gasped. It was less than half what DCP was paying already.

Barry Swenson, the city's biggest contractor, offered to make the needed improvements—carpeting and finished walls on the courts, a cover for the hot tub in the locker room—for $30,000.

Instead of begging the district for help to pay the rent, Andaluz now had a surplus in her budget. Plus, with all students in one place, she'd no longer have to pay for parking at the Y or run vans back and forth between two buildings. She'd be able to hire a regular custodian, one of her dreams.

Teachers would get their own desk and files, and a place to hang a coat, and a staff lounge without students popping in and out. The tutorial supervision burden would be less, too, since having larger rooms would mean fewer teachers would be needed to work an extra 75 minutes.

Students would have a place to eat lunch, a gym for exercise, perhaps an environmental lab by the river and a chance to work with Adobe engineers on multimedia projects. The Tech wanted to set up a partnership; Jamison had ideas for students to use the nearby arena.

The building itself was surrounded by pavement, but across the street, next to Adobe headquarters, was a minipark for outdoor activities.

"Our culture won't be fragmented," Andaluz said. "We'll have visibility at a single site. We'll have a physical address where we receive our mail instead of a post office box."

Parents would see a school that looked like a school, and that would help recruiting. Donors would see that DCP was not a fly-by-night operation. For the first time, DCP would have a sign.

DCP had made do with 10,000 square feet for 175 students, about half the recommended space. The new building would provide 27,000 square feet for 280 to 400 students.

By the time Wolff wanted the building back, San Jose Christian College—now looking at a Sacramento site—might be ready to sell its campus. Or something would turn up.

But DCP had to improvise again: Structural problems were discovered that cost an extra $100,000 and an extra two months of construction. In September 2002, DCP opened in three sites with freshmen at Saint Paul's, sophomores at the Y, and juniors at the Baptist church. Students had to shuttle back and forth for mixed classes, such as Spanish III, which included ninth, tenth, and eleventh graders. It was just as dreadful as Andaluz had imagined it would be, but it was temporary.

On October 21, 2002, Downtown College Prep—nearly 300 students, teachers and staff—left the two churches and the Y behind. For at least two years, DCP had a building.

In June 2002, Jennifer Andaluz presented a five-year operating budget to DCP's board. It predicted that per-pupil expenditures would fall as the school grew to four classes with 386 students. Over time, spending would shift away from administration and site expenses and toward teaching. In 2001, most funding came from donations and grants; by 2005, roughly two-thirds of funding would come from the state.

Downtown College Preparatory Operating Budget 2001–2005   (Operating Statistics, Fiscal Year Ending June)

	2001	2002	2003	2004	2005
Total enrollment	100	178	280	368	386
Attendance rate	96%	96%	96%	96%	96%
Average daily attendance (ADA)	96	171	269	353	371
Full-time teachers	6	12	16	22	22
Student: teacher ratio	17:1	15:1	18:1	17:1	18:1
Per pupil expenditures	$13,304	$11,392	$9,368	$8,544	$8,327
Per pupil revenues	$14,234	$11,302	$9,430	$8,669	$8,708
Per pupil rent cost	$1,612	$934	$844	$642	$612
Total budget	$1,330,427	$2,027,784	$2,622,903	$3,144,239	$3,214,263
Grants and donations	$832,298	$921,931	$1,025,000	$1,025,000	$1,025,000
Necessary to finance revenue to expense ratio	107.0%	99.2%	100.7%	101.5%	104.8%
Revenue breakdown					
Block grant	37.1%	51.2%	56.9%	63.8%	65.4%
Economic Impact Aid	0.0%	0.1%	0.4%	0.5%	0.7%
Federal Title I	0.0%	0.0%	0.0%	0.0%	0.0%
Federal Title II–IV	0.0%	0.0%	0.0%	0.0%	0.0%

Block grant *(continued)*

State categorical	1.5%	2.9%	1.3%	1.4%	1.4%
Summer school, Summer Bridge	2.9%	0.0%	2.5%	2.1%	2.0%
Grants and donations	58.5%	45.8%	38.8%	32.1%	30.5%
Total revenues	100.0%	100.0%	100.0%	100.0%	100.0%
Expense breakdown *					
Personnel	56.0%	66.0%	67.9%	59.3%	69.7%
Instructional	4.0%	6.7%	6.7%	7.0%	7.4%
Administrative	19.3%	11.8%	9.8%	9.5%	9.7%
Student services	5.3%	1.7%	3.3%	3.2%	3.2%
Site related overhead	14.8%	10.7%	10.5%	8.8%	8.7%
Capital expenditures	0.6%	3.0%	1.8%	2.2%	1.3%
Total expenses	100.0%	100.0%	100.0%	100.0%	100.0%

*Expense percentages exclude contingency

ride the carrot salad

On a warm day in May, Greg Lippman leaves the window of his office open as he works. Students on their lunch break are talking outside on a scrubby patch of dirt and grass. Rigo, a plump freshman, pokes his head in to ask a question.

"What's this meeting tonight with our parents?"

"It's a meeting for students who are at risk for having to go to summer school or repeating the grade," says Lippman.

"Why weren't we told before?" Rigo sounds indignant.

Lippman sighs. "What are you getting in English?" he asks, knowing the answer.

"F," says Rigo.

"What are you getting in math?"

"Ummm, F."

"College Readiness?"

Rigo thinks. "F."

"Science?"

Another pause. "F."

"History?"

"F."

"You're flunking all your classes," says Lippman.

Rigo nods.

"So what do you mean you weren't told?" Lippman asks. "Did you think you could flunk all your classes and pass to tenth grade?"

Parent turnout is good at the meeting, though students in the worst academic trouble are most likely to be there without a parent.

Lorenzo sits, parentless, on the fringes of the English-language meeting. Gracefully, he leaps up to give me his chair. He's a "heartbreaker," says Lippman: so much potential, so much charm, and yet he's at risk of flunking ninth grade for the second time.

Case thinks Lorenzo is too distracted by his life outside school to concentrate on doing his work. She's tried again and again to persuade him to do his homework. If he fails again, he'll have to leave DCP.

I see Dennis—another bright student with poor grades—sitting with his father and his brother. The family is moving to a San Jose suburb, and the brothers could go on to tenth grade at a new high school that would treat D as a passing grade. But, without DCP's structure, will they graduate?

Lippman explains for what must be the thousandth time that students need to pass their academic courses with a C or better to qualify for college; students who have less than a C in English or algebra will have to attend summer school, and those who can't pass English in summer school will not pass to the next grade.

Students still have time to raise their semester grades. Again, he begs parents not to make summer plans before they know whether their child will need summer school.

Parents are eager to make sure that their children can return, even if they have to repeat a grade. DCP has become their home.

This incredible year ends with an awards assembly on a warm night in June. The assembly room is decorated with silver, purple, and orange balloons. Behind the stage is a huge orange banner proclaiming, "Downtown College Prep: A Community Celebration of Academic Promise."

Jose Arreola starts it off in English and Spanish, then leads everyone in the DCP clap.

Many of the students I met in Mock Trial and Tech Challenge win awards: Rico and Rajiv are honored for photography, Bill and Clara win for Multi-Media, Rajiv again for biology.

Jack gets a leadership award from Arreola for "welcoming students, visitors, and teachers."

Art is "most improved" in second semester English I. Angela Hensley says: "At first, he never did homework. But one day, he turned it in, and I said, 'Art! You did your homework!' The whole class burst into applause. Art's done his homework every single day since then. He always checks to make sure he's got his check on the homework chart, that he hasn't missed anything."

Lorenzo wins an academic award in History of the Americas. "He's wearing the traditional loaner shirt," says Jessica Rigby. "Lorenzo was in my class for two years. He often didn't have his homework but he always prepared mentally. His interest in the History of the Americas and Mexico is inspiring."

In humanities (English and history), Jorge wins for his energy, excitement, and leadership.

Srugis honors his entire fifth-period math class. "Sometimes they locked me out of the room, but learning still happened. A couple of times I had to climb in the window, but learning still happened. One time, they locked the window. I don't know what happened, but on the next test they averaged 99 percent."

Jorge appears in a clip from a documentary. Students cheer. To be on TV is their ultimate measure of success, and there he is up on the screen.

Jorge is the youngest of 11 children, he tells the camera. "I had to change my attitude in school. Now I'm getting all B's. I want to go to Santa Clara. I want to be a teacher. I want to help my community find a better way to get to college."

Srugis returns with a guitar to lament the departure of DCP teachers. His song, "Lament of the DCP Student," uses a Counting Crows song for inspiration:

Friday 4:30 tutorial is when it hurts the most
All my friends are partying. . . .
Mrs. Zuniga and Figueroa are always chasing me to class. . . .
Hey teacher, please don't leave DCP.

Mr. Srugis' class for the second time is really a bore.
I feel like I've heard his stupid jokes one million times before.
But to get to college I better know there are two answers to the square root of four.

Arreola and the parent educator, Elena Mendez, honor parents who served on discipline, teacher recruitment, and student recruitment committees. Richard Ruiz is wearing his marine uniform.

Lippman appears when it's time to honor students for good grades—not just effort but excellence. In all, 35 students have made the honor roll with grades of 3.0 or better, representing nearly 20 percent of the school.

Some of the students I've watched over the year go up on stage: Jack, Melissa, and Armando have made it. The high honor roll—"These are students who will be going to prestige universities," says Lippman—includes Rajiv, Bill, Adam, Selena, Rico, and Neary.

Two years after he started speaking English, Roberto has a 3.01 average.

Ganas awards go to the rebels: students who didn't want to go to DCP, who quit and then returned, who fought the system. Of Lizabeta, Lippman says: "There were times when she wanted to give up but she never gave up. Sometimes she gets angry. Sometimes she gets very angry. She keeps working. She keeps working. She keeps improving."

At the very end of the program, three girls make a special appearance. They've discovered that it's Greg Lippman's birthday. He's 33 years old.

The girls begin singing a traditional Mexican celebration song, "Las Mañanitas." They start off nervously, their voices thin, tentative, and off-key.

Estas son las mañanitas
Que cantaba el rey David
Por ser dia de tu santo,
Te las cantamos a ti.

(These are the little mornings
of King David's psalms
On your special day,
we sing songs to you.)

In the audience, a father joins in, then a mother, then a whole row of parents, brothers, and sisters. Together, they find the tune and start belting it out. It is the essential DCP:

Despierta, mi bien, despierta,
Mira que ya amenecio,
Y los pajaritos cantan.

(Awake, my dear, awake.
See that the sun has risen
And the little birds sing.)

The sound fills the dingy auditorium, ruffling the colored balloons. It grows stronger and sweeter.

Despierta, they sing. Wake up.

On the last day of the 2001–2002 school year, Gallegos asked College Readiness students to write her a letter about their freshman year at DCP.

Dear Ms. Gallegos
This year was more important to me because I need to pass this year I care more, because I need to pass high school to be a cop. This job I like because I don't need to go to college for a long time. Also I can't get retain for another year. Last year I never did put attention in class or do my homework I am doing better this year better grades, I had all F's last year. This year I have better grades than last year. All I want to be is a cop. It is a job that is dangerous and their is always danger. I love danger. So I think this is a good job for me.
Sincerly,
Gil

Dear Ms. Gallegos
Thank you for helping me with the homework. I tried to do your homework but what I have time for tutorial I forget to do your homework so sometimes I do remember to do your homework and sometimes i do classwork When you say "Come Felipe do classwork" so then I do my classwork then I like your class you are nice teacher and you are cool teacher to and I like how you teach. You teach good and you tell jokes and thank you again for helping me alot and your nice with everybody and thanks again.
Sincerely
Felipe

27

lessons learned

Downtown College Prep continues to evolve, learning from experience. Four years after DCP got its start, I talked to Lippman and Andaluz separately about what they'd learned over the years and what they'd changed. Both started with the same issue.

"Our kids couldn't read," said Andaluz. "We didn't realize how serious the problems were when we started. We thought we'd get everyone to calculus as seniors. It was just a matter of engaging kids, motivating them. We discovered Marta couldn't multiply 3 times 4. Aaron Srugis brought in oranges to demonstrate. He said, 'They can't multiply, so that's where I'm going to start.'"

Lippman thought he'd been "mugged by reality" when he started teaching at Gunderson, but it hadn't prepared him for DCP students' "catastrophic" lack of reading, writing, and math skills. "We didn't understand how time-consuming remediation is. We were going to require all juniors and seniors to take AP classes. By not having remediation in place at the beginning, we set them up for failure."

"We were so winging it as a school," Andaluz said.

After adding a few remedial classes and ESL in the second year, Lippman and Andaluz faced the issue head-on in the third year: Two-thirds of incoming students had reading and math skills below the sixth-grade level; they were placed in remedial math or English or both. Those who couldn't catch up in one year would have to spend a second year in ninth grade.

Looking back, they decided they'd been too lenient in the early years. "Graduating in five years is now part of the design" for low-skilled students, Lippman said.

When the D grade was eliminated, the number of F's soared. Lippman and Andaluz didn't waver. They hadn't just promised students would go to college; they'd promised they'd be prepared to succeed once they got there. To keep that promise, they had to be willing to hold students to college-prep standards.

Raising standards raised the attrition rate: Some students transferred rather than repeat a grade at DCP. Although they worried about attrition, Lippman and Andaluz decided it was inevitable with the kind of students they were recruiting. If they discouraged the worst applicants from enrolling, they'd lose fewer students along the way and save themselves a lot of aggravation. But it wasn't DCP's mission to help students who could be successful at a conventional school.

"DCP kids often are frustrated," Lippman said. "They have to work very hard and they're not happy all the time." That's OK, he said. The hard work will pay off. "Pride in achievement is enough happiness to go around," he said.

DCP also modified its teaching techniques. At Gunderson, Lippman and Andaluz experimented with project-based, experiential learning. They realized DCP required more structure, not just to teach skills but to inculcate the culture. They'd never intended to offer such a traditional, rule-bound, step-by-step curriculum, but the students needed it, at least in the first two years. "We'll do whatever works," Lippman said.

In the early years, teachers had made up curriculum as they went along. As it became clear what was working, Lippman assembled a standard DCP curriculum that all teachers could use as a foundation.

Ganas, an idea introduced by Gallegos early on, was the core value, supplemented in later years by *orgullo* (pride) and *communidad* (community). DCP taught students to sit up straight, look people in the eye, express eagerness to learn, shake hands. It was "spiritual remediation," as Lippman called it. Getting students to take pride in their school and in themselves was a long struggle. "We try to build character," Lippman said. It's not enough to teach basic skills. Students also need to learn to solve problems and handle failure. They need to think of college as important and achievable.

By the school's third year, DCP added Advanced Placement classes in U.S. history and Spanish; 14 students passed an intensive summer class in advanced algebra and trigonometry, putting them on track to take Advanced Placement calculus as seniors.

Moving to a single building saved 40 minutes a day, since there was no need for transport periods. DCP went to block scheduling: Classes met three times a week for 90 minutes, reducing the homework burden. Students got a 35-minute lunch period and 35 minutes of silent reading every day. There was time built into the schedule for freshmen, sophomores, and juniors to meet as a class, and for activities—or detention—on Friday afternoons. Saturday study sessions were required for students who'd fallen behind.

Lippman and Andaluz also tried to reduce the burden on teachers. Instead of each teacher calling the parents of each student who'd fallen behind on homework, advisers handled the calls for the 12 students in their advisory group, creating a single contact point for parents.

As the first class of students became seniors, Lippman and Andaluz relaxed the draconian rules, trying to prepare them for the independence they'd have as college students. Seniors in good academic standing could skip tutorial to study on their own in the college counseling room, which had computers, or take after-school jobs; they were supposed to learn how to manage their own study time.

They could wear their own clothing, instead of the uniform, if they dressed "professionally," with no red or blue. I started to have trouble distinguishing young teachers from the well-dressed seniors.

With more students, it was possible to add electives, such as Latin American literature, drama, dance, and music. Physical education, which had been eliminated in the second year because of lack of space, was revived, providing an outlet for students' energies.

Enough students were eligible to allow DCP to field teams in basketball, soccer, baseball, softball, and Ultimate Frisbee. DCP sports teams began to win games against the small private schools in their athletic league. In Division III, DCP became a soccer powerhouse. Students also got the opportunity to try lawn bowling and crew.

Mock Trial didn't return. Reluctantly, Lippman and Andaluz decided there just wasn't enough student interest.

However, DCP students continued to compete in the annual Tech Challenge. After finishing fourth for three years in a row with Big Chicken Dinner, Big Chicken Dinner II, and Big Chicken Dinner III, DCP's Biggest Chicken Dinner, made up of Bill and Rajiv, won the grand prize at the 2004 Tech Challenge.

DCP students also fielded a large coed team, the Robos Lobos, in the FIRST robotics competition.

Within the school, the History Bowl, created by the U.S. history teacher, Eric Beck, became a school tradition. Teams of AP students competed for prizes by displaying history knowledge.

College planning events pulled in parents: At one meeting, 67 of 69 eleventh-graders' parents came to hear Hispanic college students talk about being the first in their family to go to college.

College counselor Evans discovered the recession had cut the generosity of financial aid, especially to C- students with below-average test scores. The C- students who didn't qualify for CSU could get into unselective private colleges but couldn't afford to go. Andaluz and her board raised the money so that every graduate could accept a four-year college offer, but it was clear that sending students to private colleges would be a huge burden on the school's fund-raising capability.

DCP adopted a new policy: No eleventh grader would be promoted to twelfth grade unless he or she was "on the matrix"—a combination of grades and test scores—for CSU admission. Eleventh graders were warned to raise their grades or prepare to spend another year as juniors; at the end of the 2003–2004 school year, about a third of the class was held back. Some were the victims of lenient promotion policies when they were ninth graders. They weren't ready.

In the future, every DCP grad would be eligible for a relatively affordable CSU. DCP would continue to help students who needed more scholarship aid to attend high-quality private or public schools and to fund undocumented students.

Evans scheduled sessions to teach college life skills: how to get and use a bank account, how to choose a meal plan, how to get along with a roommate, how to use college tutorial services, how to avoid binge drinking, drugs, and excessive partying. She promised students to keep in touch via e-mail and campus visits to make sure they stayed on track in college.

New students were entering DCP from families with less income and education: By 2003–2004, a majority of students qualified for a subsidized lunch, the official indicator of low-income status. Half of the parents were not high school graduates, one third had only a high school education, 10 percent reported some college, 5 percent had a B.A., and 2 percent had a graduate degree. Ninety percent of students identified themselves as Hispanic, 4 percent as white, 2 percent as black, and the rest as Asian, Filipino, Native American, or "other."

A quarter or more of incoming students were undocumented immigrants, but most of their parents were working on legalizing the family's status.

Recruiting new students wasn't a problem anymore, especially with an influx of younger siblings and cousins. With 165 applicants, DCP had to hold a lottery to pick the class of '09. The school enrolled 145 ninth graders to balance the unusually small senior class of 42 students and to prepare for attrition.

Unlike many educators, Lippman and Andaluz spend no time complaining about standardized tests. They know they will be judged on measurable results by their sponsor, San Jose Unified, and by their donors.

DCP started behind but is catching up.

Practice SAT scores had been so low, despite the free test-prep class, that Evans switched students to the ACT, which is a better match for the curriculum. Still, the average ACT score was only 16.2 for the first graduating class, roughly the equivalent of 790 out of 1600 on the SATs.

On the challenging California Standards Test, English and math scores are low but improving; DCP students outdo the state average in biology and ace U.S. history with 67 percent testing as proficient or advanced. Students get stronger as they go through school: In English Language Arts, 43 percent of ninth graders test at the basic level and another 24 percent are proficient or advanced; by eleventh grade, 45 percent score at the basic level and 35 percent in the proficient or advanced range.[1]

DCP jumped to a 731 on California's Academic Performance Index (API) in 2005,[2] exceeding the state average for high schools; compared to high schools with similar demographics, DCP is rated a perfect 10.[3]

Within San Jose Unified, DCP has the highest percentage of students who aren't fluent in English and vies with San Jose High Academy for the most low-income students. Yet its 2005 API score ranks third in the district.[4] When scores for Hispanic and socioeconomically disadvantaged students are compared (at the time of publication, 2004 data are the most recent available), DCP ranks second only to Leland High, San Jose's elite high school. DCP is the only district school to rate a 10 when compared to similar schools.[5]

2004/2005 API Scores for San Jose Unified High Schools

	2005	2004	2004
	All	Disadvantaged	Hispanic
Leland	862	797	709
Pioneer	777	592	630
DCP	731	638	636
Lincoln	714	610	625
Willow Glen	669	567	562
San Jose	649	530	508
Gunderson	631	566	550

—California Department of Education[6]

Passing the state graduation exam is not a hurdle for DCP students, who beat the state average. DCP's class of 2006 had the second highest pass rate in San Jose Unified.[7]

Looking at San Jose Unified's tests, the results are dramatic: DCP's first class was reading at the fifth-grade level, on average, when they started ninth grade. At the start of tenth grade, they tested at the seventh-grade level, the 29th percentile, on the district's test, known as Degrees of Reading Power. By the start of eleventh grade, DCP students tested at the 50th percentile. They'd made the long journey to average, at least on that test.

By 2003–4, 20 percent of DCP students were taking AP calculus or on track to take calculus. Ninety-five percent were taking or on track to take chemistry and physics, compared to 36 percent statewide.[8]

Boosted by a 100 percent pass rate on the AP Spanish exam, DCP more than doubled the state average of 24 passing AP scores per 100 students.[9]

All students in DCP's first graduating class were admitted to four-year colleges, as Lippman and Andaluz had promised. By comparison, only 12 percent of Hispanic high school graduates statewide completed the A-G requirements for public universities with a C or better in 2003. In San Jose Unified, which requires all students to take A-G courses, the completion rate with a C or better was 25 percent for Hispanics, 47 percent overall.[10]

Many students left DCP for academic or behavioral reasons, or because the Silicon Valley slump drove their family out of San Jose. Comparing graduation rates is difficult since DCP transfers students to district schools but takes very few transfers in return after ninth grade. Still, the *San Jose Mercury News* crunched the numbers, and found that San Jose Unified's four-year graduation rate was 77 percent for all students who'd started high school in 1999, 55 percent for Hispanics.[11]

Of DCP's original class:

- 102 students started ninth grade in 2000.
- 54 graduated in 2004; 2 who started in the class of '04 were expected to graduate in 2005.
- 29 transferred to another district high school.
- 11 moved out of the district.
- 6 left for disciplinary reasons.

DCP's board and staffers have talked for years about whether the school should add a middle school. Eastside Prep, its mentor school, now starts in sixth grade to give students more time to prepare for college. It's the one change I'd make, if anyone asked me. Many students take months, or even a whole year, to start doing the work. Then they discover they're way behind and have to work incredibly hard to catch up. They're not just climbing a mountain; they're climbing Mount Everest. If they started in sixth or seventh grade, the mountain wouldn't be quite so high and more kids would make it to the top.

Lippman has resisted the idea, fearing DCP would compromise its mission to make a difference for the neediest students. "If we got students in sixth grade, they wouldn't need DCP for high school," he said. "They could go anywhere." He wants to keep DCP's ninth grade open to students who need a fresh chance.

In a sense, however, DCP already is starting earlier. The fifth class of freshmen was a surprise. About a third were siblings or cousins of DCP students, and they were showing up already prepared to do homework and take school seriously. The word was filtering down about how to be a student. Perhaps it was just a one-year blip, but only a third of ninth graders needed remedial classes in the fall of 2004, down from two-thirds the year before. DCP had dreamed of changing the community. It seemed to be succeeding.

In 2004, San Jose Unified offered DCP a long-term lease on a closed elementary school a mile from the old Fitness 101. Andaluz agreed to use DCP's $4 million in bond money to convert Hester Elementary into a high school and raise additional money to build a technology center, library, and gym.

Hester has plenty of space for 400 students, with the possibility of adding a middle school, if the board decides to expand. There are playing fields with actual grass, an innovation at DCP.

The new DCP is across the street from district headquarters, a bit too close for comfort. It is not in the heart of downtown, but is close enough for students to take advantage of downtown cultural sites. For the first time, DCP has a permanent home.

Attrition
According to a report by the National Governors Association, more than 40 percent of high school graduates lack the skills for college or a skilled job. Of every 100 ninth graders, only 68 will graduate from high school; the graduation rate declined from 1990 to 2000, Educational Testing Service says. Forty will enter college, where more than half will need remedial English or math courses; 27 will enroll for a second year. Only 18 of the original 100 will graduate with a two-year or four-year degree within six years.[12]

28

the charter debate

Charter schools ask to be judged by results, but there's not much consensus on what the results show.

In 2004, the *New York Times* ran a front-page story, based on an analysis by the American Federation of Teachers (AFT), which charged that charter students had lower scores on the federal National Assessment of Educational Progress (NAEP) than students in mainstream schools. The union also claimed that low-income students did worse in charter schools.[1]

Charter advocates put a different spin on the data, noting that the NAEP study, which involved fourth graders at 150 schools, found charter students did as well in reading and slightly worse in math than mainstream students, despite being much more likely to come from low-scoring groups. According to NAEP, 31 percent of charter fourth graders in the study were black, compared to 17 percent of noncharter students; half lived in central cities versus 29 percent of noncharter students. Charters enrolled slightly more Hispanics (20 percent versus 19 percent) and the same number of students not fluent in English (9 percent).[2] When students of the same race or ethnicity were compared, there was no difference in reading or math performance. Jeanne Allen of the procharter Center for Education Reform called the results "a statistical dead-even tie."[3]

NAEP found 44 percent of noncharter students were eligible for a free or reduced-price lunch, compared to 42 percent of charter students, and concluded that low-income students did slightly better in mainstream schools.[4] However, a third of charter schools don't participate in the federal lunch program, skewing the poverty data.[5] A 2004 U.S. Education Department report concluded that charters serve more low-income and minority students than traditional schools.[6]

To claim that charter students do worse in reading and math, the AFT excluded scores for special education students. Eleven percent of the non-charter fourth graders had been placed in special education, compared to 8 percent of charter students.[7]

Again, there's disagreement on whether charters serve fewer disabled students. A 1998 RTI study, *Charter Schools and Students with Disabilities,* found little difference in enrollment of disabled students, and suggested charters may be less likely to identify students as disabled.[8]

In 2005, the Economic Policy Institute also released an analysis of existing research, concluding that charter students do as well as, but no better than, mainstream students and sometimes do worse.[9]

Charter advocates see the data differently, pointing to research that shows faster progress for charter students and stronger results for established charter schools.

In 2004, Caroline Hoxby, a Harvard economist, compared test scores of charter fourth graders to scores of students in nearby schools they'd otherwise attend. She found charter students 5.2 percent more likely to be proficient in reading and 3.2 percent more likely to be proficient in math than students in neighborhood schools. The longer the charter school had been in existence, the greater the advantage for charter students: After nine years, the charter edge grew to 10.1 percent in reading. In addition, achievement gains were greater for black, Hispanic, and low-income charter students.[10]

Neither study was able to track progress or look at whether charter and noncharter students started with comparable skills or motivation.

To get at that question, Hoxby compared students admitted by lottery to Chicago charter schools to applicants who applied but lost out in the lottery. Almost all the students were black and Hispanic; most were low-income. The three charter schools had been in existence for at least two years; funding was set at 75 percent of the dollars provided to students in noncharter public schools.

Charter students in kindergarten through third grade did significantly better than lottery losers: Reading test scores were 8 percentile points higher than those of the control group for those who started in kindergarten or first grade; for second or third graders, the effect was 10 percentile points in math, 4 points in reading. However, there was no effect for students who entered charter schools in fourth through eighth grade.[11]

Students who transfer from conventional schools to charters often are kids who've done poorly and need a fresh start. That's certainly true of DCP students, who have more learning problems than students of the same ethnicity and socioeconomic status.

On the other hand, charter students have parents who are committed enough to their children's education to seek out an alternative. That's normally a big advantage.

Most studies are snapshots, looking at students at one point in time, instead of finding out how well students were doing when they started a new school and how they progressed over time.

The National Charter School Research Center at the University of Washington's Center on Reinventing Public Education is attempting to provide a framework for answering questions about charter effectiveness. No single study can answer the question, concludes researcher Paul Hill, because charters differ in so many factors. For one thing, charter schools are wildly diverse in their student demographics, teaching methods, and funding: Some are experiments that don't work and won't last; others enroll high-risk students who are way behind from the start. Most charters are new and still working the bugs out.[12]

It's clear that independence alone isn't enough to create a good school. Charter starters must be able to handle the management and financial challenges of a start-up operation—finding a building, hiring staff, recruiting students, replacing the lunch lady at 11:15 A.M.—while developing a curriculum and teaching methods. Some charter operators are strong on connecting with the community but weak on education, or strong on education but weak on balancing the books. The job is very demanding. It's not uncommon for charter founders to burn out after the first few exhausting years.

The politics around charters are intense: Some founders must spend half their time and energy defending their school from political foes and from reregulation by the state legislature. Others, like DCP, exist in a more benign climate with help from the local district or, at least, neutrality.

The politics are heating up, as the No Child Left Behind Act requires changes at persistently low-performing schools; under the law, one possible sanction is to turn over a failing school to a charter operator. Potentially, many more schools could be converted to charters. However, establishment educators don't want to lose control of schools and are likely to make conversion to charter status the last resort. In addition, many charter operators prefer starting new schools to dealing with entrenched problems. They're leery of walking into a no-win situation.

I'm not hopeful charter operators will be able to turn around schools with a long tradition of failure, unless they can start with teachers and students who've made a choice and a commitment to the program.

When KIPP (Knowledge Is Power Program) agreed to take over Denver's lowest-performing middle school, it insisted on adding one class of KIPP-recruited students each year, rather than trying to turn existing students into KIPP students. That will take time, but it's likely to work. KIPP is effective because parents and students agree to follow the program.

Charters aren't a panacea. Well, what is? The question is whether to preserve the existing school system as is or to enable independent schools to compete for students. Inevitably, some charters will fail educationally or organizationally. Others will provide alternatives, empower parents, and shake up a system that needs a good shake.

Charters are experiments, and not all experiments work. What's different is that charters adapt quickly or lose students. Unlike a traditional public school, when a charter fails, it doesn't get more money. It closes its doors.

29

commencement

On June 19, 2004, a mariachi band played "Pomp and Circumstance" as 54 graduates walked out of the school and marched to a small park across the street, which had been closed to traffic for DCP's graduation. Greg Lippman, Jennifer Andaluz, the teachers, and staff members, wearing caps and gowns like their students, marched in the procession with the superintendent, the mayor, and the bishop. Every folding chair in the giant tent was filled with their family members and friends, and crowds stood or sat on the ground to watch the ceremony.

Andaluz welcomed the family and friends of DCP. A city councilwoman sat behind a grandmother up from Mexico for the ceremony. Silicon Valley executives mingled with the janitors who cleaned their buildings. "It takes hope," Andaluz said, declaring the theme of the day.

Patrick McGrath, the bishop of San Jose, gave the invocation: "Make them beacons of light and may they remain our vessels of hope for tomorrow."

"It's about hope and opportunity," said San Jose Mayor Ron Gonzales, himself the first in his family to earn a college degree.

Superintendent Linda Murray, on the verge of retirement, recalled "two bright-eyed teachers from Gunderson who said, 'We have a dream to create a charter school that will reach out to children who are falling through the cracks.' You've earned the right to be here," she told graduates. "You're here today because you've shown you have the courage and stamina to do it."

"How you start doesn't count; it's how you finish," said Michael O'Farrell, vice president of Applied Materials. His company had donated money for the graduation fiesta, which included a Ferris wheel for the younger brothers and sisters, Aztec dancers, and a picnic lunch.

Maggie Villalvazo, soon to start at Dominican University, was chosen to give the graduation speech, which recounted the hardships of the early years and how far students had come. When she'd started DCP, she said, she didn't really believe it was possible to go to college. She made a deal with her mother: If she stuck it out for a year, she could transfer to a traditional high school. She decided to stay. Maggie reminded classmates, they'd made a commitment to succeed in college, not just to get accepted. "As the first class we've faced every obstacle together. Now is the time to put our skills to the test. Thank you for all the memories we've shared, and remember this is not the end; it's only the beginning."

"All of you are the founders of DCP," Lippman said. "To the class of 2004, this is your place, this is your city. . . . You are our true founders."

Espera means "hope," he said. "DCP is the story of hope." But *espera* also means "to wait."

"First you waited for teachers to tell you what to do. You waited to do homework, if you did it at all. You waited for your parents to let you transfer to the high school you wanted. . . . We waited for you to trust yourselves enough to have hope."

In the last year, "that hope has grown muscles and strengthened into expectations."

College will be hard, he said. But they had what they needed to succeed. "Our values of *ganas, orgullo,* and *communidad* will serve you in college and the world," Lippman told his students. "You have to decide to succeed every day." He concluded, "You are college ready, and we expect you will prevail."

I saw students I'd followed for nearly four years step up to receive a diploma and, once again, shake hands with Lippman and Andaluz.

Selena, who'd joined the first Summer Bridge tutoring program, when DCP was just a gleam in the eyes of Lippman and Andaluz, walked forward. I'd volunteered that fall to help students with college essays, so I knew how hers had started: "Pulled by my mother's dreams, I walked barefoot across the border from Mexico. I was six years old." Selena wrote that she'd realized college had to be her own dream, nobody else's. The work ethic she'd learned from her mother, who worked two or three jobs to support the family, Selena turned toward school. Selena was going to Santa Clara University with the help of the scholarship Father Mateo Sheedy had persuaded the Jesuits to fund for Sacred Heart parishioners.

With his usual dignity, Roberto walked up to receive his diploma. I remembered how hard he'd worked to learn English as a ninth grader. Roberto was planning to major in agricultural business at Chico State. His English wasn't perfect, but it was good enough.

I'd helped Emilia polish an essay about her first terrified day in middle school in America. She didn't speak a word of English. Emilia was going to Mount Holyoke on a full scholarship.

Of the graduating Mock Trialers, Adam was headed to Santa Clara, his brother Bill to UC-Santa Cruz, Rajiv to Cal Poly, Barbara to San Jose State, and Jerry all the way to Goucher in Baltimore.

Byron had signed up at Sonoma State, Armando at Chico State. Selma, the smallest girl on the basketball team, was going to Monterey Bay and planning a career as a nurse. The hyperkinetic James was enrolled at Whittier College in Southern California.

Gina, who'd vowed at the start of sophomore year to regain her mother's faith, had turned D's and Fs into C's and B's and then, in some subjects, A's. She'd won a place at UC-Santa Cruz.

Eugenio and Dominga Ramirez cheered for their son, who was going to San Diego State to study engineering. Irene and Ruben Zuniga cheered for their son, soon to be a freshman at Menlo College. Richard Ruiz's son had made it to Notre Dame de Namur University.

Only one graduate wasn't going directly to college. Wesleyan had offered her admission, if she did a thirteenth year at an East Coast boarding school, on full scholarship. She took the deal.

Jorge, who'd read "ride the carousel" as "ride the carrot salad" in ninth grade, inspiring the unofficial school motto, had turned into a student strong enough to take AP and honors classes. Jorge was going to Cal State Monterey Bay.

Andaluz charged them to "further pursue the mission of DCP and thrive in college."

Then the graduates marched out of the tent to the beat of Aztec drummers, and the fiesta was under way.

Most DCP graduates went on to CSUs—San Jose State and Monterey Bay took large contingents—but three got into UC-Santa Cruz, and DCP raised $250,000 in scholarships to help students afford private colleges.

Pedro didn't make it. At the end of tenth grade, he rebelled against being told what to do. A fast learner with a short attention span, he was bored in class, sure he already knew what the teacher had to say. He was told to stop disrupting class or go home to finish the year on independent study. He chose independent study. When he failed his finals, he was offered a chance to repeat tenth grade, but he already was a year behind and didn't want to turn 20 in high school. So he tried an alternative school that promised him a chance to get two years of credit in one year. His plan was to catch up, then return to DCP to graduate with his class. He got good grades the first semester but was kicked out for bad behavior. "It was my fault," he said. "I can't keep my big mouth shut."

He continued to visit DCP, where his sister had enrolled. "Teachers here really care about your education," he said later. "They keep asking me what I'm doing, telling me I should be in school." He signed up for adult education but quit after a few weeks.

At the age of 20, working in construction, Pedro decided to take the GED test to earn an equivalency certificate and sign up for community college classes at night. His sister, by then a junior at DCP, had made the honor roll.

"DCP helped me grow," he said. "I had a reputation at DCP as the smart guy who didn't do the work. Now I make my sister do her homework. I say, 'Have you done it? Let me see it.'"

Pedro reads books he borrowed from DCP and never returned. He wears the school uniform, khaki pants and a black shirt, by choice. He still writes raps and rhymes but dropped his street name, believing "Nicknames are a gang thing." Whenever he meets someone, he shakes hands, like Greg Lippman at the schoolhouse door.

DCP's second class lost a number of students. After the Mock Trial team disbanded, Warren lost control of his behavior more frequently. To Lippman's dismay, Warren had to leave after piling up too many referrals in a single grading period.

In tenth grade, Hector also was asked to leave after repeated referrals. He earned a certificate at a vocational training center.

Felipe returned to repeat ninth grade. He was suspended for stealing from the office, came back to DCP the following year, did poorly, and left for good. He enrolled at a district-run high school but passed few classes and did not graduate. His younger sister enrolled at DCP.

As a junior, Lisa rebelled against DCP's rules and transferred to a local high school, where she found classes easy. She earned her diploma on schedule, as well as a certificate in dental assisting, and went to work as a dental assistant.

Dennis was promoted to tenth grade but transferred to a local high school after his family moved.

Gil and Art also were promoted to tenth grade but failed to pass into eleventh and left DCP. Gil gave up on high school and got a job at a drug store. Art transferred, didn't graduate on time, but returned for an extra year.

Larissa's life fell apart in tenth grade. She fought with her mother, moved in with friends, and kept going to school, but her grades slipped in the turmoil. She failed tenth grade, left DCP, and had a second child.

Of those who stayed in the class of 2005, Neary and Jack qualified for an array of colleges. Neary, who won awards for academic excellence, athletics, values, and vision, and was chosen to give the commencement speech, decided to go to Cal Poly at San Luis Obispo; she hopes to go to medical school. Jack went on to UC-Santa Cruz. Lorenzo, who'd developed into a talented artist, won DCP's Communidad Award "for embodying the values of the DCP culture." He decided to major in art at Chico State. Gonzalo, whom I'd met in Mock Trial, also enrolled at Chico State.

Lippman announced he was stepping down as principal after the 2004 graduation. Years ago, he'd promised his Hungarian wife that they'd go back to her homeland for a while. He was overdue on the promise. And he'd been working very, very hard for five years to create a school from scratch.

Lippman signed on as a consultant, spending much of his time working on strengthening the curriculum. "We're thinking of dropping the accordion paragraph," he said. "I think we can come up with something better."

The principal's job had become so demanding that the search for a new principal was a bust. Nobody could do everything Lippman had taken on. Would-be principals who were strong on curriculum were weak on leadership. It was essential to find someone who could connect with DCP parents. None of the candidates could do it all.

Before school started in the fall of 2004, Andaluz, who'd hired a full-time fundraiser to do part of her job, took over as principal. She didn't want the job on a long-term basis. The board decided DCP would continue to look for a new principal and an academic dean to take over teacher mentoring and curriculum responsibilities.

I had a hunch Andaluz would remain as principal, with Lippman returning as academic dean. I couldn't imagine anyone taking over except perhaps Gallegos. DCP isn't a start-up anymore. It can survive without its founders, if need be. The question is whether they're capable of moving on. Throughout the 2004–2005 school year, I kept running into Lippman at the school. He wasn't in Hungary, I noticed. He'd delayed so his second child could be born in the United States and then waited longer to see the second class graduate. Leaving the school of your dreams isn't easy.

The pioneer graduating class felt at home on their college campuses. From Mount Holyoke to Chico State, they made friends and leaped into campus activities. Academically, many struggled but they didn't get discouraged, Evans reported. They went to the campus tutoring center, adjusted their study styles, and picked courses they could handle. Ninety percent were going to be OK, she predicted. "They told me, 'We've been through this before.' They know what it's like to start a new school and get hammered. They can handle failure. They've done it, and survived." One graduate told her not to worry: "We learn faster now," he said.

I think of a line in the speech Maggie gave at graduation. "Slowly, our fears became our strengths."

Magdalena Villalvazo's speech

The days were long
Sweltering at Saint Paul's
Rotten bananas
Never enough ketchup
Can't stop at the food stands
Someone always sneaking off
Chips before tutorial
Two hours, too long tutorial
Endless seating charts
Talk, talk, talk
You move there

You move there
Talk, talk, talk
Don't get in the way of Mr. Lippman
Handball off the walls
Boys playing during passing period
Research papers
No library or computers
Too much homework
This same old uniform
Stanford, Berkeley, San Jose State, UCLA, Santa Clara
Bus routes
Use the crosswalk
My first referral
Everybody had detention
1–2–3 the clap
Lectures
Students
More students
Even more students
Site to site, we walked, and walked

At the beginning every student was skeptical if this school would work—if it was really possible that we could gain the skills to thrive at a four-year university. As the years progressed, I remember talking with a few of my classmates in the hall about our decision to attend DCP. We talked and talked and wondered if we had made the right choice. I didn't think this school would work since no one had ever tried before. I remember talking to my mother and I expressed to her how I felt. My mom and I made a deal: I would stay one year and if I didn't like it I would return to a traditional high school.

For some, our parents made us come to DCP. For others, we wanted to try something different. Whatever the reason, what's most important is why we stayed: We were becoming better students; we were learning about college; we were becoming a community.

As the years progressed, we slowly realized what we had gotten into. As students, we faced many obstacles. For some it was learning the English language, writing an essay, speaking in front of an audience, studying long hours, or working hard for a grade. Slowly, our fears became our strengths. The obstacle we all still faced was the fear of rejection. We didn't think a college would want any of us. As we got nearer to that reality it seemed even more surreal.

As a class we brought out the good and bad in each of us. We learned the real meaning of community. We noticed when one of us was having a bad day, when someone got a high grade on a test or a low grade on a test, who was sick, and who wasn't in class. During our freshman year it was hard to avoid each other even if we wanted to. Now we've come together as a class. Some of us know one another better than we know ourselves. Even if we didn't mean it at first, we care about each other and can't see us taking the next step alone.

There are several people that impacted our lives daily. Teachers and staff saw something positive in each of us and brought it to light. Teachers took pride in knowing our fears and weaknesses and making us stronger; always challenging us academically, socially, mentally, and emotionally. Teachers: You've helped us be part of a community that has been growing and one that we can call our very own. You've led us to the path of success. You've believed in us since the beginning, and without any of you, we would never have accomplished what we have. You've grown with us as we've grown with you. On behalf of the class of 2004, thank you for everything you've done for us and taught us.

We can thank everyone that has believed in DCP and has helped us in his or her special way. Especially our parents for always believing in us, and being willing to be part of this community with us. Family support has made it easier to let go of our fears and be ready to face whatever obstacle. Whether it was our family, teachers, staff members, donors, volunteers, board of directors, everyone has helped us and we can never thank you enough. Thank you.

To all the incoming freshmen here, we encourage and are hopeful that change will happen among students. By being here you're demonstrating that you want something, a better future. It shows your willingness to make a change not only for yourself, or family, or your community, but also for your generation. Making this commitment is hard to adjust to but never give up. We know what you will go through, but when you stand here in four years you will be a much more educated person that will have a bigger goal than just graduating high school, but being successful in college.

And to my fellow senior class, we not only made a commitment to be accepted to a four-year university but to be successful in it. The real test is out there in the world. I believe in every single one of you and can't wait to know what you will be doing after college. As the first class we've faced every obstacle together. Now is the time to put our skills to the test. Thank you for all the memories we've shared, and remember this is not the end; it's only the beginning.

appendix

how to start
a charter school

Starting a charter school is a huge undertaking. Based on DCP's experiences, here are some starting points to consider for would-be school founders.

1. Research the law

Not all states authorize charter schools, and some allow charters in theory but make it very difficult to start one in practice. Center for Education Reform (http://www.edreform.com) analyzes various state laws and provides links to state-level charter groups (http://www.edreform.com/index.cfm?fuseAction=linkpage).

U.S. Charter Schools (http://www.uscharterschools.org) provides practical advice on starting a charter school (http://www.uscharterschools.org/pub/uscs_docs/r/startup.htm).

The Charter Schools Development Center (http://www.cacharterschools.org/starting.html) also is an excellent resource.

For help with political roadblocks, contact National Alliance for Public Charter Schools (http://www.charterschoolleadershipcouncil.org/aboutus.

asp?c=2) and Alliance for School Choice (http://www.allianceforschool-choice.org/?OVRAW=Alliance%20for%20School%20Choice&OVKEY=school%20choice&OVMTC=advanced).

Finally, talk to charter founders in your area to identify obstacles and allies.

2. Build a team

Ideally, a charter team will include educators, parents, and people with business, law, and real estate experience. Look for community leaders with political connections too. Try to enlist your local university.

Building Excellent Schools (http://www.buildingexcellentschools.org/) offers a year-long, full-time training program for people who want to start an inner-city charter school. The $50,000 fellowship includes help designing the school, drafting the charter application, and preparing to manage a new school.

If you want to start a charter school based on the KIPP model, you'll be eligible for KIPP's leadership training program (http://www.kipp.org/leadakippschool.cfm?pageid=nav2), which includes business classes, residencies at successful charter schools, and assistance dealing with finding a site, fundraising, legal issues, and other activities.

The National Charter School Clearinghouse (http://www.ncsc.info/) provides state-by-state links (http://www.nationalcharterschoolclearing-house.net/mod.php?mod=userpage&menu=911&page_id=67) to charter school resources.

3. Network like crazy

One myth of charter schools features feisty founders at war with the establishment. That works if you're rich. Otherwise, no.

DCP's founders made allies in the establishment, selling their school as an asset to the school district, enlisting an influential priest, the mayor, and city council members, business leaders, the media, and ultimately school district leaders. By creating a tutoring program before they had a school, they connected with parents, students, and school counselors who could refer more students.

Charter founders need to link to existing networks, such as churches, community groups, preschools, and youth sports leagues. In the words of Don Shalvey, president of Aspire Public Schools, "In the black community, go to the Baptist and Methodist churches. In Hispanic neighborhoods, go to the Catholic churches. Go where the families are."

4. The mission matters

Most schools have vague, lofty, buzzword-laden and utterly meaningless mission statements. DCP's mission—to prepare underachievers for success at four-year colleges—clarifies priorities and drives decisions. Decide on a mission that defines what's important for your school.

5. What's the plan?

Successful charters typically are the result of one or two years of planning. Deciding on a teaching strategy, hiring a good staff, recruiting students, finding a suitable building, and raising money are the biggest challenges.

If the plan calls for substantial fundraising, start immediately. By 2003–2004, DCP was spending $11,368 per student per year; $7,083 came from state and federal funds; the school raised the rest, about $1.5 million, from donors.[1] Board members with financial expertise helped Andaluz write budgets that balanced.

6. Get real about what's not working, admit mistakes, and try something else

The greatest strength of DCP has been its leaders' willingness to abandon cherished plans that didn't work and look for different strategies to achieve the mission.

Remember that a single school won't be right for every student. Do your own thing well, and urge students who can't be served at your school to find one closer to their needs.

7. Accountability counts

A charter school has to please its parents, or they'll send their kids elsewhere. It has to satisfy donors, or they'll find other uses for their money. Prepare to prove that your school is succeeding. If you're not going to point to test scores, you'll need some other objective measure to make your case.

8. You've got to have a sense of humor, or you'll go crazy

DCP's staff stayed focused on the mission, but they could laugh together about the frustrations they shared.

notes

I

1. National Center for Education Statistics, U.S. Department of Education (Washington, D.C.: U.S. Government Printing Office, August 2000), *Average Proficiency in Reading, by Age and by Selected Characteristics of Students: 1971–1999* (Washington, D.C.: U.S. Government Printing Office, November 2000), *Average Mathematics Proficiency by Age and by Selected Characteristics of Students: 1973–1999* (Washington, D.C.: U.S. Government Printing Office, November 2001). Available at http://nces.ed.gov/programs/digest/d02/dt111.asp and http://nces.ed.gov/programs/digest/d02/dt123.asp. Accessed on June 14, 2005.
2. Jay P. Greene and Marcus A. Winters, *Public High School Completion and College Readiness Rates: 1991–2002* (New York: Manhattan Institute for Policy Research, February 2005). Available at http://www.manhattan-institute.org/html/ewp_08.htm. Accessed on June 14, 2005.
3. Mario Chacon, *The State of Latino Education in the San Francisco Bay Area* (San Francisco: Hispanic Community Foundation, June 2000), p. 11. Available at http://www.latinocf.org/espanol/resources/documents/led.pdf. Accessed on June 11, 2005.
4. Deborah Reed, *Education Resources and Outcomes in California, by Race and Ethnicity* (San Francisco: Public Policy Institute of California, February 2005), p. 5.
5. *Standardized Testing and Reporting: State of California, Hispanic or Latino* (Sacramento: California Department of Education, 2004). Available at http://star.cde.ca.gov/star2004/viewreport.asp. Accessed on June 14, 2005.
6. Education Trust-West, *Are California High Schools Ready for the 21st Century?* (Oakland: February 2005), p. 10. Available at http://www2.edtrust.org/NR/rdonlyres/819B2A7C-C749–477E-A90A–13DFA120C382/0/EdTrustWest_ReportFINAL.pdf. Accessed on June 14, 2005.
7. Chacon, *The State of Latino Education,* p. 11.
8. Education Trust-West, *Are California High Schools Ready?,* p. 7.

2

1. Chester E. Finn, Jr., *Teacher Reform Gone Astray,* Education Next, 2003, p. 13. Available at http://www.educationnext.org/unabridged/20032/211.pdf. Accessed on June 14, 2005.
2. Chester E. Finn, Jr., Bruno V. Manno, and Gregg Vanourek, *Charter Schools in Action: Renewing Public Education* (Princeton, NJ: Princeton University Press, 2000), p. 18.

3. Center for Education Reform, *Charter Schools Today: Changing the Face of American Education: Statistics, Stories and Insights* (Washington, D.C.: May 2004); e-mail from Lesley Heilman, deputy director of communications, Center for Education Reform, March 24, 2005. Available at http://www.edreform.com/index.cfm?fuseAction=document& documentID=1760&sectionID=5&NEWSYEAR=2004#%20%20. Accessed on June 14, 2005.

4. Chester E. Finn, Jr. and Eric Osberg, *Charter School Funding: Inequity's Next Frontier* (Washington, D.C.: Thomas B. Fordham Institute, Progress Analytics Institute and Public Impact, August 2005), pp. 1–2. Available at http://www.edexcellence.net/institute/ charterfinance. Accessed on September 1, 2005.

5. Kara Finnegan, et al., *Evaluation of the Public Charter Schools Program: Final Report* (Washington, D.C.: U.S. Government Printing Office, 2004), pp. 23–25. Available at http://www.ed.gov/rschstat/eval/choice/pcsp-final/finalreport.pdf. Accessed on September 1, 2005.

6. Center for Education Reform, *Annual Survey of America's Charter Schools 2004* (Washington, D.C.: December 2004).

7. Becky Morgan, CEO of Joint Venture Silicon Valley, interview by author; Ben Smith, A.T. Kearney, interview by author, San Jose, May 1999.

8. Don Shalvey, CEO of Aspire Public Schools, interview by author, San Carlos, CA, February 2001.

9. Nanette Asimov, "State school board veteran loses seat," *San Francisco Chronicle,* January 13, 2005.

10. Sam Dillon, "Charter Schools Alter Map of Public Education in Dayton," *New York Times,* March 27, 2005.

11. Center for Education Reform, Charter Schools Today, May 2004. e-mail from Heilman, March 24, 2005.

3

1. San Jose Planning Department, *Fact Sheet: Demographics, 2005.* Available at http://www. sanjoseca.gov/planning/pdf/fact.pdf. Accessed on June 17, 2005.

2. Jennifer Andaluz, interview by author, San Jose, 2001.

3. Kate Folmar, "Start-Up School Hopes High for Santa Clara County's First Charter High School as Teachers, Parents, Teens Struggle to Bring it to Life," *San Jose Mercury News,* August 25, 2000; Deborah Lohse, "A CEO's dedication to San Jose," *San Jose Mercury News,* October 29, 2004.

4. "Charters Take on LAUSD: Seven Schools Fighting District Plans to Withhold $3 Million in State Money," *Los Angeles Daily News,* August 22, 2004.

4

1. James Nehring, *Upstart Startup: Creating and Sustaining a Public Charter School* (New York and London: Teachers College Press, 2002), pp. 39–40.

9

1. Bill Evers, chairman of East Palo Alto Charter Academy board, interview by author, Palo Alto, CA, March 2001.

2. Tom Loveless, *The 2002 Brown Center Report on American Education: How Well are American Students Learning?* (Washington, D.C.: Brookings Institution, 2002), pp.

30–31. Available at http://www.brookings.edu/dybdocroot/gs/brown/bc_report/2002/ bcr_report.pdf. Accessed on June 17, 2005.

3. Jeanne Allen, president of The Center for Education Reform, "Are Charter Schools a Sound Educational Alternative? Yes," *Pioneer Press,* August 23, 2004.

12

1. "Ruling Reinstated," *San Jose Mercury News,* July 6, 1987.

16

1. "S.J. Unified, Hispanics Closer to Bias Pact," *San Jose Mercury News,* January 6, 1994.
2. "Learning To Fly in a New Language," *San Jose Mercury News,* May 3, 1998.

19

1. Kate Folmar, "Students Struggle with New Standards," *San Jose Mercury News,* February 9, 2002.

21

1. Lance T. Izumi, *California Education Report Card* (San Francisco: Pacific Research Institute, 2003). Available at http://www.pacificresearch.org/pub/sab/educat/03_ed_index/ 09_remedial.html. Accessed on June 11, 2005.

25

1. Eric Premack, *How To Calculate Proposition 39 Facilities Fees* (Sacramento: Charter Schools Development Center, 2003), pp. 1–7. Available at http://www.cacharterschools. org/pdf_files/Proposition_39_Facilities_Fees.pdf. Accessed on June 14, 2005.
2. "College Prep Is Moving Up," *San Jose Mercury News,* June 24, 2004.
3. Downtown College Prep budget, 2001–02.
4. Jennifer Andaluz, interview by author, San Jose, June 2002.

27

1. *California Standards Test Scores – 2005* (Sacramento: California Education Department, 2005). Available at http://star.cde.ca.gov/star2005/viewreport.asp?ps=true&lstCounty=43& lstDistrict=69666–000&lstSchool=4330585&rf=true. Accessed on September 5, 2005.
2. *2005 Accountability Progress Report* (Sacramento: California Education Department, 2005). Available at http://ayp.cde.ca.gov/reports/APR/2005APR_Sch_Summary.asp? AllCds=43696664330585&SchCode=4330585&DistCode=69666. Accessed on September 5, 2005.
3. *Test Scores: Downtown College Preparatory* (San Francisco: Great Schools.net). Available at http://www.greatschools.net/modperl/achievement/ca/11869. Accessed on September 5, 2005.
4. *2005 Accountability Progress Report* (Sacramento: California Education Department, 2005). Available at http://ayp.cde.ca.gov/reports/APR/2005APR_DstList.asp?cYear=& cSelect=4369666—SAN^JOSE^UNIFIED&cChoice=APR5a. Accessed on September. 5, 2005.
5. *2004 API Base Report* (Sacramento: California Education Department, 2004). Available at http://api.cde.ca.gov/API2005/2004Base_Dst.aspx?cYear=&cSelect=4369666& cChoice=2004BDst. Accessed on September 5, 2005.

6. Ibid; *2005 Accountability Progress Report* (Sacramento: California Education Department, 2005). Available at http://ayp.cde.ca.gov/reports/APR/2005APR_DstList.asp?cYear=&cSelect=4369666—SAN^JOSE^UNIFIED&cChoice=APR5a. Accessed on Sept. 5, 2005.

7. "Class of 2006 exit exam results," *San Jose Mercury News,* August 27, 2005.

8. "Latino students at Downtown Prep outscore San Jose Unified," *San Jose Mercury News,* June 18, 2004.

9. Ibid.

10. Ibid.

11. Ibid.

12. *The Educational Pipeline: Big Investment, Big Returns* (San Jose: National Center for Public Policy and Higher Education, April 2004), p. 2. Available at http://www.higheredu-cation.org/reports/pipeline/pipeline.pdf. Accessed on June 14, 2005.

28

1. Diana Jean Schemo, "Nation's Charter Schools Lagging Behind, U.S. Test Scores Reveal," *New York Times,* August 17, 2004.

2. National Assessment of Educational Progress (NAEP), *America's Charter Schools: Results from the NAEP 2003 Pilot Study* (Washington, D.C.: U.S. Government Printing Office, 2003), p. 2. Available at http://nces.ed.gov/pubsearch/pubsinfo.asp?pubid=2005456. Accessed on June 14, 2005.

3. Jeanne Allen, *Hope in the Nation's Charter Schools* (Washington, D.C.: Center for Education Reform, 15 December 2004). Available at http://www.edreform.com/index.cfm?fuseAction=document&documentID=1923&sectionID=5&NEWSYEAR=2004. Accessed on June 14, 2005.

4. NAEP, *America's Charter Schools,* p. 2.

5. Christian Braunlich and Melanie Looney, *Annual Survey of America's Charter Schools* (Washington, D.C.: Center for Education Reform, 2002), p. 5.

6. National Center for Education Statistics, *The Condition of Education 2004* (Washington, D.C.: U.S. Government Printing Office, 2004). Available at http://www.nces.ed.gov/pubsearch/pubsinfo.asp?pubid=2004077. Accessed on June 14, 2005.

7. American Federation of Teachers, *Official NAEP Reports on Charter Schools Mirror Earlier Reports' Results,* 15 December 2004. Available at http://www.aft.org/presscenter/releases/2004/121504.htm, June 14, 2005.

8. Thomas A. Fiore, Sandra H. Warren, and Erin R. Cashman, *Charter Schools and Students with Disabilities: Review of Existing Data* (Research Triangle Park, N.C.: Research Triangle Institute, November 1998). Available at http://www.ed.gov/pubs/chartdisab/enroll.html. Accessed on June 14, 2005.

9. Martin Carnoy, Rebecca Jacobsen, Lawrence Mishel, and Richard Rothstein, *The Charter School Dust-Up: Examining the Evidence on Enrollment and Achievement* (Washington, D.C.: Economic Policy Institute, 2005). Available at http://www.epi.org/content.cfm/book_charter_school. Accessed on June 14, 2005.

10. Caroline M. Hoxby, *Achievement in Charter Schools and Regular Public Schools in the United States: Understanding the Differences* (Cambridge, Mass.: The Program on Education Police and Governance at Harvard University, December 2004), p. 1. Available at

http://post.economics.harvard.edu/faculty/hoxby/papers/hoxbycharter_dec.pdf. Accessed on June 14, 2005.

11. Caroline M. Hoxby and Jonah E. Rockoff, *The Impact of Charter Schools on Student Achievement: A Study of Students Who Attend Schools Chartered by the Chicago Charter Schools Foundation* (Cambridge, Mass.: Harvard University; National Bureau of Economic Research, November 2004). Available at http://post.economics.harvard.edu/faculty/hoxby/papers/hoxbyrockoff.pdf. Access on June 14, 2005.

12. Paul T. Hill, "Assessing Student Performance in Charter Schools," *Education Week,* January 12, 2005.

Appendix

1. Joe Rodriguez, "Once Underachievers, Students Make the Grade at College Prep," *San Jose Mercury News,* June 4, 2004.

Index